Business Research Methods

S. Sreejesh · Sanjay Mohapatra
M. R. Anusree

Business Research Methods

An Applied Orientation

 Springer

S. Sreejesh
IBS Hyderabad
IFHE University
Hyderabad
India

M. R. Anusree
Department of Statistics
University of Kerala
Trivandrum, Kerala
India

Sanjay Mohapatra
Xavier Institute of Management
Bhubaneswar, Orissa
India

Additional material to this book can be downloaded from http://extras.springer.com/

ISBN 978-3-319-00538-6   ISBN 978-3-319-00539-3   (eBook)
DOI 10.1007/978-3-319-00539-3
Springer Cham Heidelberg New York Dordrecht London

Library of Congress Control Number: 2013940441

Printed on acid-free paper

Springer is part of Springer Science+Business Media (www.springer.com)

Dedicated to our elders who shaped our lives
Late Parmananda Mishra,
Late Dr. Sushila Mishra,
Dr. B. C. Mohapatra,
H. K. Mohapatra,
Kanyakumari Mohapatra (Bou)

and

Late Surendran Pillai P. (Father)
Radhamani Amma (Mother) finally,
inspiration behind all my success
Suresh S. (Brother), Sreeja Sudharman
(Sister), and Sudharman Pillai

Preface

In the globalized economy, business faces challenges that require knowledge-based solutions. The products and services that they offer need to be decisive, and precise value propositions that would meet customer's explicit and latent requirements. This means the managers need to use tools and techniques that will use research-based information to be part of decision support system. This book is about creating that information from research that can help managers to take decisions that will provide competitive edge.

This textbook provides an in-depth knowledge in the field of business research for students. Those who have made a career in practical research will also get benefits from the concepts illustrated here. It addresses all the concepts that are taught in MBA classes, explaining theoretical concepts and mapping these concepts to practical cases.

The pedagogy has been developed based on experience in teaching the subject to many batches of students. The methodologies depicted here have been used in several consulting assignments and have been proven to be useful for market researchers.

Organization of the Book

The book has been prepared in five parts. The first part explains topics related to concepts that are related to business research, second part consists of descriptive and exploratory research methodology, third part consists of causal research design, and the fourth part illustrates the approach for writing business reports. Detailed contents in the book are as follows:

Part I: Overview of Business Research

Chapter 1: *Introduction to Business Research*: Scope of Business Research—Basic Research and Applied Research—Role of Business Research in Decision-Making: Problem/Opportunity Identification, Problem/Opportunity Prioritization and Selection, Problem/Opportunity Resolution, Implementing the Course of Action—Factors Affecting Business Research: Time Constraint, Availability of Resources, Nature of Information Sought, Benefits Versus Cost—Globalization and Business Research—Business Research and the Internet: Primary Research and Secondary Research.

Case Study 1

Chapter 2: *Business Research Process*: Steps in the Research Process—Identifying and defining the Problem/Opportunity Exploratory Research, Preparing the Statement of Research Objectives, Developing the Hypotheses. Planning the Research Design, Selecting the Research Method—Surveys, Experiments, Secondary Data Studies, Observation Techniques, Analyzing Research Designs, Selecting the Sampling Procedure, Data Collection, Evaluating the Data, Analysis, Preparing, and Presenting the Research Report.

Part II: Research Design

Case Study 2

Chapter 3: *Business Research Design: Exploratory, Descriptive and Causal Designs*: The Meaning of Business Research Design—Need for Research Design—Characteristics of a Good Research Design.

Case Study 3: J & J and Cause-Related Marketing Initiatives

Part I: Exploratory Research Design: Exploratory Research Design with Secondary Data: Classification of Secondary Data, Internal Secondary Data and Published External Secondary Data, Syndicated Data; Exploratory Research Design: Qualitative Research; Rationale for Using Qualitative Research, Classification, Focus Group, In-depth Interviews, and Projective Techniques.

Video: How to Do In-depth Interviews

Part II: Descriptive Research Design: Survey methods—Telephone Methods, Personal Methods, Mail Methods, Electronic Methods; Observation Methods—Personal Observation, Mechanical Observation, Audit, Content Analysis and Trace Analysis.

Part III: Causal Research Design: Experimentation: Research Design Concepts: Dependent and Independent Variables, Extraneous Variable, Control, Confounded Relationship, Research Hypothesis, Experimental and Non-experimental Hypothesis Testing Research, Experimental and Control Groups, Treatments, Experiment, Experimental Units—Classification of Research Designs: Exploratory Studies, Descriptive Studies, Causal Studies—Choosing a Research Design—Benefits of Research Designs. Issues In Experimentation: Treatment or Independent Variable, Experimental Groups and Control Groups, Selection and Measurement of the Dependent Variable, Control of Extraneous Variables—Experimental Validity: Internal Validity, External Validity—Experimental Environment: Laboratory Environment, Field Environment—Types of Experimental Designs: Pre-experimental Designs, True Experimental Designs, Quasi-Experimental Designs, Statistical Designs, Completely Randomized Design (CBD), Randomized Block Design, Latin Square Design, Factorial Design.

Part III: Sources and Methods of Data Collection: Qualitative and Quantitative Data

Case Study 6: Launching Fruit Flavoured Soft Drinks at Fresh Cola (A)

Chapter 4: *Scales and Measurement*: Identifying and Deciding on the Variables to be Measured—Development of Measurement Scales—Types of Measurement Scales: Nominal Scale, Ordinal Scale, Interval Scale, Ratio Scale—Criteria For Good Measurement: Reliability, Test-Retest Reliability, Equivalent form Reliability, Internal Consistency, Validity, Face Validity, Content Validity, Criterion-Related Validity, Construct Validity, Sensitivity, Generalizability, Relevance—Sources of Measurement Problems: Respondent Associated Errors, Non-response Errors, Response Bias, Instrument Associated Errors, Situational Errors, Measurer as Error Source.

Chapter 5: *Questionnaire Design*: Preliminary Decisions: Required Information, Target Respondents, Interviewing Technique—Question Content—The Utility of Data, Effectiveness in Producing Data, The Participant's Ability to Answer Accurately, The Respondent's Willingness to Answer Accurately, Effect of External Events—Response Format-Open-Ended Questions, Close-ended

Questions—Question Wording: Shared Vocabulary, Unsupported Assumptions, Frame of Reference, Biased Wording, Adequate Alternatives, Double-Barrelled Questions, Generalizations and Estimates—Questionnaire Sequence: Lead-in Questions, Qualifying Questions, Warm-up Questions, Specific Questions, Demographic Questions—Questionnaire Pretesting, Revision and Final Draft.

Part IV: Multivariate Data Analysis Using IBM SPSS 20.0

Chapter 6: *Data Preparation and Preliminary Analysis*: Validating and Editing: Treatment of Unsatisfactory Responses—Coding: Categorization Rules, Code Book, Coding Close-Ended Questions, Coding Open-Ended Questions—Data Entry: Optical Scanning, Barcode Reader, Voice Recognition—Data Cleaning—Tabulation of Survey Results: One-Way Frequency Tabulation, Cross Tabulation—Data Mining: Data Mining in Management Research, The Data Mining Process.

 Chapter 7: *Experimental Analysis of Variance (ANOVA)*: Objectives, overview, relationship among techniques, statistics associated with one-way analysis of variance, Analysis of randomized block, Latin square and factorial design.

Case Study 10: Launching Fruit Flavoured Soft Drinks at Fresh Cola (B)

Chapter 8: *Multiple Regression*: Statistics associated with multiple regressions, assumptions of regression-normality, linearity, multicollinearity, heteroscedasticity, autocorrelation. How to do regression analysis using SPSS.

Case Study: ABC Group: Analysis of Sales

Videos: How to Do Regression Using SPSS

Chapter 9: *Exploratory Factor and Principal Component Analysis*: Basic concept, factor analysis model, statistics associated with factor analysis, assumptions of factor analysis, How to do factor analysis using SPSS.

Case Study: Aaron Group of Companies: A Consumer Perception Analysis

Videos: How to Do Factor Analysis Using SPSS

Chapter 10: *Cluster Analysis:* Objectives, basic concept, statistics associated with cluster analysis, steps to conduct cluster analysis. How to do cluster analysis using SPSS.

Case Study: ABC Group: Identifying Exploratory Buyer Behaviour Tendency

Video: How to Do Cluster Analysis Using SPSS

Chapter 11: *Binary Logistic Regression*: Chapter Overview, Logistic Regression, An example of logistic regression, SPSS procedure for logistic regression.

Case Study: Defaulter Prediction

Part V: Data Presentation

Chapter 12: *Business Research Reports:* Types of Research Reports: Short Reports, Long Reports—Components of Research Reports: Prefatory information, Introduction, Methodology, Findings, Conclusions and Recommendations, Appendices, Bibliography—Written Presentation: Pre-writing Concerns, Writing the Draft, Presentation of the Research Report—Oral Presentations: Initial Planning, Preparation, Making the Presentation, Delivery—Visual Aids: Tables, Charts and Graphs.

S. Sreejesh
Sanjay Mohapatra
M. R. Anusree

Acknowledgments

The book has been written after being 'class tested'. The manuscript has been possible because of class notes and several comments that we have received from different sources. As a result, the book is complete with concepts, examples and cases. We hope this will be liked by readers.

We would also like to thank our family members for their unstinted and continued support in every walk of our lives.

Finally to God, who graced us with his blessing so that we could make it all possible.

Dr. S. Sreejesh
Dr. Sanjay Mohapatra
Dr. M. R. Anusree

Contents

Part II   Research Design

Part III Sources and Methods of Data Collection: Qualitative and Quantitative Data

Part I
Overview of Business Research

Chapter 1
Introduction to Business Research

In the present fast track business environment marked by cut-throat competition, many organizations rely on business research to gain a competitive advantage and greater market share. A good research study helps organizations to understand processes, products, customers, markets and competition, to develop policies, strategies and tactics that are most likely to succeed.

Business research can be defined as a systematic and objective process of gathering, recording and analysing data that provide information to guide business decisions. It is used to understand the market trends, or find the optimal marketing mix, devise effective HR policies, or find the best investment options. This chapter provides an overview of business research and its role in decision-making. First, we shall discuss the scope of business research. Then, we shall understand the two categories of business research studies, basic research and applied research. Later, we shall discuss the role of business research in decision-making and evaluate the factors that influence the need for business research. Finally, we shall examine how globalization and the Internet are influencing business research.

1.1 Scope of Business Research

Business research is used to solve the various operational and planning problems that arise in a business organization. These may include problems related to marketing, finance, HR and manufacturing. The three major forms of business research are as follows: market research, operations research and motivational research. Market research aims at understanding and examining the marketplace in which the company operates. This helps the organization devise effective business policies and marketing strategies. Operations research involves use of mathematical, logical and analytical methods to find optimal solutions to business problems. Operations research is primarily used for forecasting demand, optimizing production and finding the best investment options. Motivational research involves analysing the reasons and motives behind people's behaviour. Motivational research is used to understand consumer behaviour. It is also used to understand employee behaviour.

S. Sreejesh et al., *Business Research Methods*,
DOI: 10.1007/978-3-319-00539-3_1,
© Springer International Publishing Switzerland 2014

1.2 Basic Research and Applied Research

Business research is conducted either to expand knowledge about a particular aspect or to find a solution to a particular problem. Business research studies can be classified into two categories—basic research and applied research.

Basic research refers to a focused, systematic study or investigation undertaken to discover new knowledge or interpretations and establish facts or principles in a particular field. In other words, it is a research aimed primarily at gaining knowledge rather than solving a pragmatic problem. The underlying motive is to increase knowledge about particular phenomena by testing, refining and elaborating theory without concern for practical application. Examples of such basic research include the following:

1. Understanding the consumer buying process
2. Examining the consumer learning process.

Applied research refers to investigation undertaken to discover the applications and uses of theories, knowledge and principles in actual work or in solving problems. In other words, it is any research that is used to answer a specific question, determine why something failed or succeeded, solve a specific, pragmatic problem, or to gain better understanding. Examples include the following: Evaluating the impact of a training programme on employee performance. Examining consumer response to direct marketing programmes Although the purpose of these two research forms varies, there is not much difference in the research methods and tools used for their conduct. Both these research forms use scientific methods in various stages of the research process. The scientific method refers to a systematic approach towards observing phenomena, drawing conclusions and testing hypotheses. Scientific methods involve systematic analysis and logical interpretation of empirical evidence to establish facts or to prove a theory.

In basic research, first the hypothesis is tested through experimentation and observation. Then, logical interpretations and conclusions are made about a particular phenomenon. These conclusions lead to the formation of general laws about that phenomenon. However, applied research involves developing alternatives to a particular problem and finding the best alternative among them.

1.3 Role of Business Research in Decision-Making

For effective planning and implementation of business decisions, accurate information about the internal business environment and the external business environment is of primary importance. The key objective of any business research is to provide accurate, relevant and timely information to the top management, so that they can make effective decisions. The business decision-making process in an organization goes through these key interrelated stages (see Fig. 1.1). They are:

Fig. 1.1 Steps in the
decision-making process

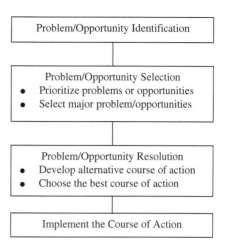

Problem/Opportunity Identification

Problem/Opportunity Selection
• Prioritize problems or opportunities
• Select major problem/opportunities

Problem/Opportunity Resolution
• Develop alternative course of action
• Choose the best course of action

Implement the Course of Action

- Problem/opportunity identification
- Problem/opportunity prioritization and selection
- Problem/opportunity resolution
- Implementing the course of action.

Business research helps the management in each of these stages by providing useful and timely information.

1.3.1 Problem/Opportunity Identification

Problem/opportunity identification involves scanning and monitoring the internal and external business environment. Such an analysis helps in identifying opportunities and threats that a company is facing and also in understanding the market trends. The role of business research at this stage is to provide information about the problems and the opportunities. For example, an Indian apparel company that wants to enter the US market can undertake business research in areas, such as identifying the fashion trends in the market, determining the brand awareness about the company among the customers, perception about the company among the potential employees, examining the competitors and their characteristics and understanding American consumer behaviour.

1.3.2 Problem/Opportunity Prioritization and Selection

In the previous step, the organizations' would have identified many possible problems and opportunities. However, it is impossible for any organization to address these problems/opportunities in one go. So at this stage, the focus would be on prioritizing the problems and the opportunities. Prioritization of the problems is based on two factors—the influence of problem on the business operations and the time factor. Top priority is given to the problems, which have a major influence on the business operations and the problems, which need to be addressed in the short term.

Another activity that organizations undertake at this stage is to gather more information about the problems and the opportunities. For example, if an organization has identified a particular problem, then research would help it to unearth the underlying causes of the problem. If the organization has identified an opportunity, then more information about the opportunity is gathered. Such an analysis provides greater clarity about the situation. Business research at this stage is used to aid the organization to prioritize the problems and identify the right opportunities. Generally, qualitative and quantitative research studies are undertaken at this stage.

1.3.3 Problem/Opportunity Resolution

After identifying the problem or opportunity, the next step is to decide on the way to resolve the problem or make use of the opportunity. Two steps are involved in problem resolution—developing alternatives and evaluating the alternatives.

Based on the problem or opportunity identified in the previous step, several alternate courses of action are considered. These alternatives are evaluated to select the best course of action. The alternatives are evaluated on the basis of certain criteria. The application of business research at this stage is mainly to help the organization in evaluating the alternatives available.

For example, a consumer electronics company that wanted to launch a new television model was faced with a dilemma regarding the advertising strategy it should adopt, as its marketing staff had suggested three different advertising programs. To evaluate the advertising programmes, the company undertook a consumer-jury test where target customers were invited to a particular location and the three alternative advertising programmes were shown to them. They were asked to rate those advertisements on various parameters like likeability, memorability, attentiveness and believability. Based on the results of the test, the company finalized the best option among the three advertising programmes. Another way in which business research aids in evaluating the alternative options is through business forecasting. For example, a company has three different investment options from among which it has to choose the best option.

By forecasting the revenue potential of each investment option, the company can select the investment option, which has the highest revenue potential.

1.3.4 Implementing the Course of Action

After deciding upon the best course of action, the organization has to effectively implement it. At this stage, business research is mainly used to monitor and control the programmes that are being implemented. Evaluative research studies are undertaken at this stage. One type of evaluative research study used is performance research. In this type of research, the performance of a particular activity is measured, so that it can be compared with the objectives set for that activity. For example, if a company has offered a discount coupon scheme in the market, the coupon redemption rate at the end of the scheme is measured and compared with the objectives that were set for this scheme. This helps in evaluating the performance of the scheme.

Companies also monitor the performance of a particular activity continuously so as to identify the opportunities and detect the problems at an early stage. This helps a company in altering the plans or developing new programmes. For example, certain companies continuously track the sales at retail stores, so that they can identify which products are registering higher sales, the buying behaviour of consumers, and consumer preference towards the company's products.

1.4   Factors Affecting Business Research

Although business research provides many benefits to an organization, it is not a panacea for all the problems that an organization faces. And conducting business research also involves cost, time and effort. Therefore, an organization should decide upon the option of conducting business research after considering various factors. These include time constraints, availability of resources, availability of data, nature of information that the organization is expecting and the costs involved.

1.4.1 Time Constraint

Time constraint is a key factor that influences a company's decision regarding whether to conduct a business research study or not. In certain cases, lack of time prompts a company to take decisions without making any research study. Sudden changes in competitors' strategies, regulatory changes, change in the market environment, or changes in the company's operations, require immediate action.

For example, P and G drastically cut the prices of its detergents in India, in May 2004. HLL responded to the price cuts without making any study on the implications of the price cuts on its product sales or image.

1.4.2 Availability of Resources

Another factor that influences the decision to undertake business research or not is the availability of resources. The availability of resources can be either in terms of budgetary allocations or human resources. Lack of financial resources may lead to improper conduct of a business research study. The results obtained from such research, in turn, will be inaccurate. Lack of financial resources forces a company to compromise on the way its research project is undertaken, such as taking a smaller sample size where the project demands a larger sample size, using cheaper methods of data collection and even comprising on the data analysis process that is crucial for any business research study. Therefore, before conducting the business research, the company needs to consider the issue of availability of financial resources.

A company also needs to consider the availability of human resources while taking a decision about the business research study. Lack of qualified personnel may affect the data collection and data analysis processes in a business research study. Lack of qualified personnel may lead to selection of improper sample, improper filling of data and inaccurate analysis of data. Therefore, a company needs to look for well-qualified and well-trained personnel before conducting a business research study.

1.4.3 Nature of Information Sought

The information or input that a company wants to obtain from the research study also influences the decision of whether to conduct the business research study or not. If the information that a company wants to obtain from the research study can be obtained from the internal records of the company, or from prior studies conducted by the company, then conducting business research is a waste of time and effort. For example, if a company like Pepsi is launching a new fruit drink in India and wants information about the market potential of the product, it can use its knowledge and its prior studies regarding the beverages market in India, rather than conducting a new market study. In certain cases, the management's experience and intuition is enough to take a particular decision and there is no need for a business research study.

1.4.4 Benefits Versus Cost

The benefits of a research are many. However, a research demands significant efforts and that requires allocation of sufficient budget for the same. Therefore, every manager has to make a cost-benefit analysis before taking a decision regarding the conduct of a business research study. Unless the benefits of the research, in the form of the information to be gained that would serve to improve the quality of the decisions to be made, outweigh the expenditure on the research, the research proposal should not be approved.

1.5 Globalization and Business Research

Globalization of business and the formation of regional trading blocks have had a major impact on all aspects of business and especially, on business research. Companies are increasingly looking out for international markets due to various compelling reasons. As firms overcome the geographic barriers of their operations to cash in on the opportunities in the global market, the need for timely and relevant information from a broader and more diverse range of markets is increasing. An organization or a market research company, conducting international business research requires a different set of capabilities and approaches as compared to the ones involved in domestic research. Some of the issues that an organization needs to consider before venturing into international business research are as follows:

- Global business research efforts need to be more closely associated with market growth opportunities outside the industrialized nations.
- International business researchers need to devise new creative approaches to understand the international markets.
- Researchers should make use of technological advances in order to undertake international business activities effectively.

Until now, the focus of international business research has been confined to industrialized markets including North America, Europe and Japan. However, these markets are saturating while emerging markets like Latin America, India, China and Southeast Asia are showing a high growth potential. Therefore, multinational firms should concentrate on understanding these markets by devoting greater time and effort in conducting research activities in these markets.

However, conducting research studies successfully in emerging markets requires different approaches than the usual approaches. These markets do not possess well-developed business research infrastructure. Moreover, the literacy rate is low. Therefore, researchers while designing the response formats and research instruments for the emerging markets need to keep these aspects in mind. Researchers should also develop innovative tools to understand these markets.

Unlike in western markets where quantitative research techniques are used more, qualitative and observation studies are effective in emerging markets.

Researchers can use innovative tools like videotaping techniques to understand consumer behaviour in these markets. Researchers can use focus groups to understand views, preferences and cultures.

Companies can also use projective and elicitation techniques like collage, picture completion, analogies and metaphors and psycho drawing to gain a deeper understanding about these markets.

Use of technology can aid the researchers in effectively implementing the research activities. Researchers can make use of technologies like Computer-Assisted Telephone Interviewing (CATI), and Computer-Assisted Personal Interviewing (CAPI) and the Internet to make the research process faster, efficient and effective.

1.6 Business Research and the Internet

Use of the Internet in business research studies is increasing. The declining costs of conducting online research activities coupled with the increasing number of Internet users have made the Internet a cost-effective alternative to traditional research methods for business research organizations. The following sections discuss the role of the Internet in primary and secondary research.

1.6.1 Primary Research

Primary data are collected directly from respondents using data collection methods like survey interviews, questionnaires, measurements, direct observation or tabulation. Use of the Internet for primary data collection is still in its infancy. Although there have been satisfying results of its initial implementation and the future prospects look good it is still used cautiously. There are various advantages in conducting online surveys compared with traditional survey methods. These include the following:

- The responses and feedback can be obtained faster.
- Costs for conducting online surveys are less compared with traditional survey methods.
- Questionnaires can be delivered to the respondents faster.
- Confidentiality is maintained as only the recipients read the questionnaire.
- Respondents can reply to the questionnaire at their convenience.
- Apart from online surveys, organizations are also conducting online focus group studies.

- Although there are several advantages in using the Internet, there are certain drawbacks as well. Online surveys lack face-to-face interaction. Also, lack of accessibility of the Internet among the population compared with other media is a major limitation.

1.6.2 Secondary Research

Secondary data are the data that already exist which have been collected by some other person or organization for their use and are generally made available to other researchers free or at a concessional rate. Major use of the Internet in business research is in the area of secondary research. The research reports and databases maintained by major research companies are also available on the net. This makes it faster, economical and reliable for companies to know about competitor activities. The very essence of the Internet as a major source of secondary information probably springs forth from the advantages of its broad scope, covering virtually every topic and the reasonable cost in acquiring them.

1.7 Summary

Business research can be defined as a systematic and objective process of gathering, recording and analysing data to guide business decision-making. Business research is mainly used to reduce the uncertainty of decisions. Business research encompasses various facets of business in an organization including marketing, finance, human resources and manufacturing. Three types of business research studies are mainly employed by organizations: market research, operations research and motivational research. Business research studies can be classified into two categories—basic research and applied research. Basic research refers to a focused, systematic study or investigation undertaken to discover new knowledge or interpretations and establish facts or principles in a particular field. Applied research refers to investigation undertaken to discover the applications and uses of theories, knowledge and principles in actual work or in solving problems. The key objective of any business research is to provide accurate, relevant and timely information to the top management, so that they can make effective decisions.

In business, decision-making goes through four key interrelated stages: problem/opportunity identification, problem/opportunity selection, problem/opportunity resolution and implementing the course of action.

Business research helps the management in each of these stages by providing useful and timely information. Organizations should decide upon the option of conducting business research after considering various factors. These include time constraints, availability of resources, availability of data, nature of information that the organization expecting and the costs involved.

Globalization of business and the formation of regional trading blocks have had a major impact on all aspects of business and especially, on business research. Companies are increasingly looking out for international markets. As firms overcome the geographic barriers of their operations to cash in on the opportunities in the global market, the need for timely and relevant information from a broader and more diverse range of markets is increasing. The role of the Internet in business research studies has also been discussed in the chapter. The declining costs of conducting online research activities coupled with the increasing number of Internet users have made the Internet an attractive option for business research organizations.

Chapter 2
Business Research Process

The business research process involves a series of steps that systematically investigate a problem or an opportunity facing the organization. The sequence of steps involved in the business research process are as follows: problem/opportunity identification and formulation, planning a research design, selecting a research method, selecting the sampling procedure, data collection, evaluating the data and preparing the research report for presentation. The above steps provide a broad outline applicable to any business research project. However, the number and sequence of activities can vary as per the demand of an individual research project.

The process of business research can be primarily divided into three phases—planning, execution and report preparation. The planning phase begins from problem/opportunity identification and leads to selection of the sampling procedure. Data collection and evaluation can be described as the execution phase of the business research process, while report preparation can be considered as the last phase. In this chapter, we will discuss each of these phases in detail.

2.1 Steps in the Research Process

The steps in the research process, namely identification and definition of the problem or opportunity, planning the research design, selecting a research method, selecting a sampling procedure, data collection, evaluating the data and finally preparing and presenting the research report have been shown in the Fig. 2.1. Each of these steps in the research process is discussed below.

2.1.1 Identifying and Defining the Problem/Opportunity

The initial step in the research process is the identification of the problem or opportunity. As businesses today operate in a highly volatile environment governed by various macro environmental factors, they need to constantly assess their

S. Sreejesh et al., *Business Research Methods*,
DOI: 10.1007/978-3-319-00539-3_2,
© Springer International Publishing Switzerland 2014

Fig. 2.1 Steps in the
Research Process

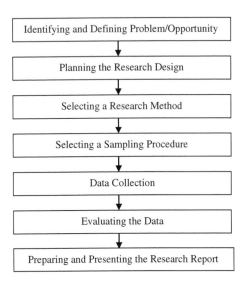

relative position and identify the various problem areas or opportunities they need
to work upon in order to sustain themselves competitively in the market. The
managers need to analyse the changing dynamics of business and to evolve a
strategy to adapt to the changes taking place in the external environment. Whether
these are potential problem areas or opportunities, it is very important for the
manager to identify them accurately and at the earliest. Problem identification
precedes the problem definition stage. For instance, a company producing cell
phone wave protectors (devices that protect the cell phone from harmful radiations) may realize that its new product is not selling, but it may not know the
reason for this at the outset. Although it has identified the problem in a broader
perspective, it needs to define the problem specifically in terms of what is to be
researched.

It is important to define the problem in a precise manner. A well-defined problem
gives the researcher a proper direction for carrying out investigation. It also helps in
utilizing the resources provided for the research effectively. A researcher can focus
his efforts on collecting relevant information, if the problem is defined properly.
Some research problems such as conducting a survey on the newspaper reading
habits of a given set of the population can be clearly defined. But if a company
wants to define a research problem such as declining sales, it needs to explore the
research problem further through exploratory research.

2.1.2 Exploratory Research

Exploratory research aims at understanding the topic being researched. Through
exploratory research, one arrives at a set of questions that are to be answered in

order to solve the problem or cash in on an opportunity. Exploratory research is undertaken in the initial stages of the research process. It is an informal process that helps in defining the identified problem. This process involves evaluating the existing studies on related topics, discussing the problem with experts, analysing the situation and so on. At the end of this process, the researchers should be clear about what type of information needs to be gathered and how the research process should proceed.

Secondary data analysis and pilot studies are the most popular tools used in exploratory research. Secondary data are the data that have already been collected previously for some other research purpose. It can be obtained from magazines, journals, online articles, company literature and so on. Data from these secondary sources needs to be analysed so that the researcher has the knowledge to define the problem. For our problem of low sales, since it is a new product in the market, it may be difficult to obtain information. But a researcher can get some related information, which may help him to a certain extent in defining the problem. Pilot studies involve collecting data from the actual respondents in order to gain insight into the topic and help the researcher in conducting a larger study. Here, data are collected informally in order to find out the views of the respondents. The researchers may casually seek the respondent's opinion of the new cell phone wave protectors. Once the research problem is identified and clearly defined, and a formal statement containing the research objectives must be developed.

2.1.3 Preparing the Statement of Research Objectives

Once the problem is clearly defined, it becomes absolutely essential to determine the objectives of the research. The objectives of the research should be stated in a formal research statement. The statement of objectives should be as precise as possible. Objectives act as guidelines for various steps in the research process, and therefore, they have to be developed by analysing the purpose of the research thoroughly. The objectives of the research must be brief and specific; also, it is preferable to limit the number of objectives. The research objectives comprise the research question/s and the hypothesis. If the objective of the research is to study the perceptions of the customer, a typical research question could be: 'Do the customers perceive the radiations from their cell phones to be hazardous to health?'. Once the objectives and the research questions are identified, a researcher has to develop a hypothesis statement that reflects these research objectives.

2.1.4 Developing the Hypotheses

A hypothesis is a statement based on some presumptions about the existence of a relationship between two or more variables that can be tested through empirical data. For instance, the exploratory research for the above problem may have resulted in the hypothesis that consumers perceive that the radiations emanating from the cell phone are harmful. When a researcher is developing a hypothesis, he/she will try to assume an answer for a particular research question and then test it for its validity.

A hypothesis normally makes the research question clearer to the researcher. For instance, if the research question is—'Why are the sales of refrigerators going up in winter? In this case, the hypothesis could be—'The sales of refrigerators are going up during winter due to off-season discounts' This makes the research question much clearer. The formulation of a hypothesis allows the researcher to make a presumption or 'guess' and can thus ensure that all the relevant aspects of the research are included in the research design. For instance, the above example gives the researcher scope to include a question on off-season discounts in the questionnaire during the research design phase.

If a research study is to be conducted about the consumption patterns of tea and coffee in India, the hypothesis could be: 'Consumption of tea is higher in North India and coffee in South India because of the varying lifestyles of these two regions'. This hypothesis adds factors of geographic location and lifestyle to the research problem. For any research question, several hypotheses can be developed, but there are limits to the number of hypotheses that can be validated. Researchers should avoid including any hypothesis that has already been validated by other similar studies.

However, a hypothesis cannot be developed for every research question. Moreover, a vague hypothesis may be of no use at all. For example, if a company wants to know whether its sales will increase, then a hypothesis—'The sales will increase' versus 'The sales will not increase' will add little value to the research question as they are almost the same as the research question itself. Once the hypothesis is developed, the next stage in the research process, the research design phase, begins.

Before proceeding to the next stage, it is essential to consider two points. The first one is to assess the value of information that is being sought. In this stage, it is important to conduct a cost-benefit analysis, wherein the costs incurred on obtaining the needed information are compared with the benefits accruing to the organization. If the costs are more than the benefits, then it is better to halt the research, while the subsequent phases of the research process can be carried on if the benefit is greater than the cost. The second point is to ensure that the required information does not already exist as it would make the research effort futile.

2.1.5 Planning the Research Design

Once the problem or opportunity identification and definition stage is complete, the process of research design begins. Planning the research design is a crucial step in the research design process. A research design is the actual framework of a research that provides specific details regarding the process to be followed in conducting the research. The research is designed based on the objectives formulated during the initial phases of the research. The research design includes all the details regarding the research such as where the information should be obtained from, the time and budget allotted for conducting the research, the appropriate measurement techniques and the sampling process. Factors like the research objective, the importance of the decision, costs involved in conducting the research and the availability of data sources determine the selection of an appropriate research design. The design and implementation process for business research have been discussed in Chap. 3.

2.1.6 Selecting the Research Method

After developing an appropriate research plan, it is important for the researcher to select a proper research method. There are four basic methods of conducting a research study—secondary data studies, surveys, experiments and observation. The research design method is chosen based on the objectives of the study, the costs involved in conducting the study, the availability of the data and finally the importance and urgency of the decision. We will now discuss the four basic research methods.

2.1.7 Surveys

A survey is a research technique, which is used to gather information from a sample of respondents by employing a questionnaire. Surveys are normally carried out to obtain primary data. Primary data are the data that are gathered first hand to answer the research question being investigated. Surveys are conventionally conducted by meeting the respondents in person or contacting them through the telephone. In the past few years, the Internet has started being widely used for conducting surveys through email. A researcher can personally meet the respondents to survey their preferences of television channels. Another researcher may use a telephone to ask the consumer about his satisfaction levels related to a newly purchased product. Yet another researcher may send an email to a respondent to check whether he is interested in a new insurance policy. These methods have their own advantages and disadvantages. Researchers adopt any of these methods depending on their requirement.

2.1.8 Experiments

In business research, experiments can be conducted for studying cause-and-effect relationships. Analysing the changes in one variable, by manipulating another variable, helps one identify cause-and-effect relationships through experiments. For instance, analysing the sales targets achieved by individual salespersons by manipulating their monetary rewards is a typical example of experimentation. Test marketing conducted by companies to test the viability of their new product in the market is a form of business experimentation.

2.1.9 Secondary Data Studies

A secondary data study is concerned with the analysis of already existing data that is related to the research topic in question. In secondary data studies, secondary data are studied in order to analyse the future sales of a product. For instance, for the cell phone wave protector research, secondary data regarding the telecommunications set-up, mobile networking, the waves used for communication in wireless telephony and its effects, may be essential for assessing the future sales trends of the cell phone wave protector. Secondary data studies help in projecting future sales trends using some mathematical models.

2.1.10 Observation Techniques

Observation technique is a process where the respondents are merely observed without any interruption by the observers. For instance, the shopping patterns of customers in supermarkets assessed by the observers or by counting the number of vehicles passing through a junction can qualify as observation research. The advantage of this method is that the observers do not depend on the respondents for their responses as they are only observed and are not asked to participate in the research process. Although the observation technique is useful, it cannot be used for studying several other factors such as motivations, attitudes and so on.

2.1.11 Analysing Research Designs

Although several research designs are available for a researcher to choose from, it is very difficult to say that a particular research design best suits a particular business research problem. Therefore, researchers should be cautious while selecting a research design. The best method to select a research design is to work backwards; that is, a research design should be selected based on the end result that needs to be obtained. For instance, to study the cell phone usage patterns of customers in public places, an observation technique would be a better method than a survey research as it would save on research costs and would not require the researchers to rely on the responses of the respondents.

Once the researcher selects a research method that is most appropriate for the research, he now needs to develop a sampling procedure. Sampling is the most important activity pertaining to the planning phase of the business research process.

2.1.12 Selecting the Sampling Procedure

Sampling is generally a part of the research design but is considered separately in the research process. Sampling is a process that uses a small number of items or a small portion of a population to draw conclusions regarding the whole population. Alternately, a sample can be considered as a subset of a larger set called the population. A well-defined sample has the same characteristics as the population as a whole, and therefore, when a research is conducted on such sample, the results obtained will represent the characteristics of the whole population. But if errors are made in selecting the sample, then the research results will be wrong, since a wrongly selected sample does not represent the characteristics of the population as a whole. For instance, to study the petrol and diesel consumption patterns of people, if a sample is selected from a list of vehicle owners, it may not represent the whole population, since there are several others who use petrol or diesel for running generators or for purposes other than travelling. It is therefore very important to define the population before selecting the sample; otherwise, the research results may not be helpful for the manager in taking effective decisions. For example, a television manufacturing company wanting to assess its future sales potential may select a sample from a population of households having no TV sets at all. But there may be several TV owners who may want to buy a second TV set or replace the existing one, and if they are not included in the population, then the research results may not be accurate.

Another important aspect of sampling is to decide the size of the sample. How big should a sample be? The bigger the sample size the greater will be its precision. But for practical reasons, it is not feasible to select large samples. Therefore, a sample that is selected using probability sampling techniques will be sufficient for getting effective results. A sample can be selected in two ways from a population—through probability sampling, or through non-probability sampling. When the subsets of a population are chosen in such a way that it ensures a representative cross-section by giving every element in the population a known chance of being selected, it is called probability sampling. When subsets of a population in which little or no attempt is made to ensure a representative cross-section are chosen, it is called non-probability sampling. Sampling has been extensively discussed in Chap. 6.

All the steps in the business research process till selecting the sampling procedure constitute the planning phase. The execution phase of the research process begins with data collection that is the next logical step following the sampling procedure. Once a researcher decides on a sample, he needs to obtain data from this sample. We will discuss this process in the following section.

2.1.13 Data Collection

After preparing a suitable sample, the researcher collects the data from the units in this sample. As there are several research techniques, there are a number of data collection methods as well. For instance, in the survey method, the data are collected by asking the respondents to fill out a questionnaire administered to them, while in the observation technique, the respondents are just observed without their direct participation in the research. Whatever the method used to collect the data, it is very important that the data are collected without any errors. Errors may creep in during the data collection process in several forms. Potential data collection errors may arise if the interviewee does not understand the question or if the interviewer records the answers inaccurately. The various types of data collection errors are discussed in Chap. 4.

Data collection is done in two stages—pre-testing and the main study. Pre-testing involves collecting data from a small subsample to test whether the data collection plan for the main study is appropriate. This helps the researchers to minimize any potential errors that may crop up during the main study. The pre-test results may also be used to decide on a way of tabulating the collected data. If the results of a pre-test are not appropriate for decision-making, then the researcher may consider altering the research design.

Once the data are collected to the satisfaction of the researcher, the research process enters the next stage, which is evaluation of the data.

2.1.14 Evaluating the Data

Once the data have been collected, the next important phase in the research process is evaluating the data. The most important aspect of data evaluation is to convert the data collected into a format which will facilitate the manager in effective decision-making. The reason for analysing the data is to obtain research results and to prepare the research report. Several mathematical and statistical models are used to evaluate the data. Evaluation of data normally starts with editing and coding of the data. Editing is undertaken to verify the data and check for any potential errors or for any inconsistencies and so on. Another task of editing is to remove any errors that may have cropped up during the interview such as recording the answers under the wrong columns of a questionnaire and so on. Coding is a process of assigning different symbols to different sets of responses. The coding process is done so that the data can be fed in and interpreted easily using computers. These days, technological advances have made it possible for data to be collected and directly fed into computers, removing the possibility of human error. For instance, an interviewer may question respondents through telephone and record the answers directly into a computer, where the data are processed almost immediately, thus eliminating the scope for errors which may arise if conventional methods of data collection are used.

2.1.15   Analysis

The interpretation of the data that have been collected by using different analytical techniques according to the requirements of the management is called analysis. Several statistical tools are used for data analysis, in order to make the analysis suitable for effective decision-making. The statistical analysis of the data may range from simple frequency distribution tables to complex multivariate analysis.

2.1.16   Preparing and Presenting the Research Report

After the evaluation of the data, the last and the major phase that comes into picture is the preparation of a research report. The research reports can be presented either in oral or in written format. The research report should contain a brief description of the objectives of the research, a summary of the research design adopted, a summary of the major findings and conclude with the limitations and recommendations. The purpose of conducting any research is to obtain information that can aid in efficient decision-making. Therefore, it is very important to carefully analyse the information obtained and present it according to the requirements of the management of the company. At this stage, the research report should be developed most efficiently and it should portray the research findings most effectively. Most often researchers fill the research reports with all the technical details. This should be avoided to the maximum possible extent, as the management is more interested in the actual research results and they have to be presented lucidly in a concise format. The amount of information provided in the research report should be based on the requirements of the manager. A research report also acts as a historical document, in the sense that the manager may refer to this document in the future if a research on the same lines is being conducted sometime in the future.

2.2 Summary

The business research process can be considered as the framework of the entire topic of business research. It involves a series of steps starting from the identification of the problem or opportunity to the stage of preparing the research report. These stages are as follows: identification and definition of the problem or opportunity, planning the research design, selecting a research method, selecting a sampling procedure, data collection, evaluating the data and finally preparing and presenting the research report. Any business research is primarily conducted for taking effective managerial decisions regarding various problems or opportunities identified by the organization.

Whenever a company identifies a potential problem or opportunity, it recognizes the need for conducting a research study. Once the problem is clearly identified, the manager can check whether the required information is already present; if such information is easily accessible, then the manager need not spend a lot of resources in obtaining the same information again. After clearly identifying the problem, it needs to be defined accordingly, and subsequently, the objectives of the research are determined. Development of the hypothesis plays a crucial role in the research process. Once this is done, the research boundaries are defined followed by estimating the value of information to be obtained against the costs incurred on conducting the research. At this stage, the most important part of the research begins, that is, planning the research design and involves the selection of the sample and the measurement technique. After this, the data are collected and evaluated and are later presented in the form of a report to the company's management for decision-making.

Part II
Research Design

Chapter 3
Business Research Design: Exploratory, Descriptive and Causal Designs

Learning Objectives

After reading this chapter, the reader should be able to:

1. Understand the meaning of research design, select and develop appropriate research design to solve the concerned management dilemma.
2. Understand the basic difference between the three research designs: exploratory, descriptive and causal research designs.
3. Identify the mode, techniques and plan for data collection for collecting necessary information to solve business research problem.

S. Sreejesh et al., *Business Research Methods*,
DOI: 10.1007/978-3-319-00539-3_3,
© Springer International Publishing Switzerland 2014

Chapter Overview

The objective of this chapter is to define and explain research design in detail. In this chapter, we discussed three major types of research designs, such as exploratory, descriptive and causal research designs. We also explained the mode of data used in each of these designs and the techniques to collect these data, which would ultimately helps the researcher to decide appropriate analysis technique. This chapter concludes with budgeting and scheduling of a business research project and elaborated the guidelines for writing a business research proposal. This chapter designed in such a way that the reader can appreciate these concepts by considering the examples and cartoon illustrations, which would better elicit and convince the concept understanding.

3.1 Introduction

Once the researcher has identified and established the broad approach to the research problem, the next step is to prepare a framework or blue print of the study, which specifies the procedures necessary for achieving the stated objectives in a robust manner. This framework helps the researcher to lay foundation for conducting business research project. A well-prepared framework will ensure that the business research project is conducted in an efficient and effective manner.

Research design can be defined as a framework or blue print for conducting business research project in an efficient manner. It details the procedures necessary for collection, measurement and analysis of information which helps the researcher to structure/or solve business research problems.

Typically, a good and well-planned research design consists of the following components, or tasks:

1. Selection of appropriate type of design: Exploratory, descriptive and/or causal design.
2. Identification of specific information needed based problem in hand and the selected design.
3. Specification of measurement and scaling procedures for measuring the selected information.
4. Mode of collection of information and specification of appropriate form for data collection.
5. Designing of appropriate sampling process and sample size.
6. Specification of appropriate data analysis method.

Some important characteristics of a good research design are flexibility, adaptability, efficiency, being economy and so on. A good research design should minimize bias and maximize accuracy of the data obtained and should have as few errors as possible. The most important requirement of good research design is that it should provide adequate information so that the research problem can be analysed on a wide perspective. An ideal design should take into account important factors like:

1. Identifying the exact research problem to be studied
2. The objective of the research
3. The process of obtaining information and
4. The availability of adequate time and financial resources.

Case 1: Johnson & Johnson and Cause-Related Marketing Initiatives

Product failures and litigations is not a new story for Johnson & Johnson. In September 1982, the company faced a tragedy when seven people died from ingesting Tylenol capsules that had been laced with cyanide. Soon after the tragedy, the company stopped the advertising and recalled all Tyenol products from the market. The FDA investigations found that the tampering had been done at the retail level rather than during manufacturing. In the next 2 weeks after these deaths, the company's stocks dropped 18 % and its major competitors products Datril and Anacin-3 were in such demand that supplies were back ordered. The company was able to restore its losses and confidence among the masses via several marketing strategies. The company ran a one-time advertising that explained how to exchange Tylenol capsules for tablets or refunds and worked closely with the press, responding directly to reporter's questions as a means of keeping the public up to date. The company also placed a price reduction offer of $2.50 to any Tylenol products in newspapers across the country.

In 2002, the company introduced Ortho Evra birth-control patch, considered to be good hit in the market, because of its benefits to younger women as a convenient alternative to the pill. Time magazine quoted this as 'coolest inventions' of the year. But at the end of 2005, the first lawsuits were filed against J&J claiming that the patch cause blood clots that could lead to heart attack or stroke and that the company misled the doctors and regulators for years by withholding data on those risks. Figure 3.1 shows that there are around 40 women died after using this patch. One victim was Ashley Lewis a 17-year-old high school girl who died in 2003, leaving behind a 1-year-old son. Reports shows that of the 4,000 lawsuits the Ortho Evra patch has spawned, most have either been settled under confidential terms with admitting the liability or dismissed.[1] In response to FDA regulations, J&J strengthened the patch in several time since 2005. However, without considering these rules and regulations, the patch remains on the market, and J&J is still defending against patent lawsuits over the product.

In this context, the company decided to restore its decaling image about its product among public through introducing cause-marketing programmes. Cause-related marking is a strategy in which a 'for-profit' organization aligns itself with a worthwhile cause. There are several incentives for a company to use a cause-related marketing strategy. First, a company can improve its public image by showing that it is interested in more than just making profits. Second, a company can also increase demand for its goods and gain a competitive advantage. For instance, consumers would be more willing to purchase something from a company that they know donates a portion of their proceeds to a charity than from a company that just keeps all the profits for itself.

---

[1] By David Voreacos, Alex Nussbaum and Greg Farrel, Johnson and Johnson reaches a band-aid, Bloomberg Business week.

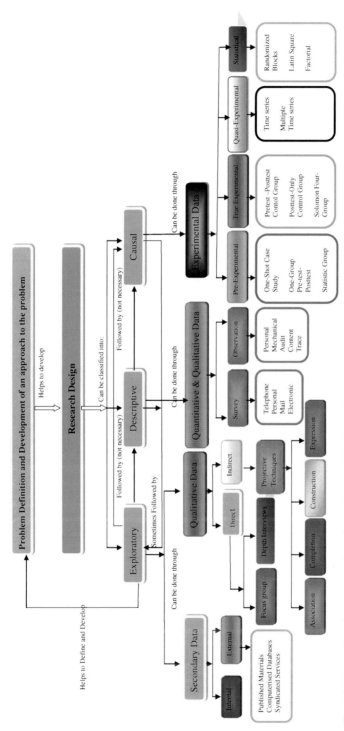

Fig. 3.1 Research design: an overview. *Source* Prepared by the Author

As part of its introduction of cause-marketing activities, the company conducted an exploratory research in the form of secondary data analysis and focus groups. The main objective behind this exploratory analysis was to identify the major factors that determine the social causes that a pharmaceutical company should be concerned about. From the exploratory investigation, the company found that the major social causes that the industry concerned about are the following: child care, drug abuse, public education, hunger, crime, the environment, medical research and poverty.

After the exploratory findings, the company decided to conduct a conclusive research that was in the nature of a descriptive cross-sectional survey. The major objective behind this survey was to understand how and why cause-related marketing influences consumers' perception of company's brand and to identify the relative importance of each attribute identified in the exploratory research. The company uses a random sample of 1,000 Indian consumers and conducted a telephonic interview. The findings of the study showed that about 50 % of the respondents stated the fact that when price and quality of the pharmaceutical products are equal, they would switch to a brand that supports good causes, protect the environment and caring about the public. The survey also support the fact that more than half of the people that the company surveyed would be able to pay a premium to those brands or products which is linked to a good cause. In short, the overall survey revealed the fact that the general public in India would give more image and greater trust to those companies and products that is linked to a good cause (see Table 3.1: Findings of the survey, Social Issues Johnson & Johnson should concern about).

After this survey, company has been working hard towards becoming more environmental friendly by: reducing generated hazardous waste, decreasing water use, and using alternative sources of energy for production. This is a smart move for Johnson & Johnson, because they were one of the first one to recognize the environmentally friendly social movement that has been happening all around the world. Another way that Johnson & Johnson is improving its image is by partnering with organizations such as UNICEF to provide medical care for women and babies in India and by contributing millions of dollars each year to humanitarian works all around the world. Even though companies that implement cause-related marketing strategy exercise their social responsibility, some critics see this as 'cause-exploitation'. This is because cause-related marketing allows a company to improve its image, increase sales and gain a competitive advantage; some companies may choose to implement this strategy not to exercising their social responsibility, but just to have its benefits.

Table 3.1 Findings of the survey, social issues Johnson & Johnson should concern about

Social issues	Relative importance
Public education	0.10
Crime	0.05
Environment	0.35
Poverty	0.05
Medical research	0.05
Hunger	0.05
Child care	0.20
Drug abuse	0.15

3.2   Part I: Exploratory Research Design

Exploratory research is carried out to make problem suited to more precise investigation or to frame a working hypothesis from an operational perspective. Exploratory studies help in understanding and assessing the critical issues of problems. It is not used in cases where a definite result is desired. However, the study results are used for subsequent research to attain conclusive results for a particular problem situation. In short, exploratory research can be used to obtain necessary information and to develop a proper foundation for conducting detailed research later. Exploratory studies are conducted for three main reasons, to analyse a problem situation, to evaluate alternatives and to discover new ideas. Consider for instance that the top management of a company has ordered the research department to evaluate the company's production pattern. This is not a clearly defined problem situation for researchers. Therefore, they will first conduct exploratory studies to understand all aspects relating to the company's production process right from purchasing raw materials, inventory management, processing them into finished goods and stocking them.

3.2.1   Exploratory Research Design: Secondary Data

A classification of secondary data at this stage will give a better understanding into the usefulness of the various sources of secondary data. Classification of secondary data is based on source, category, medium and database. A diagrammatic representation of the classification is provided in Fig. 3.2.

3.2.1.1   Classification by Source

This is the simplest way of classifying any sort of data. The source of data can be either internal or external. Internal sources of secondary data are those that are available within the organization. Examples of internal sources of secondary data are departmental reports, production summaries, financial and accounting reports

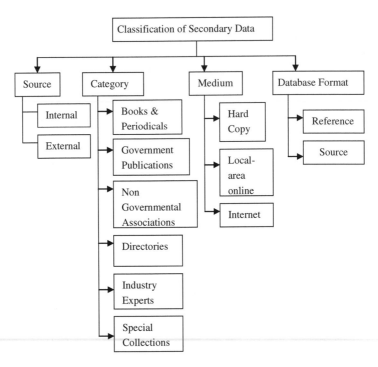

Fig. 3.2 Classification of secondary data

and marketing and sales studies. Internal sources might be the only source of secondary information in some cases, whereas in others it might just be the starting point. Internal records can be obtained from every department of the company where they are generated and stored. Sales records can be a source of valuable information regarding territorywise sales, sales by customer type, prices and discounts, average size of order by customer, customer type, geographical area, average sales by sales person and sales by pack size and pack type, trends within the enterprise's existing customer group, etc. Financial data records have information regarding the cost of producing, storing, transporting and product lines. Such data prove to be useful in the measurement of the efficiency of marketing operations and also estimation of the costs attached to new products. Miscellaneous reports that include researches conducted in the past, unique audits and outsourced information may also have significance for current researches. For example, if Hindustan Lever Limited which deals in diversified products carries out an analysis of media habits or advertising effectiveness for one of its products, then it is likely that the information will also be useful for other products appealing to the same target market. Though these data sources hold great potential, it is surprising to note that companies and researchers frequently fail to look into these valuable records.

External sources of secondary data are those that exist outside the company in the form of books and periodicals, government sources, computer-retrievable databases, trade and manufacturers' associations, publications, media sources, commercial sources, syndicated services, directories, external experts and special collections. These sources can also provide valuable information pertaining to research.

3.2.1.2 Classification by Category

Classifying secondary data by category, we put the sources under books and periodicals, databases, government documents, publications, associations, external experts, directories, media sources, commercial sources and special collections.

Books and periodicals

Books and periodicals procured from various sources are a typical source for a desk researcher. A researcher who locates the right book pertaining to his research gets off to a good start. Journal of Business Research, Journal of Accounting Research, Journal of Marketing Research, Financial Analysts Journal are some of the professional journals that contain much needed and useful information that serve as rich sources of secondary data.

Business Week, Business World, Economist, Fortune and Harvard Business Review are some of the magazines that feature research surveys and cover general business trends both nationally and internationally. Fortune magazine brings out a list of the top 500 companies in the world in terms of sales volumes, revenues generated, best practices, etc. which are of great help to researchers in garnering vital information.

Most metropolitan areas have periodicals and journals specific to the developments in that particular area. Most business and consumer magazines can also be a boon for secondary research as they obtain updated data through their research departments and make them available in the marketplace.

Newspapers can also be a vital source for market research information. All major newspapers have a business section that brings out industry-specific information and also the general trends in the market. In India, we have newspapers like the Economic Times, Business Standard, The Financial Times, etc. which provide only business-related news. Such sources prove to be of great help for researchers in anticipating trends in various businesses.

Government publications

Government agencies and their publications can be a vital source of secondary information for the market researcher. Taking the case of our own country India, we have a number of government agencies and publications that can be a source of secondary data for research.

In India, we have the reports and publications from The Registrar General of India, The Central Statistical Organization (CSO), Planning Commission, RBI, Department of Economic Affairs, Ministry of Food and Agriculture, The Indian Labour Bureau, etc. The Registrar General of India conducts a population census for the whole country every 10 years that gives a huge report about the demographic data. Another government agency called The CSO has various publications such as 'Estimates of National Product, Savings and capital Formation'—

which come out annually and compile the estimates of national income for several years, and the 'Statistical Abstract, India'—which is also an annual publication containing economic statistics for various sectors usually for 5 years which includes additional statewise statistics for the previous year. It has also a publication called, 'Annual Survey of Industries'(ASI), which compiles detailed data on the performance of the industrial sector in terms of the number of companies in an industry, employees (workers and non-workers), productive capital employed, total production by product types, fixed and variable costs. The data collected through ASI relate to capital, employment and emoluments, consumption of fuel and lubricants, raw material and other input/output, value added, labour turnover, absenteeism, labour cost, construction of houses by employers for their employees and other characteristics of factories/industrial establishments. Another important publication of the CSO is the Monthly Statistics of the Production of

---

Exhibit 3.1: Useful Governmental Publications

- The Wholesale Price Index numbers by The Office of the Economic Advisor, Ministry of Commerce and Industry which is weekly and covers various products such as food articles, food grains, minerals, fuel, power, textiles, chemicals, etc.
- All-India Consumer Price Index by the Government of India.
- Basic Statistics Relating to the Indian Economy by the Planning Commission.
- Reserve Bank of India Bulletin, Currency and Finance Report, which are monthly and annual journals, respectively, by the RBI, covering currency and financial aspects in general.
- The Economic Survey, a yearly publication of the Department of Economic Affairs, Ministry of Finance. This is published on the eve of the presentation of the national budget.
- Agricultural Situation in India by the Department of Economic Affairs, Ministry of Food and Agriculture. This monthly journal compiles reports and assessments of the agricultural situations in the country.
- The Indian Labor Journal a monthly publication of The Indian Labour Bureau, which contains detailed statistics on price indices, wages and earnings absenteeism, etc.

Adapted from Beri (1989)

The Director General of Commercial Intelligence, brings out monthly statistics of foreign trade in two parts, that is, export and import. This report also contains vast past records that help researchers to learn about the changing face of India's foreign trade. The National Sample Survey (NSS) is another important source, also worth mentioning in this context, as it publishes data regarding social, economic, demographic, industrial and agricultural statistics on an elaborate and continuing basis. Some other publications that are useful to researchers are given in Exhibit 3.1.

As in India, we also have a number of useful government publications in other countries. These publications would be useful for those companies that are planning to venture into the international markets. Taking the case of United States, we have the Internal Revenue Service (IRS) from the Department of Treasury which provides information on the IRS strategic plans for coming years, annual performance plans and other budgetary information; The Bureau of International Labour Affairs from the U.S. Department of Labour publishes The International Price Programme through Import Price Indexes (MPI) and Export Price Indexes (XPI) which contains data on changes in the prices of non-military goods and services traded between the United States and the rest of the world. Some of the major state department publications in the Unites States are 'Battling International Bribery' which is the Department of State's report on enforcement and monitoring of the OECD Convention and 'Country Reports' submitted annually to the Congress by the Department of State regarding the status of internationally recognized human rights practices.

Other government agencies in the United States which bring out useful secondary information are The Bureau of Alcohol, Tobacco, Firearms and Explosives, Bureau of Industry and Security from the U.S. Department of Commerce, The U.S. Food and Drug Administration, etc. The U.S. Environmental Protection Agency brings out the publication 'Waste management reports—selected publications related to climate change and municipal waste management' The Economic Report of the President is an annual report written by the Chairman of the Council of Economic Advisors which gives the nation's economic progress using text and extensive data appendices.

Non-governmental associations

Apart from the official publications, there are also loads of non-governmental or private organizational reports that can be useful to researchers. Various industry and trade associations are worth mentioning in this context. The Indian Cotton Mills Federation publishes statistics on the cotton textile industry. The Bombay Mill Owners' Association similarly publishes in its annual report statistics on the performance of its member units. Other non-governmental sources of publications are the annual statistics by The Market Research and Statistical Bureau of the Coffee Board, Bangalore; 'India's Production, Exports and Internal Consumption of Coir and Coir Goods' an annual publication by The Coir Board, Cochin; The Rubber Statistics, an annual report by The Rubber Board, Kottayam; the Indian Sugar Year Book by the Indian Sugar Mills Association, Delhi and a quarterly publication entitled 'Wool and Woolens of India' by The Indian Woolen Mills Federation. Apart from bringing out the latest statistics and details about the industry, these industrial and trade reports also provide an insight into the problems of the industry as a whole. The Steel Authority of India Ltd. also brings out, on a quarterly basis, a statistical publication relating to the functioning of the iron and steel industry in India.

Apart from these non-governmental associations, there exist several chambers of commerce. These include the Federation of Indian Chambers of Commerce and Industry (FICCI), Associated Chambers of Commerce and Industry of India and the Indo-American Chamber of Commerce, which have their own periodic publications highlighting the functioning and latest trends of a specific industry and the problems it faces.

Similarly, in the United States too, there are several non-governmental associations that publish industry-related information. 'The American Statistics Index' published monthly, quarterly and annually by LexisNexis, brings out indexes and abstracts of a wide range of statistical publications produced by the US government. 'FedStats' provides access to the statistics and information produced by more than 70 US federal agencies. Other non-governmental associations in the United States which provide statistical information are 'The Digital National Security Archive' which is a collection of primary documents central to US foreign and military policy since 1945. More than 35,000 declassified documents—totalling more than 200,000 pages—have been gathered through use of the US Freedom of Information Act (FOIA). LexisNexis Statistical Indexing and abstracts for over 100,000 U.S. government and non-government statistical publications with links to selected full text documents and agency web sites are available on the Net. Selected tables can be imported to spreadsheets, etc.

The governmental and non-governmental associations mentioned here are only a few of those available and illustrate the point that an ample amount of secondary data is always available at hand. One should make good use of these sources for various research purposes

Directories

While framing its marketing strategy, a company needs to take serious note of its potential competitors and customers. As such, the company has to be aware of the latest developments and market strategies of the major players in the industry. It is possible for the company to access such information through industry-specific directories. These directories give first-hand information about the existing players, their products and strategies. Researchers often make use of directories when they are preparing sampling frames. Stock exchange directories can be a handy source for detailed information on the corporate sector. For example, The Bombay Stock Exchange Directory is unique in providing detailed data on the financial accounts, key profitability and other important ratios of listed companies. The presentation makes it easy for earlier data to be replaced with the latest data without much difficulty.

Trade show directories are another useful source of secondary data. They help in identifying trade shows linked with a specific industry, along with information on individual companies including addresses, names of executives, product range and brand names. This facilitates establishing contact with sponsors and various exhibitors who participate in these exhibitions. Some Indian directories are '121 India' (Portal with news, entertainment, matrimonials and business), 'The City as it Happens' (detailed information about major metros, people and their lifestyles, pubs, latest fashion trends, etc.) and 'Tata Yellow Pages' (Guide offering classified information of products, services and organizations in major Indian cities).

Every country has its own Yellow Pages on the Internet. Some major directories in other countries include 'The Thomas Register of American Manufacturers' (New

York: Thomas Publishing Co.) which has data on more than 150,000 companies, 'Who Owns Whom' (North American Edition) lists 6,500 parent companies and 100,000 domestic and foreign subsidiaries and associated companies.

Industry experts

Looking out for industry experts for specific information is another means of collecting secondary data. These experts specialize in their own domain and so getting information from them is often highly useful for research. These experts give expression to their expertise knowledge through published articles and through consultation services. Hence, the best way to contact them would be by tracing published information articles to their authors or contacting consultancies offering specialized services. Examples of such expertise consulting services are Price Waterhouse Coopers (PWC) that has expert financial consultants; Data-monitor's Business Information Centre which provides services to the world's largest companies in the fields of automotive and logistics, consumer markets, energy and utilities, financial services, and healthcare and technology sectors and ACNielsen for industrial services.

Special collections

Special collections consist of diverse materials that include reference books; university publications consisting of master's theses, doctoral dissertations and research papers; company publications such as financial reports, company policy statements, speeches by eminent personalities, sales literature, etc. Miscellaneous data available from organizations that publish statistical compilations, research reports and proceedings of meetings also come under special collections. Finally, there are personal, historical and other social science research reports which find an occasional place in business studies.

Classification by Medium

Secondary data classified by medium include hard copy and Internet. Hard copy refers to non-database information. This comprises of all books, magazines, journals and special collections contained in hard-copy libraries. It is very difficult to get detailed indices for all hard copies.

With the advancement in technology in recent times, huge databases and information have become available on the Internet and these facilitate the new trend of data collection over the old tradition of spending long hours in the library. In fact, there is so much data available on the net that researchers at times do not need to go to other sources. Not only does it facilitate the retrieval of online data pertaining to the research, but also helps in gathering information from respondents via e-mail. Browsers such as Microsoft's Internet Explorer and Netscape's Navigator make it possible to access sites and user groups of all those connected through the Net.

There are two reasons which keep the researchers glued to the internet—first it makes it easy for the researcher to gather information regarding the advertising, promotions and communications of various products and services from the websites created by companies, and secondly, it acts as an interface between the user groups interested in a particular subject and the researcher. There are many databases available online which contain certain research papers, articles, etc., and a researcher can find data relevant to his topic in some database or the other. These can be accessed for a fixed amount or on a pay-as-you see basis. These data are updated regularly by those who provide and maintain them. All governmental and non-governmental associations, companies and publishing companies have their specific websites which one can surf through at a minimum cost to gather useful data. Such online databases are a resource to be converted to useable data for improved decision-making and analysis. Each of these websites has hypertext links to other useful data for similar purposes. Some websites also offer membership options. A person wanting to be a member pays a fixed amount of money and is then able to access the information stored in the database. Another form of multimedia database is the vast number of CD-ROM business databases that interrelate audio, video and text and provide search and download capabilities.

Classification by Database Content

Classification of secondary data by database content is useful for a better insight into the subject matter. A database is a collection of information in a detailed and standard format. A classification of database by the content of information includes online, internet and offline databases. Online databases consist of a central databank accessible by a terminal via a telecommunications network. Internet databases are those that can be accessed on the net and can also be downloaded if required. Offline databases are those which make the information available on diskettes and CD-ROMs. A further classification of these three highlights two common aspects. We will now look into each of these types in detail.

Reference database

A reference database provides a bibliography of documents, abstracts or locations of original information. Since they provide online indices, citations and abstracts, they are also referred to as bibliographic databases. Wide varieties of bibliographic databases are available for a variety of business research applications. Abstract Business Information (ABI) contains 150 word abstracts and 1,300-business publications worldwide. Reference databases enable the researcher to use natural-language key words to search for abstracts and summaries of a wide range of articles appearing in various business magazines, government reports, trade journals and research papers.

Some examples of reference databases are Predicasts Overview of Markets and Technology (PROMPT), Marketing and Advertising Reference Services (MARS), Aerospace/Defence Markets and Technology (A/DM&T), PTS Newsletter Database, F and S Index, etc. These databases contain index, word abstracts and full-text records, including competitor information and emerging technologies from trade and business publications worldwide.

Source databases

Source databases usually publish numerical data, full text or a combination of both. They include full texts of various economic and financial databases. Unlike reference databases, which are limited to providing indices and summaries these databases provide complete text and numerical information. Census-based numeric databases are often found to be useful for studies dealing with market potential, segmentation and site location evaluations. Time series data available online are also useful for tracking and forecasting.

Source databases provide data relating to economy and industries. They can be classified into full-text information sources, economic and financial statistical databases, online data and descriptive information on firms. Harvard Business Reviews Online, Hoovers Online, LexisNexis and EBSCO are good examples in this case. EBSCO facilitates access to various business databases and also special newspapers, periodicals, books and company annual reports.

3.2.1.3 Advantages of Secondary Data

Secondary data are used by managers as it is cheaper and takes less time to gather, thus saving them a lot of money and time that they would have otherwise spent in gathering primary data. Apart from these, there are other distinct advantages of using secondary data, which are as follows:

Secondary data can help identify, clarify and redefine the research problem: In situations where the actual problem in a research study cannot be defined or is defined in an ambiguous way, the use of secondary data can help clear the confusion with a clear definition of the problem to be probed into.

Secondary data might also hold a solution to the problem: Research problems might not require the gathering of primary data each time. Many a times, it happens that precise data regarding the current research is already available as secondary data that had been collected for some other research purpose. Hence, it might not be necessary to conduct a primary data collection exercise at all.

Secondary data may provide alternatives methods that can be used for primary research: Every research situation has a custom-made primary research designed for it. If such published reports are gathered from secondary sources, then it gives a push to the initial stages of the similar current research at hand by outlining the possible research alternatives.

Secondary data generate requisite information for better creativity: Secondary data can provide insights into the means to identify potential customers, industry trends and proper language usage. This prior knowledge helps in the design and progress of the current research. This provides a better chance of creativity in the research.

Although secondary data have many advantages to its credit, it has its own share of pitfalls and disadvantages. A close look at the utility of secondary data reveals the following limitations and disadvantages.

Lack of availability: Even though secondary data might be available for many research studies, it might so happen that there is no secondary data available for special cases or that the organization holding such data are not willing to make it accessible to outsiders. If a company like General Motors would like to conduct a research for the market potential of its cars in particular cities in India, then it is very unlikely that any secondary data would be available in this context.

Lack of relevance: Secondary data might be irrelevant because of the changes in competitive situation, changing trends and other variables in the research environment from the time the data were initially collected. Thus, its usage for a current research study might be limited. Relevance might be reduced due to difference in units of measurement, use of surrogate data in the secondary sources, difference in definition of classes and time.

Inaccurate data: Secondary data can be subject to doubt because of the errors that can occur in any of the steps or due to personal bias. Errors of this sort can make the secondary data inaccurate and therefore unusable. It is possible that the secondary source of data might have been custom made to avoid some specific realities and as such fail to mention the sources of error. Hence, an effort should always be made to trace the secondary data to its original source.

Insufficient data: Secondary might be available but they might not posses all the required data useful for the current research at hand.

3.2.1.4 Syndicated Data

Syndicated data are data produced by a market research firm, which provides a body of similar data compiled from a large number of sources, organized into a common format for a fee to its subscribers. This data are neither available nor can be gathered from any internal source. Such data are not client-specific, but are flexible enough to be custom made to suit particular researches. A brief classification of syndicated data has the following three inclusions that are also shown below in Fig. 3.3. Syndicated data can be collected using the following.

- Surveys
- Audits
- Panels
- Warranty cards.

Surveys
Commercial surveys undertaken by research organizations fall under three categories, that is, periodic surveys, panel surveys and shared surveys.

Periodic Surveys
These are surveys that are conducted at regular intervals—weekly, monthly, quarterly or annually. The sample respondents are different each time the survey is conducted. Though the sample population differs, the topic of the survey remains the same allowing the researcher to analyse the changing trends. This type of survey does not facilitate the study of trends at the individual level as the respondents of the survey change over a period of time. These surveys can be used to study changing trends in the competitive environment or consumer behaviour. Mail, personal interviews and telephonic interviews are some of the methods of conducting commercial surveys.

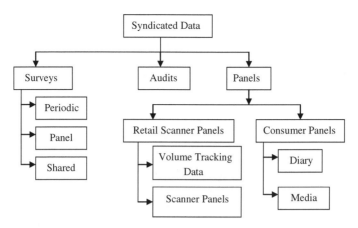

Fig. 3.3 Syndicated data

Panel Surveys

Panel surveys are those surveys that are conducted among a group of respondents who have agreed to respond to a number of mail, telephone and personal interviews over a period of time. Unlike random online surveys, panel surveys are more effectiveness as the participants' key demographics; behavioural patterns and selected product ownership information are readily and voluntarily available. This allows the researchers to have quick access to a nationally representative sample, core target audiences or both.

As the researcher can draw samples with varied specifications from the same panel, it is possible to survey the same panel members over and over again within the reference time period to find the changes in their response to various marketing stimuli. The agreement of the panel members to be interviewed repeatedly saves the researcher from the tedious task of generating new sample frames each time leading to wastage in time and resources. Thus, the panel survey method scores over random sampling. Data are collected mainly by mail, but the use of personal interviews, telephonic interviews and focus groups are also prevalent in panel surveys.

Interval panels are mostly used for cross-sectional, that is, one-time surveys where no attempt is made to replicate the conditions of the previous surveys excepting that the actual questions posed to the respondents may differ in vocabulary or meaning, and the sampling and field procedures may not be the same as in previous surveys. The essential feature panel surveys offer is that they make it possible to detect and establish the nature of individual change. A major advantage is the high response rate obtained. Various types of panels and their uses are discussed later.

Shared Surveys

Shared surveys conducted by a research firm use questionnaires that contain a pool of questions that are of interest to different clients. Hence, these are known as multi-client surveys and are sometimes called omnibus surveys. The questionnaire features standard demographic questions along with other questions asked by each client. Clients do not have any sort of access to either the data or the questions asked by other clients. The findings of the survey are tabulated according to the needs of the client. Such surveys are mostly conducted through mail, telephone or personal interviews. Respondents are selected from interval panels or selected randomly from a larger population.

Shared surveys offer several advantages. Firstly, since the fixed cost of sample design and other variable costs are borne by many clients, the cost per question is usually low. The pricing is based on the number of questions asked by each client. The cost per question decreases as the number of questions increases. Sampling consisting of interval panel members offers extra benefits as the extensive demographic data associated with each panel member can be used in the analysis of the responses. Surveys can be generally used for market segmentation (with psychographic and lifestyle data for establishing consumer profiles), product image determination, price perception analysis and evaluation of the effectiveness of advertising.

Surveys are advantageous in that they are flexible enough to collect data from different segments of the society regarding consumers' motives, attitudes and preferences. They even help to locate intergroup differences based on demographic variables and even help to forecast the future. But their utility may be limited due to respondent bias. There may be a difference between what the respondent says and what he does, or he might be influenced to give socially desirable responses.

Audits

An audit involves an in-depth analysis of the existing situation in a firm. In business, there are many activities that can be subject to an audit. Audits are carried out by the physical inspection of inventories, sales receipts, shelf facings, prices and other aspects of the marketing mix to determine sales, market share, relative price, distribution and other relevant information. A performance audit is an objective and systematic examination of evidence in order to provide an independent assessment of the performance of an organization, programme, activity or function, so that information to improve accountability and facilitate decision-making can be made available to the parties responsible for overseeing or initiating corrective action. Audits are of different types such as store audits, product audits and retail distribution audits.

Store audits examine the quantity of a product that is being sold at the retail level. Nielsen Retail Index provides such audited data. Generally, such audits provide data on the total sales of all the packaged goods carried by the different types of retail stores sampled for auditing. The packaged goods considered for store audit include food, tobacco, pharmaceuticals, beverages, etc. Retailers and wholesalers who participate in the auditing get cash and the much-needed auditing reports as incentive. Store audits allow the marketers to measure the performance of their brands against the competitors. They can also help marketers to evaluate the main reasons for the product being off-shelf on the basis of supply/distribution problems, incorrect master data and store replenishment issues.

Product audits are similar to store audits in the information provided but focus on covering all types of outlets that store a particular product. For example, a store audit for Close-up toothpaste can help to estimate the total potential market and distribution of sales by type of outlet and various regions. The product audit for the same would include grocery stores, mass merchandisers and retail chain stores. Retail distribution audits are also similar but they differ in their mode of operation. Auditors enter a retail shop unannounced, without permission, record the stock holdings, shelf facings and collect other relevant data for selected product categories. Pantry Audits are special audits used to find out customer preferences by studying the quantity, price and type of goods being purchased by the consumer. The method studies the buying pattern of the consumers relating to which type of consumers purchased what products and could be followed by a questioning session to find the exact reasons for the purchases done by the consumers. The limitation of this method is that it is difficult to specifically identify consumer preferences through this method if used as a stand-alone method especially in cases where promotional schemes are being run.

Auditing data find their uses in:

• Assessing brand shares and competitive activity
• Identifying inventory problems
• Developing sales potential and forecasts
• Determining total market size
• Monitoring promotional budgets based on sales volume.

Audit data provide accurate information on the sale of various products at various levels. However, they have the disadvantage of limited coverage and time factors. Unlike scanner data, audit data cannot be associated with consumer characteristics and advertising expenditures.

Panels

A panel is a group of individuals or organizations that have agreed to provide information to a researcher over a period of time. This section relates to continuous panels, which consist of samples who have agreed to participate in a survey and provide specified information or report specified behaviours on a regular basis within a reference time period. Panels are of various types such as:

• Retail Scanner Panels
• Consumer Panels.

Retail Scanner Panels

Retail panels consist of sample retail outlets, and retail panel surveys provide information based on sales data from the checkout scanner tapes of a sample of supermarkets and retailers that use electronic scanner systems. Supermarkets and big retail chains carry products that have barcodes, which make it easier to capture (using scanners), the details of the products sold by the retail stores on a real-time basis. Scanner data are obtained by passing merchandise over a laser scanner that optically reads the Universal Product Code (UPC) from the packages.

Another technology related to UPC is the Electronic Point-of-Sale (EPOS) systems. These are used extensively by retailers like K-Mart, Wal-Mart, Toys'-R'Us, Food World, etc. The mode of operation in both is similar. ScanTrack (A. C. Nielsen), InfoScan (IRI) and SRI (INTAGE) are some popular scanning services available to researchers. These panels have their own samples of retail chain outlets having the requisite technology. These samples consist of super-markets, drugstores, mass merchants and other smaller retail chains.

There are two types of scanner data that are available. They are volume-tracking data and scanner panels. Panel members are selected in a systematic way so as to ensure that they are representative of the total population. Detailed data are collected and stored for each of the participating households or individuals.

Volume-Tracking Data: In volume-tracking data, the UPC of all purchases made by customers is scanned by electronic scanners. These codes are then linked to their corresponding prices held in the computer memory after which the sales slip is prepared. The data are then analysed to deliver reports on purchases by brand, size, flavour and market share as against time, area and store classification, as specified by the client. These panels focus on exclusive markets and geographic regions for specified time periods. Retail scanner panels have been able to put down deep roots because of their flexibility and efficiency. Retail chains too can make use of this data to detect price elasticities, placement of products in the store and effects of in-store advertising and merchandising.

Scanner panels: Scanner panels are a little more advanced than the retail scanner panels and are used by IRI, NPD/Nielsen. In scanner panels, each household member of the selected sample household is given an identity card that has a code specific to the individual and which can be read by the electronic scanner. Thereafter, along with the scanning of all the products purchased, the customers are required to swipe their ID cards at the checkout counters. In this way, consumer identity is linked to the purchased products along with the time and date. Some firms alternatively provide their customers with hand-held scanners. Once back home, the selected consumers are required to scan the codes of the products they purchased. But in comparison with the automatic ID scanning, this requires more effort on the part of the consumer as, apart from the scanning at home, the store name, prices and other data have to be fed in manually. This is also known to create problems as for example in the case of goods consumed before reaching home, wrong entries of prices and unscanned data due to time pressures, which can affect the accuracy of the data entered.

Consumer Panels

Continuous consumer panels are those that monitor shifts in individual or specific household behaviours and attitudes over a period of time. They are helpful in gathering relevant data pertaining to competitors' strategies or own marketing strategy efficiency. They also make use of UPC or consumer diaries. The following sections will give a better insight into each of these functionalities.

Diary Panels: A diary panel as the name suggests is a panel of households who continuously record their purchases of selected products in a diary. Records are generally maintained for products frequently purchased like food items, household goods and personal-care products. Nielsen Household Services, MRCA and IN-TAGE are some of the famous suppliers of diary panel data. The number of product categories on which information is sought might vary from one service provider to another. Each panel of the vast sample of families and non-family households are required to report information on purchase of selected items, including the following data:

- Dates of purchase
- The number and sizes of the packages
- The total amount paid
- Payment mode, whether cash, credit or coupons
- Whether purchase was influenced by any promotional methods
- The store where the purchase was made.

Apart from these information sample respondents are also required to answer certain special questions that are specific for each product category. Recent developments are slowly replacing paper diaries by electronic diaries, where the sample respondents make their purchase entries online or by automatic electronic devices provided to them. Data provided by diary panels prove to be useful in sales forecasting, market share estimation, assessment of brand loyalty and brand switching and measuring advertising effectiveness. This method is not yet used extensively in India.

Media Panels: Media panels are used by researchers who are interested in knowing the media habits of their target customers. Media panels consist of sampled households whose television viewing behaviour is recorded through special electronic devices. This electronic device is a household meter wired to the TV and connected to a central computer by a telephone line. This arrangement automatically starts recording the specific channels that were being tuned to when the TV is switched on. But the limitation of this system is that the researcher cannot find out the number of viewers and their demographic characteristics.

To overcome this limitation, Nielsen Media Research came up with the Nielsen People Meter. These meters can be placed on the TV sets of the sample households which recorded two things, that is, the channel being tuned to and the person(s) watching. The operation is also simple. The meter is linked to a remote control that records the age and gender of each of the family members when they press the identifying button. The records are automatically fed into the central computer that already has the demographics of each of the family members. Thus, data for each day are stored.

Apart from these electronic meters, TV diaries and booklets are also used to collect the media habits of the households. This data are used by various service providers like A. C. Nielsen, INTAGE to estimate the number and percentage of all TV households viewing a specific show. This data are also disaggregated into various demographic and socioeconomic characteristics such as household income, size and age of members, education levels and geographic locations as per client specifications.

This technology has also stepped into tracking home video (cable, VCR, DVD players) and Internet indexes. Data gathered from media panels serve to be useful in establishing advertising rates by TV and radio networks, the selection of appropriate programming and profiling viewer and listener groups. Diary and media panels have distinct advantages over surveys. Respondents participate due to their own willingness and as such provide more and higher quality data than sample respondents. Secondly, the use of electronic devices that records at the time of purchase and TV switching eliminates human error in both diary (recall error) and media panels, respectively. These methods also have disadvantages in the form of lack of representativeness, maturation and response bias, refusal and attrition.

Warranty Cards

These postcard-sized cards are used commonly by dealers in the consumer durables industry. The dealer sends the card to the consumers who post them back, so that the dealer can gather information about the products from them.

3.2.2 Exploratory Research: Qualitative Data

The exquisiteness of qualitative research lies in its flexibility to adapt to different situations. Not only can it help in probing the sub-conscious mind of the respondent, but it also finds extensive use in brainstorming sessions that often pave the way for embarking upon product development or solving marketing problems. The participation of the customer in the brainstorming sessions can have a deep impact on the objectivity of the research.

Increase the Value of Subsequent Quantitative Research

Qualitative research can serve as a prelude to quantitative research. A quantitative research generally has a pre-designed set of responses. A respondent has to choose from the limited answers irrespective of whether or not they represent his true feelings. Such responses may have little value for the research. A better method would be to make use of qualitative research prior to conducting a more analytical quantitative research and try to include the most relevant responses in the questionnaire.

Obtain Visceral Feedback Instead of Just Number Crunching Data

Qualitative researches, unlike quantitative ones are not data centric. In addition to the ability of generating richer data, they also have the advantage of observing the respondents (in face-to-face interviews), which helps in probing the mind of the respondents and interpreting the information given by them.

Group Dynamics Enhance Results

Qualitative researches involve group dynamics where participants can interact with one another. This interaction has the inherent tendency to draw out responses that may not have been obtained in a one-to-one confrontation with the interviewer.

Customers are People, Not Pie Charts

Unlike quantitative research, which depicts the findings in the form of graphs and charts, qualitative research strives to expose the human perspective behind the findings. This makes it easier to understand and end-users find themselves more comfortable with the reports.

Qualitative research methods can be sub-divided into the following types and classified as represented in Fig. 3.4.

- Depth interviews
- Focus groups
- Projective techniques.

3.2.3 Depth Interviews

A qualitative approach in which a trained moderator conducts interviews with individuals, rather than with groups, to obtain information about a product or brand is known as a depth interview. These interviews are primarily conducted on a one-to-one basis. Therefore, they are also known as individual depth interviews. Depth interview is simply the routing of an ordinary conversation that permits both the researcher and the interviewer to interact and explore an issue.

A depth interview can serve as a prelude to a more analytical questionnaire design for quantitative research. Therefore, such interviews are used to unravel theoretical issues at an early stage in the development of a questionnaire.

Individual in-depth interviews can be subdivided into three types depending upon the amount of guidance extended by the interviewer. These are:

- Non-directive or unstructured interviews
- Semi-structured interviews
- Standardized open-ended interviews.

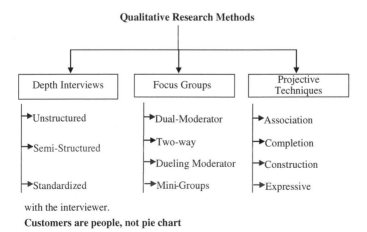

with the interviewer.

Customers are people, not pie chart

Fig. 3.4 Classification of qualitative research methods

3.2.3.1 Unstructured Interviews

Unstructured interviews take the form of a natural conversation and the interviewer brings up various topics that are of interest to him during the course of the conversation. The respondent is given the freedom to decide the direction of the conversation while expressing his opinions or narrating his experiences relating to a topic. This unstructured characteristic of the interview enables the interviewer to develop a rapport with the interviewee and understand him better. Unstructured interviews are also known as non-directive interviews as there are no pre-formulated set of questionnaires and no pre-determined paths to route the interviewee responses.

The success of a non-directive interview depends upon the interviewer's expertise in giving an informal touch to the interaction, his ability to probe into and elaborate on specific responses and in bringing back the discussion to line whenever it deviates from the relevant topic. Such interviews normally extend anywhere between an hour and two and can be tape recorded with the prior consent of the interviewee. Although flexible and responsive to individual and situational changes, this method is known to generate less systematic data and it is very difficult and time-consuming to classify and analyse such data.

3.2.3.2 Semi-Structured Interviews

These types of interviews are more structured than the non-directive interviews. While allowing some amount of flexibility to the interview, the interviewer ensures that he keeps the interview limited to the topics that are essential to the research. The interviewer at his discretion can make use of appropriate wordings and allocate a specific time for each question. This lends him sufficient flexibility to adapt to different responses. At this stage, probing techniques can be used to encourage the respondents to provide details for relevant responses. This technique is primarily used to interact with busy executives, technical experts and thought leaders. As the technique calls for interactions with experts, the interviewer must possess knowledge of the latest trends in technology, market demand, legislation and competitive activity. This will enable him to apply probing techniques better. Therefore, much depends upon the inherent skills of the interviewer.

Recording the answers may be a problem in case the interviewee dislikes it. To counter this, a group of interviewers, probably 3–4 can alternatively ask questions and note down the answers. Although advantageous in many respects, the technique is known to have no provision to permit the interviewer to probe into unanticipated issues cropping up during the interaction, which were not a part of the basic checklist. Even the flexibility regarding the choice of words of the interviewer may lend bias, leading to different responses from different individuals.

3.2.3.3 Standardized Open-Ended Interviews

This is different from the two interview methods described above with respect to the flexibility in the questionnaire. Here, the questionnaire contains a set of sequential ordered, carefully worded, open-ended questions. This reduces the differences in responses from different individuals due to the choice of words on the part of the interviewer. This technique is appropriate when two or more interviewers conduct the interviews. It minimizes the variation in the questions posed by them to different interviewees. These types of interviews enable the evaluator to collect data systematically, thus facilitating comparison of responses collected from different respondents. This method, however, limits the use of substitute questioning to probe into individual differences.

3.2.3.4 Techniques for Conducting Depth Interviews

Marketers rely on surveys, and demographic information to help them develop marketing strategies and tactics for their products. These marketers fall back on depth interviews when they do not have much knowledge about a population and desire to explore the same. This preliminary information can be gathered through three different interview techniques as recommended by Durgee. These are as follows:

Laddering

An interviewing technique that enables the interviewer to gain an insight into the subject's personal reasons for purchasing certain products is known as laddering. In this technique, the interviewer starts the interview with questions related to product attributes and slowly starts probing into user characteristics as the interview progresses. In other words, a tactful set of closely related questions probe into the product attributes, consequences and personal values behind a consumer's preferences for a product/service.

For example, a respondent may be asked to give the distinguishing features for his preference of supermarket A over supermarket B. The main motive in this technique is to trace the tangible aspects of the product/service to the intangible aspects of the respondent's mind to gain an insight into decision-making at an individual level. If the factors are 'ambience' and 'better service', the respondent is further probed on the specific ambience or service factor, to trace the linking of that factor to the sub-conscious mind of the respondent. The traceability of the tangible product attributes to the intangible aspects helps to determine the key factors in the sub-conscious mind that affect the buying behaviour of the respondent and to identify the hurdles preventing the greater diffusion of certain goods and/or services.

This technique, aims at obtaining cognitive maps, or Hierarchical Value Maps (HVMs) and is the most widely used method to uncover consumers' cognitive structures. The interviewer needs to have expertise in specific probing techniques to enable him to read the sub-conscious mind of the interviewee and frame the questions accordingly. The key to conducting successful laddering is practice. The following steps are necessary for a laddering interview to be successful.

- Choose a brand-loyal respondent who is uniquely capable of articulating the key aspects of the product he likes most.
- Start out with questions that get the customer talking about the product. This tends to put the respondents at ease and gets them accustomed to answering your questions about the product.
- Questions should always link to the previous response given by the interviewee, to construct a ladder establishing links between the attributes, consequences and values.
- The second round of questions begins by probing why certain attributes are important. Upon a specific response, the interviewer should keep probing deeper into that consequence to find the underlying value to identify the real reason behind the purchase.

Hidden-Issue Questioning

This interview technique aims to identify significant personal views that would otherwise not be revealed by respondents during a direct approach. This technique tries to probe into the hidden issues and items like daydreams, anxieties, fascinations and hopes in peoples' lives that do not surface in their day-to-day schedule. Turner refers to these fallback thoughts as 'liminoid' or, 'the state of marginality occurring when normal structural constraints—limits imposed by work, family, ones own abilities and attributes—are removed'.

The key point here is to unravel the 'second life' captured in the liminoid condition. Respondents tend to take interest in such topics and answer questions not only with speed but also in detail. Therefore, questions like 'what would you do if you get 10 crores?' or 'How do you see yourself as a celebrity?' are typical questions in such techniques. Questions under this method probe into the respondent's attitude towards work, home, leisure pursuits and the like.

3.2.3.5 Advantages and Disadvantages of Depth Interviews

Advantages

- Depth interviews attribute independent responses directly to the respondents, unlike focus groups where it is difficult to trace responses to a particular respondent.
- Attitudes and emotions of the test persons can be explored in detail and are close to reality as there is no social pressure to conform to group responses, as is the case of focus groups.

- It is possible to determine the motivations and resistance towards certain markets, products and services.
- Mutual interaction between the interviewer and the interviewee helps to generate an informal atmosphere that facilitates the discussion of sensitive questions or 'taboo themes'.

Disadvantages

- It is difficult and expensive to find and employ skilled interviewers.
- Lack of structure in questionnaires in non-directive and semi-structured interviews introduces interviewer bias.
- Quality of the results depends on the skills of the interviewer.
- The cost and the length of the interviews combined do not permit more number of interviews to be conducted.

3.2.4 Focus Group Interview

A focus group is defined as group of individuals selected and assembled by researchers to discuss and comment on, from personal experience, the topic that is the subject of the research. This type of interviewing is particularly suited for obtaining several perspectives about the same topic. According to the late political consultant Lee Atwater, the conversations in focus groups 'give you a sense of what makes people tick and a sense of what is going on with people's minds and lives that you simply cannot get with survey data'. A focus group consists of a group of anywhere between 6 and 12 members. This size of the group encourages the participants to give their views on the specific issue. The very essence of the focus group as a technique lies in tapping the unexpected findings that result from an interactive session between the members of the group.

These members take part in the discussion for about 2 h, which is the normal time for a focus group interview. These members are selected from a planned sample. It should be ensured that the participants have ample knowledge and experience of the issue/topic to be discussed. Prior to conducting the focus group discussion, the participants are updated, over the phone, regarding the purpose of the focus group and the confidentiality of the members and their information. At the onset of the discussion, the moderator reiterates the same things in addition to introducing any co-moderators and explaining how and why these group members were invited to participate and stating the purpose of note taking and recording.

It should be ensured that the focus group is homogeneous with the participants having common interests, experiences, or demographic characteristics. This would facilitate proper blending among the members resulting in a productive discussion.[2] However, in doing so, it should be ensured that people who know each other or are in some sort of command chain are not recruited into the same sessions. For this purpose, the researchers segregate the participants into different groups based on the difference in views (for or against) or some other parameters.

The effectiveness of a focus group depends on the person who moderates the discussion. A moderator should balance a directive role with that of a moderator, which calls for the moderator to be skilled in establishing and upholding group dynamics and being able to provoke intense discussion on relevant issues. This is important as the quality of data collected is directly proportional to the effectiveness with which the moderator monitors the discussion by asking questions and keeping the discussion targeted on the research objectives. A moderator external to the research organization but with sufficient expertise can also be invited to preside over and facilitate the discussions. If there are different groups then the moderator is expected to be flexible enough to customize his style to each of them.

As the group consists of a number of participants, the format of the questioning plays a major role in eliciting responses from the participants that are cumulative and elaborate than individual responses. The questions should be open-ended, clearly formatted, neutral and sequential. Close-ended questions and leading questions (questions that favour a particular response from the participants) should be avoided. Focus group questioning is not a serial interview. It is rather a discussion of a specific topic that follows from the interaction of the group members. Not only does the discussion prove to be useful in comparing the responses of the different members but also helps the researcher to know what the members think and why. The responses of the members of the group are also affected by the immediate physical surroundings. Therefore, the provision of a relaxed, informal atmosphere should be ensured.

As the focus group involves the interaction of different participants, it becomes difficult to gather the information generated during the course of the discussion. Therefore, some of the techniques that are used to keep a track of the responses of the participants in combination with manual note taking are audio/video recording and multiple methods of recording. Although videotaping is costly, if used, it can capture the details of the discussion including the facial expressions of the participants.

3.2.4.1 Variations in Focus Groups

Focus groups can be of different types depending on the subtle variations incorporated into the standard procedure. These variations are necessary as members differ widely across various groups and some amount of variation helps in eliciting

---

[2] Due of lack of representativeness it is not possible to compare the results from different groups in a strict quantitative sense.

a multiplicity of views and emotional processes within a group context. Some of the variations in focus groups are discussed below.

Dual-moderator group: These types of focus groups are presided over by two facilitators or moderators. There is simple division of labour between the two moderators. One of them takes charge of the smooth flow of the interactive session and the other ensures that the topics in the basic checklist are discussed.

Two-way focus group: This type of focus group consists of two groups. One of the groups discusses the relevant topics with the other group monitoring their words and responses. The second group then analyses the observed interactions and conclusions.

Duelling-moderator group: This consists of two facilitators who preside over the group discussions. The unique feature of this group is that the moderators take opposite stances against one another on the specific topics. In doing so, they ensure that all the topics in the checklist are covered during the discussion and they get to analyse both sides of a controversial issue. In taking opposite stances, they push the members to come up with more information than they would have otherwise done.

Mini-groups: These usually consist of three to six respondents with a single moderator. They may not assist the collection of as private and highly insightful data as in the case of individual depth interviews, but nevertheless, the presence of less number of members facilitates better and extensive probing into the subject matter. Therefore, they prove to be more competent when compared to larger groups, in the case of discussion of narrower issues. The duration of these discussions is usually for an hour.

3.2.4.2 Advantages and Disadvantages of Focus Groups

Advantages

- *In-depth synergism*: Focus groups can, by putting together a number of people, get information about the subjects that cannot be obtained through individual depth interviews.
- *Snowballing*: Participants not only discuss their own opinions but they also have an opportunity to react to the ideas of others. This can uncover issues that would not emerge in a one-to-one interview.
- *Hands-on*: There is also an opportunity for extensive direct investigation. Products can be tried out, concepts can be reviewed, and reactions observed and probed.
- *Timely*: Post-group debriefings with moderators and clients can create shared insight and reduce selective hearing or premature conclusions.
- *Security*: The homogeneity among the members regarding their experiences and feelings place them at a comfortable position where they willingly communicate their ideas. Ideas arise more unexpectedly in a group than in individual interviews.

- *Speed*: Interviewing a large number of people at the same time makes the data collection and analysis faster than usual.
- *Structure*: A focus group interview permits the interviewer to have in-depth discussions on varied topics.

Disadvantages

- *Misuse*: People often tend to consider focus group results a replacement for survey data. It needs to be clarified that focus group researches probe the nature of attitudes and motivations, not their frequency in the population.
- *Misinterpretation*: The spontaneous responses from the members pose a difficulty for the researchers to decide which responses can be generalized. This can lead them to use their own conclusions, resulting in bias.
- *Poorly managed group dynamics*: Conducting focus groups require skill, insight and experience. It is often difficult to find a moderator with the requisite skills.
- *Messy*: As the members answer in an unstructured manner, it becomes difficult to code, analyse and interpret the responses.

3.2.5 Projective Techniques

Every individual has a sub-conscious mind that holds a lot of attitudes and motivations that even the individual may not be aware of. Use of direct questions to unravel these attitudes and motivations are least effective. Therefore, researchers use special techniques to venture into the private worlds of subjects to uncover their inner motives. These special techniques are known as projective techniques.

The projective technique is an unstructured, indirect form of questioning that encourages respondents to project their underlying motivations, beliefs, attitudes or feelings regarding the issue of concern. The respondents are exposed to various scenarios and asked to interpret them. A close observation of the way the respondents describe a situation or a scenario reveals their own motives, attitudes, values and motivation.

Projective techniques find applications in various fields and are not limited to the exclusive study of consumer motivation. They are not used to measure (which is more the territory of other techniques such as surveys), but to uncover feelings, beliefs, attitudes and motivation that many consumers find difficult to articulate. The underlying principle of projective techniques is that the unconscious desires and feelings of the respondents can be inferred by presenting them with an ambiguous situation in which the respondent has to use the ego defence mechanism of projection.

The following are some of the projective techniques used by researchers to tap the feelings in the sub-conscious minds of the subjects.

- Association techniques
- Completion techniques
- Construction techniques
- Expressive techniques
- Sociometry.

3.2.5.1 Association Techniques

In this technique, subjects are presented with a stimulus and are asked to reveal the first word, image, or thought elicited by the stimulus. *Word association* is the most popular type of association technique used, where a respondent is asked to respond to a word spelt out with the first word or thought that comes to their mind. This is known as free word association where the subject has to share his first word of thought. Successive word association is a slight variation in which the subject shares a series of words or thoughts that strike his mind in response to the stimulus. For example, the word 'ambience' asked by the interviewer can have varied responses from individuals like 'sales men', 'building' and 'cleanliness'.

The researcher records the responses and the time taken to respond to each word. This helps in analysing the frequency in which the subject gives a particular word or thought in response to the stimulus. These responses are analysed by calculating the following:

- The frequency of the words given in response
- The time elapsed before the response
- The number of non-respondents.

Association tests are especially useful in consumer research used for discovering brand image or product attributes. Brand personification is one such area. Association tests can also be extended to measure attitudes about specific brands, their attributes, packaging and even advertisements.

3.2.5.2 Completion Techniques

These are somewhat similar to association techniques in that the subject is required to complete an incomplete stimulus. Completion techniques are of two types, that is, sentence completion and story completion.

In *sentence completion*, a subject is asked to fill up the blank in a sentence. The subject uses his/her intuitive ideas to do the job and in the process leaves clues that are traceable to his/her underlying attitudes, thought process and feelings. This technique scores over word association in that the subjects can be given more directive stimulus. These statements are usually in the third person and are somewhat ambiguous. Interpretation is usually informal and qualitative, rather than quantitative. Sentence completion is useful when time is limited, but depth of feeling still has to be tapped.[3] A slight modification in this technique is the *paragraph completion* where the subjects are required to fill in an incomplete paragraph.

Story completion is also similar to the above two variations with the exception that the respondent is required to fill in the conclusion of the story. The story contains enough clues to direct the responses of the subject but gives no hints at the ending. The choice of words and the way the respondent concludes the story helps the researcher to form an idea about the feelings and personality of the respondent.

3.2.5.3 Construction Techniques

In construction technique, the subject is asked to construct his responses in the form of a story, description, dialogue or a picture. In construction techniques, the respondent is supplied with less initial structure that in turn requires more complex and controlled intellectual activity on his part. Construction techniques are of two types, that is, picture response and cartoons.

Picture response techniques originated from the Thematic Apperception Test (TAT) that is based on Henry Murray's Personality Theory. The participants in this technique are given one or more pictures and asked to interpret the background situation, discussion, or direction of the story from the moment the picture is captured. It is for this reason that it is also known as the picture interpretation technique. It is used to identify the unspoken thoughts of the characters.

Cartoon techniques also serve a similar purpose. Here, the statements or a thought of one of the cartoon characters is given in the box above his head. This is supposed to evoke certain responses in the mind of the other cartoon. This is exactly what the subjects have to identify. This evokes varied responses from different subjects, which in turn help the researchers to understand their unique mindset and personalities. Other variations in this technique are the third-person techniques, fantasy scenarios and personification.

3.2.5.4 Expressive Techniques

This is a technique that involves role-playing, where the respondent is given a verbal or visual situation and is asked to play the role of a specific character like a sales executive, a manager, or a political leader. The respondent, for example, is asked to assume that he is a political leader who has been invited to an interactive session with the public on TV. The people tend to pour out their woes and

---

[3] Green.

objections against the government. The manner in which the respondent copes with the situation, tackles the grievances and makes statements reveals a lot about the personality of the subject.

3.2.5.5 Sociometry

Sociometry is a method that was devised by Jacob L. Moreno for assessing group structure. Moreno defined Sociometry as the mathematical study of psychological properties of populations, and the results obtained by the application of quantitative methods.

Sociometry is based on the fact that people make choices in interpersonal relationships. Whenever people are in a group, they chose where to sit or whom they speak to etc. It studies patterns of affection and loyalty that bind some group members more closely than others and can be applied to situations involving study of group behaviour in business research.

3.2.5.6 Advantages and Disadvantages of Projective Techniques

Advantages

- As the respondent is aloof of the purpose of the study, he tends to give responses that would otherwise have not been possible.
- Respondents do not perceive right or wrong answers to the exercise and are encouraged to respond with a wide range of ideas. This results in an increased amount of data collection that is rich and accurate.
- Projective techniques help in generating hypotheses regarding why consumers behave as they do.
- They are useful in 'breaking the ice' in focus group discussions.

Disadvantages

- Complexity of the techniques requires trained interviewers and skilled analysts, who are difficult to find, to analyse the responses.
- The employment of highly skilled staff is expensive which makes it difficult to administer the techniques.
- Getting subjects for role-playing is difficult, as not all subjects may feel comfortable with the idea.
- The reliability of measures is difficult to establish.

3.3 Part II: Descriptive Research Design

3.3.1 Descriptive Research Design: Survey and Observation

The method of collecting information by asking a set of pre-formulated questions in a predetermined sequence in a structured questionnaire to a sample of individuals drawn so as to be representative of a defined population is known as survey research. A researcher conducting a survey has to deal with sampling, questionnaire design, questionnaire administration and data analysis. These questionnaires are administered to an individual or a group of individuals through interviews. These interviews can be either face-to-face, over the phone or through any other communication media which has to be decided in advance. Typical survey objectives involve describing or learning from an ongoing activity by studying the changes in behavioural patterns of the subjects of interest to the researcher. Thus, surveys tend to be descriptive in nature, although they are often quantitative in nature surveys also entail some qualitative aspects as in research concerning consumer satisfaction surveys and new product development.

3.3.2 Classifying Survey Research Methods

Having looked at the essential features of surveys in general, we can now classify surveys into their different types. Surveys can be classified on basis of the method of communication, the degree of structure and the amount of disguise in a questionnaire and the timeframe for data collection. The next section deals with the classification in terms of questionnaire structure, disguise and the timeframe, following which the classification based on mode of communication will follow under the section on survey methods. For a detailed classification of survey research methods, refer Fig. 3.5

3.3.3 Questionnaire Design

Questionnaire design is a vital issue in interviewing. A properly designed questionnaire can tap the necessary information from the respondent. Therefore, researchers always design a tactful set of questions to probe and prompt the interviewee to give useful answers. Questionnaires fall under various categories, such as structured, unstructured, disguised and undisguised. But in this section, we will limit our discussion to the study of structured and disguised questions.

A structured question is one that has a specified number of responses. Hence, the interviewee has to choose from among the alternatives given. Structured interviews are for the most part, orally administered questionnaires. Such

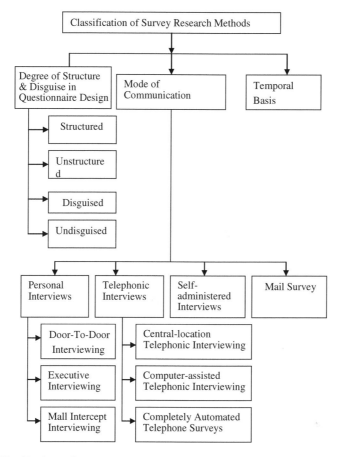

Fig. 3.5 Classifications of survey research methods

questions restrict the interviewee from giving his own answers and require him to choose from among the alternatives given. This saves a considerable amount of time as the respondent is quick to choose from among the options given to him. Thus, rather than going off the track, the interviewer takes the interview in the required direction. The structured questionnaire makes the interview somewhat 'funnel' shaped, wherein the interviewer consciously guides the interviewee through a sequential, pre-formulated set of tactful questions to extract the 'factual' responses without any influencing factors. This leads to the goal of the interview being accomplished. Some common features of structured interviews are as follows:

- A common vocabulary for all interviewees.
- Question formats have the same meaning for all.
- All respondents are interviewed in exactly the same way.

- The questions are set in advance with their order and the range of possible responses the same for all respondents.

These features enhance the effectiveness of a structured questionnaire in the following ways:

- Structured questions are easy and the interviewee can answer them quickly.
- Similar questions and a uniform format make the answers easy to decode and analyse.
- The factual information has a high degree of reliability.
- The possibility of any interviewer bias is reduced.

Although structured questionnaires help the researcher in eliciting programmed responses, they fail to probe into the actual motives of the respondent. This drawback can be overcome by including some unstructured questions in the questionnaire. Unstructured questionnaires are usually open-ended and try to probe into the mind of respondent, allowing the interviewee to express his own thoughts rather than restricting him to the available response options.

Sometimes, it might happen that a questionnaire has a set of personal and sensitive questions to which the respondent might give incorrect answers. These are a set of questions to which the interviewee might take offence or questions that might threaten his ego or prestige. In such situations, interviewee may knowingly give the wrong information. To nullify such instances of deliberate falsification, the interviewer frames the questions in a disguised manner. These disguised questions framed in a tactful manner help to elicit the right information from the respondent in an indirect manner, thus leading to the accomplishment of the research objective.

Depending upon the degree of structure and disguise involved, questionnaires can be further categorized as structured-undisguised, unstructured-undisguised and structured-disguised.

However, these classifications have a number of limitations. Firstly, the variance in the degree of structure and disguise in the questions makes them less straightforward and liable to misunderstanding by the respondent. Secondly, since the number of responses is limited, interviewees feel forced to choose one even if it does not divulge their true feelings. Thirdly, since surveys have a mix of personal and general questions they tend to adopt a hybrid style of questionnaire format including structured, unstructured, disguised and undisguised questions. This leaves no alternative other than response bias to creep into the research data.

Since some research projects have a limited purpose, the data required can be gathered in a single survey. However, there are other research studies that require multiple surveys for a consensus on data and conclusions to be reached and hence extend over a longer period of time. Classifying research surveys based on the time period over which they extend, we have cross-sectional and longitudinal studies, which are discussed below.

3.3.4 Cross-Sectional and Longitudinal Studies

Most cross-sectional surveys gather information at a single point in time. Most surveys fall into this category. In this type of survey, the total target population is divided into various segments, and then data are collected from all these segments using a sampling method. Data collected are then analysed to define the relationship between the various variables based on cross tabulation.

For example, a study designed to establish the relationship between ethics of parents and their views on internet filtering is likely to bring in varied responses from different sections of society who are studied at the same time.

The advantages of cross-sectional surveys lie in the fact that they are more representative of the population. These surveys can be used to study the differences in the consumption levels or trends in income, job changes and buying behaviour of individuals hailing from various groups and sub-groups of the population. But when it comes to defining the same research objectives over a period of time, cross-sectional studies cannot be used. Here, longitudinal studies are required.

Longitudinal studies are those research studies that use multiple surveys to gather data over a period of time. They help in monitoring the behavioural changes taking place in the population that is of interest to the researcher. This type of survey is flexible and can over a period of time, interview different respondents provided the new subjects are also from the same group or sub-group originally interviewed. Hence, longitudinal surveys are essential not only to learn about current social situations, but also to measure their variation over a time period.

A number of different designs are available for the construction of longitudinal surveys. They are:

- Trend studies
- Panel surveys
- Cohort panels.

Trend Studies: Longitudinal surveys consisting of a series of cross-sectional surveys conducted at two or more points in time, with a new sample on each occasion are known as trend studies. But it should be ensured that the new sample is from the same category or segment of population originally surveyed, as trend studies focus on the changing patterns of a particular population. Since each survey brings out the existing trend at a particular point of time, data from several cross-sectional studies of the same population can be integrated and a time trend analysis can be established into the longitudinal survey. This can be done by using consistent questions in each of the cross-sectional studies.

Panel Surveys: A longitudinal survey that involves collecting data from the same sample of individuals or households across time is called a panel survey. The selected sample is called a panel. Panel surveys enable the researcher to detect and establish the nature of changes occurring in the population over a period of time. These changes can be traced to the level of the individual as the surveys are conducted on the same panel over a period of time. A particular sample of interviewees might respond or react to an impulse in a certain way, which might differentiate them from others over a period of time. The very basis of longitudinal surveys lies in detecting these changes. Although they provide highly specific information, they have certain drawbacks. They are time-consuming, expensive and are also known to have high attrition rates as people often drop out of the study.

Cohort Panels: A cohort is defined as those people within a geographically or otherwise delineated population who experienced the same significant life event within a given period of time. Cohort panels can be considered as a specific form of panel study that takes the process of generation replacement explicitly into account. Thus, one or more generations are followed over their life course. The study usually probes into the long-term changes and the individual development processes. If in each particular generation the same sample people are investigated, a cohort study amounts to a series of panel studies whereas, if a new sample of respondents is drawn in each generation, in each period of observation, a cohort study consists of a series of trend studies.

3.3.5 Survey Methods

Surveys are conducted through interviews and are generally classified based on the method of communication used in the interview. The following are some of the common methods of conducting surveys.

- Personal Interviews
- Telephonic Interviews
- Self-Administered Interviews
- Mail Surveys.

3.3.6 Personal Interviews

Based on the respondents to be interviewed and the means to contact them, the different methods of personal interviews can be classified into the following types:

- Door-to-door Interviewing
- Executive Interviewing
- Mall Intercept Surveys.

Personal interviews are characterized by the presence of four entities, that is, the researcher, the interviewer, the interviewee and the interview environment. The first three participants have some inherent and acquired characteristics specific to each of them. As such, they are able to influence the interviewing process in some way or the other. The choice of the fourth entity, that is, the interview environment is chosen by the researcher based upon the type of data to be collected. Before we move on to discuss the various personal interviewing methods classified according to the interview environment, it would be prudent to look at the advantages of personal interviews.

3.3.6.1 Advantages of Personal Interviews

Face-to-face personal interviews have a number of inherent advantages over non-personal interviews. These advantages are discussed below.

Feedback Opportunities: The opportunity to clarify the doubts of the interviewee is one of the features that put personal interviews ahead of other methods of gathering data. A respondent hesitant to provide sensitive information can be assured of the confidentiality of the information provided.

Probing: The interviewer, in a personal interview, has the advantage of probing the respondent for complex answers. A respondent might reveal her likes/dislikes for a certain soft drink which is of no use to the researcher. But with the interviewer present, the actual reason can be traced back to any of the product attributes. The interviewer, by asking further questions, can probe respondents to zero-in on the specific product attribute that they like/dislike. This kind of information is more useful to the researcher.

Length of Interview: *As compared to other survey methods, the length of interview is appreciably better in personal interviews. This is so because* it is easy for a reluctant respondent to hang up the phone or not respond to a mail rather than avoid someone in a face-to-face interview. Hence, the chance of the respondent answering all the questions is greater as compared to other non-personal survey methods. Some respondents, though reluctant to participate in a non-personal survey method, feel comfortable about sharing information with an interviewer present right in front. This leads to an increase in the length of the interview and an improvement in the quality of response in the case of personal interviews.

Door-To-Door Interviewing

This traditional survey method, supposedly the best, involves consumers being interviewed in their homes. There are a number of reasons why this method is considered the best. Firstly, door-to-door interview involves a direct, face-to-face contact with the interviewee. Therefore, it has the inherent advantages of instant feedback and explanation of complex and difficult tasks. Secondly, special questionnaire techniques requiring visual contact to improve data quality can be used in this method. Thirdly, where complex product concepts are to be explained to the customer, door-to-door interviewing is an obvious choice. Fourthly, it is also helpful to the interviewer since as the customer being at home is at ease and is likely to reveal factual information.

Another advantage is that it provides a sample that is more representative of the population as compared to mail questionnaires. Even people who do not have a telephone or whose numbers are not listed in the telephone directory can be reached by door-to-door interviewing. It is the best possible way for in-home product tests, which require either establishing facts about the product or explaining complex product features to the customer. Since it involves direct face-to-face interaction, it reduces the chances of non-response error. However, owing to the large number of drawbacks involved, there has been a slow decline in the usage of door-to-door interviewing. Some of its drawbacks are listed below.

i. The number of potential respondents is low in a population where both adults work outside the home.
ii. Unsafe areas, distance and lack of accessibility pose a hindrance in reaching the desired sample.
iii. Dearth of qualified interviewers.
iv. Fluctuations in weather conditions, vehicle breakdown or sickness are also factors that might pose a hindrance to reaching the target samples.
v. It might not be possible to interview individuals who reside in high-rise apartments or are too busy to entertain personal interviews. Hence, these individuals have to be excluded from the list.

Although door-to-door interviewing does not enjoy the status it once had, yet it will remain in use for the variety of reasons for which it is particularly useful.

Executive Interviewing

Executive interviewing is similar to door-to-door interviewing with the only difference that it is specific to workplace respondents. Executive interviewing is concerned with finding out information related to some industrial product or service and hence requires the interviewing of business people who use these products in their offices.

If an ERP solutions provider seeks to identify the latest user preferences, then it should at first identify and get in touch with the end users of its ERP products. After making a list of suitable names, the interviewer should contact the respondents over the phone asking them to spare some time for the interview. The process is expensive but it is worth it. This is because the users more often than not, make time for the interview, as they too are interested in expressing their opinions and learning more about the products and services they use at work. The interviewer should ensure that he reaches the venue on time. Often, the interviewees are busy at work and the interviewer might be required to wait for the meeting; at other times, the appointment might be postponed due to time constraints. Since executive interviews are similar to door-to-door interviews, they share the same advantages and disadvantages as door-to-door interviews.

Mall Intercept Surveys

Marketing practitioners and advertising researchers base vital business decisions on available market research information. The concept of mall interviewing (a predominant type of personal interview in the United States today) has become a popular way to collect survey data. The technique gained popularity in early 1960s when big, enclosed shopping centres attracted a large number of people from various sections of society (something of an ideal sample for researchers).

Mall intercept interviews are often viewed as an inexpensive substitute for door-to-door interviews. Shopping *mall intercept* interviewing involves exactly what the name implies—stopping or intercepting shoppers in a *mall* at random, qualifying them if necessary, asking whether they would be willing to participate in a research study and conducting the interview right on the spot or taking them to the research agency's interviewing facilities located in the mall. Prior to the mall intercept, surveys were conducted in other places having a high concentration of people, such as supermarkets, discount stores, theatres and railway stations.

Since its inception, mall intercept surveys have come a long way. The present period is witnessing huge developments and advancements in mall intercept surveys with enterprising researchers opening permanent offices and test centres in malls. Today, some mall research facilities are equipped with complete food preparation/storage facilities for conducting taste tests, focus group facilities, video tape equipment, etc. Since each mall has its own customer characteristics, the chances of deriving biased information is more as compared to door-to-door sampling.

Mall intercept interviews are useful when the chances of demographic influences are negligible or the target group is a special population. It comes in handy for surveys that require coordination and timing such as cooking and tasting food products and for products that need to be demonstrated. Purchase intercept technique is a special case of mall intercept interviewing. This technique involves an in-store observation and in-store interviewing, where consumers are intercepted and interviewed while buying a specific product. The interviewer then probes into the reasons for selecting the particular product. Mall intercept surveys score over other modes of survey interviews in the following respects: cost of research and degree of control, time taken for execution and the quality of information collected. Mall intercept interviews have the following advantages:

- Depth of response is greater for mall intercept interviews than for any other face-to-face interview.
- The interviewing environment is controlled by the researcher.
- Interviewer can notice and react to the non-verbal indications of the interviewee.
- Various types of equipment are available to analyse the responses.
- The memories about the shopping experience are fresh, and hence, the situation is conducive for studying purchase behaviour.

Although the advantages of mall intercept interviews are considerable, yet their adoption without recognition of their shortcomings is not prudent. Some of the drawbacks of mall intercept interviews are as follows:

- Getting personal information from respondents is not easy and involves many problems.
- Social desirability effect.
- Interviewer bias.
- Shoppers and respondents who are in a hurry might respond carelessly leading to wrong information.
- Samples drawn may not be representative of the population.
- Lower completion rates of questionnaires.
- Inapplicability of probability-based sampling techniques.

- The respondents might be in a hurry to leave the mall.

Disadvantages of Personal Interviews

Although personal interviews have a number of advantages, they are also known to have some disadvantages such as high cost, lack of anonymity of respondent and necessity for callbacks. These points are discussed below.

Cost: As compared to mail, internet and telephonic surveys, personal interviews are generally expensive. The costs are directly related to the number and the quality of the workforce employed; the reach of respondents; the length and complexity of questionnaires and also the extent of non-response due to non-availability and ignorance.

Lack of Anonymity of Respondents: A respondent in a personal interview may hesitate to provide the right information as his identity is known to the interviewer. Questions like smoking habits during driving and extra marital affairs are sure to fetch falsified answers. Thus, the interview suffers from social desirability bias. To overcome this issue, interviewers spend a lot of time in framing questions in the best possible way so as to be able to prompt the true responses from the interviewees even for sensitive issues.

Necessity for Callbacks: We have already discussed that the characteristics of those who remain at home like (non-working women and retired people) are different from those who go to work. Hence, it becomes necessary to recontact people who were unavailable at the first call. This requires a systematic procedure and often turns out more costly than interviewing the individual in the first call itself.

3.3.7 Telephonic Interviews

Telephonic interviews, once thought of as 'quick and dirty', providing less reliable or valid data, have finally come of age and are currently judged as one of the best cost-effective alternatives to face-to-face interviews and mail surveys. The shift of focus to telephonic interviews of late has happened for several reasons, prominent among which are:

- Plunging response rates in face-to-face interviews in certain urban areas.
- Lower cost of telephonic interviews as interviewer travel time and mileage are eliminated.
- Introduction of random digit dialling as a remedy to previous problems (cited below) of telephonic interviews and
- Adoption of new technology in telephonic interviewing in the form of computer-assisted telephone interviewing (CATI) and computer voice activated telephonic interviewing.

The use of random digit dialling as a sampling procedure eradicated many problems associated with telephonic interviews. Instead of sampling from existing telephone directories, it used sampling via a random number procedure. This ensured that even those individuals in the sample who had shifted or changed their telephone numbers could be included. But the sampling frame for telephonic interviews is not restricted only to directories. Researchers are also known to make use of student registers, hospital and clinic records, census tract information and employee lists of corporations as sampling frames for telephonic interviews. Before we move on to discuss the various developments in telephonic interviewing, we take a quick glance at the advantages and disadvantages of telephonic interviewing.

3.3.7.1 Advantages

- Speed in data collection.
- Potential to produce a high-quality sample through improved techniques.
- Increased co-operation and quality of data as individuals reluctant to respond to face-to-face interviews feel more comfortable with telephonic interviews.
- Ability to interview respondents in high-crime areas, which is a limitation for face-to-face interviews.
- Facilitation of collection of socially undesirable responses which is a drawback in face-to-face interviews.
- Making callbacks is easier.

3.3.7.2 Disadvantages

- The absence of face-to-face contacts which results in the inability of the inter-viewer to display products, concepts and advertisements, or to judge the respondent on demographic characteristics.
- Time length of interviews is less and it is easy for a reluctant respondent to hang up the phone rather than avoid someone in a face-to-face interview.
- Interviews on sensitive topics, although they may exceed the expected length of time give rise to doubts regarding the quality of data.
- Greater tendency among respondents to give shorter answers generating 'not ascertained' responses as compared to face-to-face interviews.
- Absence of face-to-face contact also results in the respondent continuing to speak without realizing that the interviewer is still engaged noting the previous response.
- Uses of screening devices such as Caller ID and answering machines have increased the non-response rates for telephonic interviews, with respondents more willing to participate in a legitimate survey rather than entertaining callers who wish to sell products.
- Samples are usually not representative when the interest group consists of the general population, and directories are used as sampling frames.

Adoption of advanced techniques in telephonic interviews has helped interviewers to overcome many of the problems associated with this method. These advanced techniques are discussed below.

3.3.7.3 Central Location Telephone Interviews

For central location telephone interviews, the interviewers make calls from a centrally located marketing research facility to reach and interview respondents. Wide-Area Telecommunications Service (WATS) lines are used for making the calls. These lines facilitate unlimited long distance calls throughout the country or geographical area at fixed rates. The superiority of CLTI can be attributed to one factor, that is, control. The whole interviewing process can be monitored by supervisors using special monitoring equipment. This means that interviewers who do not conduct the interview properly can either be corrected or removed. This also facilitates editing and checking interviews for quality on the spot. Interviewers can be appraised of any deficiencies in their work. Finally, since interviewers report in and out of the workplace, it helps to scrutinize and control their work hours.

3.3.7.4 Computer-Assisted Telephone Interviewing

The process in which the telephonic interview responses can be directly entered into the computer is known as computer-assisted telephone interviewing. Here, the telephonic interviewer is seated at a computer terminal while interviewing qualified respondents. The questions are usually close-ended. The questions along with their possible response options appear on the computer screen (one at a time) in front of the interviewer. The interviewer reads out the questions and enters the corresponding answers of the interviewee into the computer. Once the answer to the question is entered, the computer automatically skips to the next question. Since the interview consists of close-ended questions with possible options for each, the questionnaire needs to be highly structured.

The processing of the CATI has become much easier with the use of latest technology. This technology includes telephone management systems that take care of everything, starting from selecting telephone numbers at random to dialling them. Another call management feature is automatic callback scheduling where the computer is programmed to make the necessary recalls as per the desired timings. Thus, timings can be set to recall 'busy numbers' after 15 min and 'no-contacts' after 1 h. The computer can also be programmed to fill a certain quota and to deliver daily status reports according to the quota. Even though this process can be done in the traditional way using pencil and paper, there are many advantages attached to CATI. A separate step of editing is not required as data can be edited with their subsequent data entry. Moreover, tabulations, which would require a week or more to compile in the traditional way, can be done at the click of a button using CATI. This speed in tabulations also proves to be advantageous in indicating clearly whether certain questions need to be deleted or added to the existing questionnaire to make it more specific.

3.3.7.5 Completely Automated Telephone Surveys (CATS)

This process that combines computerized telephone dialling and voice-activated computer messages makes use of Interactive Voice Response (IVR) technology to record the responses of the interviewees. The need for an interviewer is eliminated since CATS involves a voice-synthesized module controlled by a microprocessor. The questions are highly structured and close-ended with response options. The functioning of the technique is explained as follows.

The computer uses the recorded voice of a professional interviewer to ask the questions. Interviewees are required to answer by choosing from the options available and then pressing a number button on their telephone sets to mark their choice of options. The options selected are thus recorded by the computer. The system is so designed that if a respondent does not answer the first couple of questions the computer moves on to dial the next respondent. The use of CATS is handy for short, simple questionnaires. CATS technology is known to produce quality data at good speed and is also considered to be much economical compared with other telephonic methods. Since the computer handles the entire interview, CATS shares the same advantages as CATI. The flexibility of the system extends its usability to various research needs such as customer satisfaction surveys, monitoring service quality, in-home product testing and electoral polling.

The Direct Computer Interview is another related method. This is very similar in functioning to the other computer-assisted interviewing methods with the only difference being that the interviewee is intercepted in a mall, made to sit in front of a terminal in the mall and given basic instructions as to the filling of the questions. Here, however, the interviewee enters the answers instead of the interviewer.

3.4 Self-Administered Interviews

An interview where the questionnaire is filled out by the respondent without the intervention of an interviewer is known as a self-administered interview. Respondents of such interviews are not assisted by interviewer or the computer. These self-administered interviews are mostly conducted in shopping malls, supermarkets, hotels, theatres and airlines as these locations provide captive audiences. Passengers and regular customers are given brief questionnaires to enquire about their views of the quality of service offered in an airline or hotel. The absence of the interviewer, however, results in a limitation, namely clarifications on responses to open-ended questions cannot be obtained. A customer might just indicate his/her liking as a reason for buying a particular product/brand, which is of no utility from a managerial perspective. The absence of the interviewer thus makes it difficult to trace the buying decision of the customer to any of the product/brand attributes. Even the quantity of information generated is limited. However, the absence of the interviewer proves to be a boon in disguise as it eliminates the possibility of interviewer bias.

The use of kiosks is another recent improvement in self-administered interviews. Kiosks are multimedia, touch-screen computers contained in freestanding cabinets. The capacity of these pre-programmed computers to administer complex surveys is enhanced by their ability to display full-colour scanned images, play stereo sound clips and show videos. These kiosks having been successfully tested at trade shows are now being tried in retail stores due to their numerous applications. Kiosk interviewing is less expensive and is known to derive more honest results than methods that involve an interviewer.

3.5 Mail Surveys

A survey where questionnaires are sent to qualified respondents by mail or e-mail is known as a mail survey. Two types of mail surveys are used in business research. They are ad hoc mail surveys and mail panels. The only difference between the two is that there is no prior contact in the case of ad hoc mail surveys. A questionnaire is just sent to a sample selected from an appropriate source and responses are awaited. The selected sample is used only for a single project.

The functioning of mail panel surveys is explained below.

- The process starts with obtaining mailing lists from various sources after ensuring that they have the current, complete address of potential participants. It should be ensured that the list of participants is closely related to the group under study.
- The next step involves contacting the sample participants through mail, postcards, letters or telephone. The purpose of their participating in the panel survey is explained to the participants. If the participants contacted agree to take part, they are required to fill in an initial questionnaire pertaining to their background and demographic details, which may be used to determine whether the participant qualifies for inclusion in the survey.
- On successful selection, the panel participants are sent questionnaires from time to time.
- Participants are thereafter contacted by various means to remind them to mail back the completed questionnaire.

An essential feature in mail panel surveys is that it is a type of longitudinal study where the same respondents are surveyed at different points of time to note specific changes pertaining to the topic of research. The advantages are similar to those of self-administered interviews. The method is cost-effective as the need to recruit, train, monitor and pay the interviewers is eliminated. The questionnaire can be administered from a single location for better control. It is even possible to contact respondents who are hard to reach. Respondents can spend as much time as they like answering the questionnaires and can complete them at their convenience. Thus, the respondents tend to give more detailed responses. However, the absence of a qualified interviewer gives rise to the same limitations in mail surveys as for self-administered interviews. Mail surveys are, however, characterized by a high rate of non-response. Typical ways to cope with non-response in mail surveys are outlined below.

- Monetary incentives
- Stamped, self-addressed return envelope with a persuasive covering letter
- Premiums such as pen, pencil and other small gifts
- Promise of contributions towards charity
- Entry into drawings for prizes
- Emotional appeals
- Reminder that the respondent participated in previous surveys.

3.5.1 Factors Determining the Choice of Survey Research

The choice of the survey method is influenced by a number of factors. An ideal survey method should provide the researcher with the required data with the specified quality at the lowest possible cost. The various factors that come into play in the choice of a survey method are outlined below.

3.5.1.1 Sampling Precision

The required level of sampling precision varies from research to research. Therefore, the researcher can select a research survey that suits the accuracy needs of the research. For example, if the researcher requires the results of the sampling survey to be very accurate he can select central location telephone interviewing. On the other hand, mail surveys can be used when there is not much emphasis on the accuracy of the data. A central location telephone interviewing employing a random digit dialling sampling procedure is more likely to deliver a better sample than a mail survey. Hence, the trade-off between the costs and accuracy of a sampling procedure that a researcher is willing to make plays a major role in the selection of the survey method.

3.5.1.2 Budget

The financial resources available to the researcher to conduct the research have a direct impact on the selection of survey method. A research project supported by huge amounts of funds can include an appropriate survey method irrespective of its costs. Thus, when a low budget is set apart for the survey, the researcher cannot employ a costly survey method like door-to-door interviewing. In some cases, even if accuracy of the data is important, the researcher may have to settle for a telephonic interview rather than door-to-door or mail surveys to minimize the cost of the research.

3.5.1.3 Quality of Data

The validity and reliability of the data required plays an important role in the choice of survey methods. Validity refers to the research surveys ability to produce results that are relevant to the researcher. Reliability refers to the consistency with which the results are produced under the same conditions with the same or comparable populations. Quality of data in a survey is affected by factors like choice of questionnaire design, sampling methods, scaling techniques and interviewer qualification and training. It is also affected by the inherent pros and cons of the selected survey method.

For example, an exploratory research study involving an open-ended questionnaire would rather prefer a door-to-door interview over a mall intercept since people on a shopping spree would not be interested in answering open-ended questions.

3.5.2 Need to Expose the Respondent to Various Stimuli

Surveys that need to expose the respondent to certain marketing stimuli like product concepts, components and demonstrations have no better option other than to choose a face-to-face survey method. For example, when a cola major wants to test its customers' response to a new soft drink flavour it is planning to launch, a taste test is necessary and this requires the researcher to select a face-to-face survey method. Similarly, researches aimed at product testing, advertising research, shopping behaviour, etc. require direct contact with the customer. Thus, the type of stimulus that is to be provided to the interviewee as part of the interview decides the type of survey method required to conduct the interview.

3.5.3 Incidence Rate

The percentage of households or persons out of the total population that fit the qualifications of people to be interviewed in a particular study is known as the incidence rate. It might so happen that the incidence rate for a research study is very low. Hence, the researcher cannot afford to employ expensive methods like door-to-door interviewing where the cost of searching the respondents would exceed the costs incurred for actual face-to-face interviewing. Hence, the choice here would be definitely a combination of survey methods that could provide desired results at a reasonable cost. People might be screened using telephone or mail surveys, and later, an interviewer can be sent to meet the selected respondent in person.

3.5.4 Accuracy of the Resultant Data

The accuracy of the data collected by the survey methods can also influence the choice of survey method in a business research. It might be happened that the questionnaire involves sensitive questions or the involvement of the interviewer might bring in some interviewer bias. Personal interviews may not be the right choice in these cases. Mail and self-administered survey methods would be more appropriate. CATI or CATS might also be a choice option since the interviewer would not be in direct face-to-face contact with the interviewee.

3.6 Errors in Survey Research

Technological advancements have led to remarkable improvements in survey techniques and standards. A proper evaluation of the research methodology employed coupled with the standard techniques can give precise results. But survey research can still result in errors in findings and their application. The different types of possible errors in a research study are shown in Fig. 8.2. The two major sources of survey error are

- Random sampling error
- Systematic error.

3.6.1 Random Sampling Errors

Random sampling error is the error caused by a particular sample not being representative of the population of interest due to random variation. Sampling as an integral part of any survey process exposes a representative cross-section of the target population. Even though a representative sample is taken, there is always a minimal deviation between the true population value and the sample value. This is due to statistical error as the sample selected is not perfectly representative of the test population due to chance variation. Therefore, a small random sampling error is evident. This error cannot be altogether avoided, but it can be brought under acceptable limits by increasing the sample size.

3.6.2 Systematic Errors

Errors that occur due to the nature of the research design and the precision of execution are known as systematic errors. The use of wrong techniques or wrongly calibrated instruments leads to systematic errors. When the results of a sample show consistent deviation, in a direction away from the true value of the population parameter, it is known as a sample error or bias. There are many sources of systematic errors, which can be classified under two broad categories, that is, administrative errors and respondent errors. The following section contains the discussion of these errors.

3.6.3 Administrative Errors

An error caused by improper administration or execution of the research task is known as administration error. These are caused due to sample design error or due to other factors on the personal front such as carelessness, confusion, negligence, omission, etc. The different types of administrative error are given below:

- Sample Selection Error
- Sample Frame Error
- Population Specification Error
- Data Processing Error
- Interviewer Error.

3.6.3.1 Sample Selection Error

A systematic error that occurs because of an inaccuracy in either the stage of sample design or the execution of the sampling procedure resulting in an unrepresentative sample is known as sample selection error. It can even surface in cases involving a proper sample frame with the population correctly defined. Nonadherence to appropriate sampling procedures and use of incomplete or improper sampling procedures are the main reasons for errors in sample selection. For example, mall intercept interviewers may choose to interview only those customers who they think are neatly dressed or only families with children. As a result, they might not take the opinions of other potential customers or respondents. A political leader during a election campaign in a potential area might wrongly select telephone numbers at random and corresponding names for a door-to-door campaign, rather than ensuring that he pays a visit to all the registered voters in that area. In this case, the leader might miss out on several potential and eligible voters.

3.6.3.2 Sample Frame Error

The list of population elements or members from which units to be sampled are selected is known as the sampling frame. A sampling frame error is said to occur when this list of members does not correspond exactly with the target population. For example, if the target population is defined as 'all the supermarkets in Hyderabad' and the sample frame does not list all the supermarkets, then it would result in a frame error.

3.6.3.3 Population Specification Error

An error that results from an incorrect definition of the universe or population from which the sample chosen is known as a population specification error. For example, a small electronic car manufacturer trying to estimate the market potential for its cars in Hyderabad might select only other small car users for interviewing. This is a case of population specification error where the actual population should have been all car users in Hyderabad. In this case, the mistake is made, because of uncertainty as to whether only small car users will switch to the new electric car segment. It might happen that with the rising price of petrol or due to personal preferences, other classes of car users might also choose to buy the new electronic car. If other classes of car users who are very different in terms of their interests are excluded then it will result in biased sample results.

3.6.3.4 Data Processing Error

An error that occurs because of incorrect data entry, incorrect computer programming or any other error during data analysis is called data processing error. Data entry into the computer is usually done manually. Hence, there are chances of errors creeping in during the transfer of data from the document to the computer. Programming too is done manually. Hence, the accuracy of data processing by a computer depends on the accuracy of data entry and programming. Data processing error can be minimized by a meticulous verification of each step in the data entry and processing stage.

3.6.3.5 Interviewer Error

Interviewer error is an administrative error caused by mistakes committed by the interviewer while administering the questionnaire or recording the responses. This is due to the interaction of the interviewer with the respondent. Different interviewers differ in their characteristics and abilities. The respondent might be influenced by the interviewer to give untrue or inaccurate data. It might also happen that an interviewer is unable to record the answers correctly as his/her writing speed is not very good. Selective perceptions of the interviewer might also influence the way they interpret and record them. It is possible that the interviewer might record the view of a respondent in the way he understands (specific to his attitudes and perceptions), leading to an error. Tone of voice and verbal cues from the interviewer can also influence telephone respondents. These errors are caused due to improper selection and training of the interviewers. Interviewers should be trained to remain neutral throughout in order to collect answers that are devoid of any influence by the interviewer. Cases of interviewer cheating have become another major cause of survey errors. This is particularly prevalent in door-to-door interviews, where the interviewer in order to save time or avoid asking sensitive questions, deliberately skips questions or fills in the answers to certain questions, resulting in wrong information. Some might even submit false reports of having visited the respondents. This can be checked by forewarning the interviewers that a small number of respondents will be called upon to confirm the authenticity of the answers and whether the interviewer visited them.

3.6.4 Respondent Error

Respondent error as the name suggests are those errors that are observed on the respondents' side. A survey requires the respondents' cooperation in giving answers that contain the correct information. In practice, it is very difficult to get the interviewees to cooperate with the interviewer or reveal their true opinions. Hence, the two common types of respondent errors that arise are non-response error and response bias.

3.6.4.1 Non-Response Error

It is very difficult for any survey to achieve a 100 % response rate. The statistical difference in results between a survey that includes only those who responded and a perfect survey that would also include those who failed to respond is known as non-response error. A non-response occurs when a person is not at home both at the time of preliminary call and the subsequent callback. This problem, rampant in mail and internet surveys, is also confronted in telephonic and door-to-door interviews. The number of 'no contacts' is on the rise with the increased usage of caller ID and answering machines. Refusals in telephonic, mail and face-to-face interviews are also prevalent and occur due to personal preference or due to the respondents being too busy with other important engagements. Fear is assumed to be the main reason behind people refusing to participate in a survey.[4] Concealing privacy and sensitive issues are among other reasons for refusing to participate in a

---

[4] See Ref. Sudman (1980).

survey. One way of measuring response bias is to compare the demographics of the sample with that of the target population. If a certain group of the population is underrepresented, then additional efforts are put into gather data from the under-represented categories through personal interviewing rather than telephonic interviewing.

The success of mail surveys is dependent on the extent to which the respondent is involved in the survey. This is referred to as self-selection bias. Thus, a customer who has had good or bad experience with the service of any particular airlines is more prone to fill up a self-administered questionnaire on board or at the airport counter than a person who is indifferent about the airline's service.

3.6.4.2 Response Bias

A survey error that results from the inclination of people to answer a question falsely, either through deliberate misrepresentation or unconscious falsification is known as response bias. Thus, response bias can occur in two basic forms, that is, deliberate falsification and unconscious misrepresentation.

Deliberate Falsification: It might be difficult to reason out why people knowingly misrepresent or give false answers to questions when they are not certain about facts. But there are many reasons why this happens. People might tend to give false answers in order to appear intelligent or to conceal information they consider personal or embarrassing. Time pressure, social desirability bias, courtesy bias and uninformed response errors are among other reasons why a respondent would knowingly provide wrong information.

For example, a respondent might remember the number of times he visited a supermarket in the last 6 months, but he might not be able to exactly recollect which supermarkets he visited and how many times to each of them. Thus, rather than to say a clear cut 'Don't Remember', the respondents might provide details banking on their memory. Such responses are also prevalent in employee satis-faction surveys where the employees might conceal their true responses towards the efficiency of their unit or the supervisor. They put themselves in a safe situation thinking that revealing the truth might put them in a difficult situation. This type of respondent behaviour is the result of their urge to be perceived as person with opinions in close proximity to that of the average person.

Unconscious Misrepresentation: Unconscious misrepresentation is a situation where a respondent gives wrong or estimated information due to ignorance and forgetfulness even though he has no intention of doing it. Such situations can arise due to question format, content, etc. It might happen that respondents misunder-stand a question and give a wrong or biased answer in the process. Prior inex-perience to a subject or activity is also a reason why unconscious misrepresentation on the part of the respondent occurs. Some respondents may also consider it to be a prestige issue and try to answer every question thrown at them in the best possible way rather than admitting that they do not know the answer to a question. A response bias may also pop up when a respondent is taken aback by an unexpected question by the interviewer. Thus, we see that there might be mis-representation of answers consciously or unconsciously due to a number of factors. These factors are a by-product of different types of biases in the nature of the respondent such as:

Acquiescence Bias. It might arise from the respondent's inclination to be of the same/opposite mind as that of the interviewer and tend to say a 'yes' or a 'no' respectively to everything that the interviewer says.

Extremity Bias. These are individuals who either use extremes to answer questions, or who tend to remain neutral in all answers. But this depends on individual characteristics and differs from person to person.

Interviewer Bias. This occurs due to the interaction between the interviewer and the respondent, where the presence of the interviewer influences the respondent to give untrue or modified answers. The physical characteristics of the interviewer like facial expressions, age, gender, tone, etc. also play a role in inducing inter-viewer bias into the survey.

Social Desirability Bias. Social desirability is the tendency for respondents to give answers that are socially desirable or acceptable, which may not be accurate. A social desirability bias may occur either consciously or unconsciously to gain prestige or build a socially acceptable image. Information about educational qualification and salary might be overstated to gain prestige. Here, the respondent tries to create a favourable image or 'save-face' and prefers to give a socially desirable answer rather than the correct information.

3.7 Observation Methods

Unlike the methods discussed earlier, observation methods do not involve any verbal communication with the respondents. Observation methods involve recording the behavioural patterns of respondents without communicating with them. Some of the most popular observation methods used by researchers are discussed below.

3.7.1 Direct Observation

Direct observation is a method where the observer tries to gain an insight into the behaviour of a shopper in a tactful manner so as not to be noticed. This has applicability in studying merchandising effects in a supermarket and compliance to traffic rules by motorists. In tracking the behaviour of a shopper in a supermarket, the observer can either remain in a passive state as a silent observer (structured) or disguise himself as another shopper and engage in a shopping spree in close association with the subject (unstructured). In both the cases, the observer notes down certain specific behaviours related to the subject. This makes it possible for the observer to find the appealing factors in the buying behaviour and service problems faced by the subject. This is a highly subjective task and requires the observer to record certain noticeable behavioural features useful for the study. It can often be a rapid and economical way of obtaining basic socio-economic information on households or communities.

Be it structured or unstructured, it is imperative for the observer to ensure that he is not identified; else it would lead to an alteration in the behaviour of the subject and introduce subject bias. Various ways that facilitate in direct observation are one-way mirrors and disguised and hidden cameras. However, while using one-way mirrors or hidden cameras, it should be ensured that there is no invasion into the privacy of the subject. Direct observations make it possible to identify the exact timing and length of continuation of an activity. There is instantaneous recording of the observations, which eliminates the necessity of having to recall later. This method is, however, prone to observer bias where the observer may wrongly assign a specific demographic characteristic to the subject.

3.7.2 Contrived Observation

An observation in which the subject under study is unaware of being scrutinized for specific behaviour is known as a natural observation. The subjects under study have little knowledge that they are being observed for specific behavioural aspects and demographic characteristics. This method uses more of a disguised observer who inconspicuously records the specific behaviour he has to scrutinize. This method of natural observation has little relevance for researchers who desire to analyse special behaviour, which may be rare among individuals operating in natural circumstances.

Here, in the concept of contrived observation, the subjects in this case have some advanced knowledge of being participants in the observation study. Although the subjects are aware of their involvement in the study, they still have no idea as to which aspects of theirs are being scrutinized and observed. However, it may be advantageous, the artificial setting and the awareness of the subject that he is being observed can bring in respondent bias.

A corollary concept to contrived observation is mystery shopping. Here, the main motive of the observer is to analyse the behavioural aspects of participants primarily, in the service sectors. The following are some situations, where this concept is used.

Pizza Hut claims to deliver orders for home-delivery within 30 min. The company may authorize any person to pose as a customer and place an order to observe the timeliness in the delivery process. Similar procedures can be applied to analyse the quality of service offered in hotels and banks.

An observer may desire to analyse the variety of responses that can be available to a set of questions. For example, an observer pretending to be an airline passenger throws unnatural questions at an executive at the enquiry counter to notice and analyse the set of responses he gets in return.

3.7.3 Content Analysis

Written materials like advertising copies and news articles, and TV and radio programmes have many implicit and explicit meanings. Therefore, their content has to be thoroughly analysed for any mismatch or misrepresentation in communications. This is where the technique of content analysis comes into play. These written materials need to be analysed, based on words used, themes, characters and space, to enable the smooth flow of the intended communicational aspects. This helps the management to introduce the required changes in the communication process, as may be deemed necessary to generate a better response rate.

3.7.4 Physical Trace Measures

Physical trace measures refer to exposure to advertisements, computer cookie records, records of credit card usage and dirt on the floor to determine store traffic patterns. In other words, it is the process of looking systematically into the immediate surroundings for any evidence of human interaction with one another or the environment. This method usually helps in unravelling the space usage patterns of people. Two types of traces are observed and measured. They are:

- Erosion traces are shown by deterioration or wear and tear that provides a look at the usage pattern. This refers to the traces of selective wear and tear of certain parts or things in a space that shows evidence of being used.
- Accretion traces are a build-up of a residue or an interaction. Traces of lumps of dirt in close proximity reveal the piling up of shoes. Similarly, a number of glasses together reveal their use for drinking purposes.

3.7.5 Participant Observation

A process in which a researcher establishes a many-sided and long-term relationship with individuals and groups in their natural setting, for the purposes of developing a scientific understanding of those individuals and groups is known as participant observation. At the first look, it may seem as a process concerned with looking, listening, experiencing and recording the same. However, in reality, it is more demanding and analytically difficult. This method of observation requires the researcher to be involved in the day-to-day activities of the subjects or the social settings that are under investigation. This involvement can be categorized into three types depending upon the degree of involvement of the researcher. These are as follows:

Complete participant: The researcher immerses himself fully in the activities of the group or organization under investigation. It supposedly produces accurate information, as the intensions of the researcher are not disclosed to the subjects or social settings under investigation and is least likely to guide researchers to enforce their own reality on the social world they seek to understand.

Participant as observer: The researcher in this case keeps the group informed about his intensions, but does not actively involve himself in the social settings.

Complete observer: The researcher is uninvolved and detached, and merely, passively records behaviour from a distance.

The presence of the researcher can cause some initial sparks of discomfort. Language and cultural dissimilarities can pose barriers in this method. This requires the researcher to negotiate access into the social settings after a thorough study of the power relations within the setting, the relations of people to their physical environment, as they perceive it, and the social openings and barriers. The compatibility of observation and interviewing in this method makes it highly flexible. Apprehensions about observations pave the road to questions that are later clarified during interviews to understand the significance of the observations. The interview in this case is highly unstructured.

3.7.6 Behaviour Recording Devices

Human observation is prone to deficiencies or errors. To overcome such errors, machine observers in the form of behaviour-recording devices are used. This sort of mechanical observation include

- On-site cameras in stores and at home for eye-tracking analysis while subjects are shopping or watching advertisements using coulometer to identify what the subject is looking at and pupil meters to measure how interested the viewer is.
- Electronic checkout scanners that record the UPC on the products as those used by A.C. Nielsen and INTAGE. These are used to record purchase behaviour of the subjects under investigation or in general (refer this chapter on 'Secondary and Syndicated Data').
- Nielsen People Meter for tracking television station watching (refer this chapter on 'Secondary and Syndicated Data').
- Voice pitch meters that serve to measure emotional reactions.
- Psycho galvanometer that measures galvanic skin response.

It may be easier for these machines to record the behaviour of the subjects, but measuring the precise level of arousal and reaction through them is questionable. Therefore, calibration and sensitivity is a limitation with the mechanical devices.

3.8 Part III: Causal Research Design

3.8.1 Causal Research Design: Experimentation

The basic aim of causal studies is to identify the cause and effect relationship between variables. For instance, studying the effect of price, advertising and marketing on sales comprise causal studies. It is therefore essential for researchers to have a thorough knowledge of the subject area of research. The basic premise of the causal relationship is that when we do a particular thing (cause), it gives rise to another thing (effect). It is highly impossible to prove a causal relationship scientifically. Researchers develop evidence to understand causal relationships. For instance, if researchers want to establish a relationship that good nutrition (cause) leads to intelligence (effect) among children, they should then be able to prove that good nutrition precedes intelligence.

3.8.2 Causal Relationships

The causal analysis is the process of determining how one variable influences the change in another variable. As far as business research is concerned, the cause and effect relationship is less explicit. Three types of possible relationships can arise between two variables—symmetrical, reciprocal and asymmetrical.

3.8.2.1 Symmetrical

A symmetrical variable is one in which two variables fluctuate together. However, it is assumed that the changes in either variable are not due to changes in the other. Symmetrical conditions usually occur when the two variables become alternate indicators of another cause or independent variable. For instance, the low attendance of youth in martial art clubs and active participation in discotheques and parties is the result of (dependent on) another factor such as lifestyle preferences.

3.8.2.2 Reciprocal

When two variables mutually influence or reinforce each other, we can say that there is an existence of a reciprocal relationship. For instance, a reciprocal relationship exists when a person goes through a particular advertisement, which leads him to buy that brand of product. Later, after usage, it consequently sensitizes the person to notice and read the successive advertisements of that particular brand or company.

3.8.2.3 Asymmetrical

Asymmetrical relationship exists, when changes in one variable (independent variable) are responsible for changes in another variable (dependent variable). There are four types of asymmetrical relationships,

(1) *Stimulus response relationship.* It represents an event that results in response from some object. For example, an increase in product price may lead to fewer sales.
(2) *Property–disposition relationship.* A property is the enduring nature of a subject, which does not depend on circumstances for its activation. A disposition is an inclination to respond in a certain way under certain circumstances. For instance, family status, age, gender, religion and so on can be considered personal properties. Attitudes, opinions, values, etc. are part of disposition. For property–disposition, examples include the effect of age on attitude with regard to savings, gender and its impact on attitude towards social issues, etc.
(3) *Disposition–behaviour relationship.* Consumption patterns, work performance, interpersonal acts, etc. are part of behaviour responses. Examples include a person's perception about a brand and its purchase, job satisfaction and productivity, etc.
(4) *Property–behaviour relationship.* The family life cycle and purchase of goods, social class and family saving patterns, etc. are some examples.

3.8.3 Experimental Designs

An experiment refers to the process of manipulating one or more variables and measuring their effect on other variables, while controlling external variables. The variable, which is manipulated, is called the independent variable and the variable whose behaviour is to be measured after experimentation is called the dependent variable. For instance, if a company wants to test the impact of advertising on product sales, researcher conducts the experiment by manipulating the advertising frequency to study its impact on product sales in a particular region. Here, the variable, which is being manipulated, is advertising, and therefore, it is the independent variable. The impact of change in advertising frequency on product sales is measured and analysed. Thus, a product sale is the dependent variable.

The aim of experimentation is to establish and measure the causal relationship between the variables studied. A well-executed experiment can depict the causal relationship between variables by controlling extraneous variables.

In this chapter, we will discuss the experimentation process. First, we will study various aspects to be considered by the researcher while conducting an experiment. Then, we will look at experimental validity and the threats to it. Later, we will move to experimental environments and the pros and cons of laboratory and field experiments. Finally, the chapter ends with a brief note on different types of experimental designs that are widely used by researchers.

3.9 Issues in Experimentation

To make an experiment successful, a researcher has to take decisions regarding various aspects. There are four key issues a researcher has to consider while conducting an experiment. They are the following:

- Treatment of independent variable
- Experimental groups and control groups
- Selection and measurement of the dependent variable
- Control of extraneous variables.

Let us now discuss them in detail.

3.9.1 Treatment of Independent Variable

An independent variable is a variable over which the researcher is able to exert some control for studying its effect upon a dependent variable. Experimental treatment refers to the manipulation of the independent variable. For example, consider a company planning to test a change in package design in terms of its impact on product sales. To test the relationship between package design and sales, it has decided to expose customers to packs of three different designs, A, B and C. These packs are placed on the shelves of select outlets. The consumer's response is measured. Here, package design is the independent variable, which is manipulated, and there are three treatment levels (A, B and C) of the variable.

3.9.2 Experimental Groups and Control Groups

In a simple experiment, a researcher uses two groups—the experimental group and the control group. The *control group* is a group of test units that are not exposed to the change in the independent variable. The *experimental group*, on the other hand, is exposed to a change in the independent variable. In the package design example discussed above, a group of supermarkets (experimental group) are selected and each package design is displayed for a month. Another group of supermarkets (control group) continue to carry the regular package design for that particular period. Then, the sales of the product are measured in each case, and the difference between the measurement (sales) in the experimental group and the control group is analysed to determine whether the design change has affected sales.

3.9.3 Selection and Measurement of the Dependent Variable

Selection of the dependent variable and its measurement is another important decision the researcher has to take. The dependent or response variable is the variable whose behaviour is to be measured as a result of an experiment. Dependent variable is the variable that may change due to the manipulation of independent variable.

By using the same example of package designs, the sales volume of the product is considered as the dependent variable. Selecting a dependent variable may not be easy in all cases. For example, if a company wants to do research to evaluate the effectiveness of various advertising programmes, the dependent variables can be brand-image, brand awareness and product sales. The researcher has to select the dependent variable depending on the purpose for which the experiment is being conducted. Proper problem definition will help the researcher select the appropriate dependent variables.

3.9.4 Control of Extraneous Variables

Other extraneous variables, which influence the dependent variable, have to be controlled to determine the real effect of manipulation in the independent variable on the dependent variable. The presence of these variables in the experiment will put the researcher in dilemma as to whether the change in dependent variable is due to the change in the independent variable or due to extraneous variables. This is why extraneous variables are also called confounding variables. Researchers use various methods to control extraneous variables. They are randomization, physical control, matching, design control and statistical control.

Randomization is the most popular method to control extraneous variables. Randomization refers to the process of assigning test units randomly to experimental treatments and assigning experimental treatments randomly to test units. This process helps researchers to spread the effects of extraneous variables equally over the test units.

Another approach is to physically control the extraneous variables. This is achieved by keeping the level of extraneous variables constant throughout the experiment.

Another variant of the physical control approach is matching. In this method, the researcher adopts judgmental sampling to assign test units to both the experimental group and the control group. This ensures that both the groups (experimental and control groups) are matched in terms of characteristics of test units.

Design control is another approach to control extraneous variables. Selecting appropriate experimental designs to conduct the experiment helps researchers to control particular extraneous variables that affect the dependent variable.

Statistical control can also be used to control the effect of extraneous variables. Here, extraneous variables that are affecting the dependent variable are identified and measured using appropriate statistical tools like analysis of variance. Then, the effects of extraneous variables on the dependent variable are adjusted statistically, cancelling out the effects of extraneous variables.

Exhibit 3.2 shows the required characteristics that a good experiment should have.

3.10 Experimental Validity

Validity is the extent to which a research process is accurate and reflects actual market conditions (i.e. it is free from systematic error). There are two types of validity that are considered in experimentation—internal validity and external validity. Internal validity measures to what extent the change in a dependent variable can be explained by the independent variable. External validity measures to what extent the inferences derived from experiments can be generalized to the real environment.

Adapted from ASQ Statistics Division Newsletter (2000)

Exhibit 3.2: Prerequisites for Conducting Experiments
There are certain characteristics that a good experiment should possess.

- The experiment's objectives need to be well defined. This means that problem definition, the independent variable(s) and their treatment levels, dependent variable, the experimental design and process should be clearly defined.
- The effect of independent variables should not be influenced by extraneous variables. The experiment needs to be designed in such a way that the influence of extraneous variables is minimized.
- The experiment should provide a measure of precision (experimental error), unless it is known from previous experimentation. Replications provide the measure of precision while randomization assures the validity of the measure of precision.
- The expected precision of the experiment should be sufficient to meet defined objectives. There generally is a trade-off between the expense of additional experimentation and the

---

3.10.1 Internal Validity

Internal validity refers to 'the approximate validity with which we infer that a relationship between two variables is causal or that the absence of a relationship implies the absence of cause'.[5]

---

[5] See Ref. Cook and Campbell (1979).

In other words, internal validity indicates to what extent the change in dependent variable in an experiment is caused by the manipulation of independent variable or due to extraneous variables. If extraneous variables have an influence on the dependent variable, then establishing the causal relationship between the dependent and independent variable becomes difficult. Any findings or conclusions drawn from experimentation in the absence of internal validity will be superficial and deceptive. Hence, while developing experimental research designs, researchers should take adequate care to include the influence of extraneous variables to improve the experiment's internal validity. Let us now examine six major types of extraneous variables that are sources of threat to internal validity. They are the following:

- History
- Maturation
- Testing
- Instrumentation
- Selection bias
- Statistical regression
- Mortality.

3.10.1.1 History

History here means something different from the general sense. History here refers to a specific event in the external environment that is historic (rare occurrence) in nature and occurs at the same time an experiment is being conducted. Such events may impact the dependent variables. Consider a situation where a company conducts an analysis to market new farm equipment in a south Indian state. If the major agricultural belt in that state is affected by flash floods, the results of the test will be influenced by this historic event. Similarly, an experiment aimed at assessing the impact of a new promotional campaign for a car may be influenced by the steep spurt in petrol prices due to a historic event like the Iraq war. An occurrence of an event, which is beyond the control of the researchers, will have an impact on the dependent variable (sales in this case).

3.10.1.2 Maturation

The maturation effect refers to the change in the test units, not due to the influence of independent variable but due to the passage of time. During the course of the experiment, people may become older, hungrier or tired. For example, if a pharmaceutical company is conducting drug trials on a sample of patients over a longer period of time, there may be some difference in the effect of the drug on patients due to physiological changes in them. This impacts the experiment's internal validity.

3.10.1.3 Testing

Another extraneous variable that affects experimental results is the testing effect. This refers to the subjects becoming alert when they are exposed to experimentation. For example, when employees are made to answer a questionnaire that tests their knowledge and skills before attending a training programme, they are alerted that they are being studied. This prompts them to pay more attention to the training modules. Thus, they obtain better scores in the test conducted after the training programme. Thus, there will be change in experimental results between the first test and the second test.

3.10.1.4 Instrumentation

A researcher can vary the measuring instrument used for pre-testing and post-testing to minimize the test effect. However, this may lead to the introduction of a new effect called the instrumentation effect. This refers to the effect on experimental results due to change in the measurement instrument, measurement values or the researcher's process of recording measurements during the course of the experiment.

For example, a researcher has to record observations from morning till evening. During the morning hours, the researcher will record observations enthusiastically and the measurements will be accurate. In the evening, due to fatigue, he or she may not show the same interest in recording the observations. Such an instrumentation effect will impact experimental results.

3.10.1.5 Selection Bias

Selection bias refers to improper assignment of respondents to treatment conditions. Selection bias occurs in two ways. One is the wrong selection of test units in experimental group. As a result, it does not represent the population from which the test units are drawn. Another is that test units assigned to experimental groups differ from test units assigned for the control group. The difference will result in selection bias. For example, a company may have included more heavy users of the product in the experimental group and moderate and light users in the control group. The outcome of the experiment may be favourable to the company as a result.

3.10.1.6 Statistical Regression

Statistical regression refers to the phenomenon where extreme values of the sample tend to converge near the mean value of the sample during the course of the experiment. This can be either positive extreme values or negative extreme values. Consider an experiment aimed at ascertaining consumer perception on the customer service levels of a financial institution. In a pre-test measurement, some consumers may rate the customer service as highly exceptional, and some may rate it as very poor. However, in a post-treatment (a pilot launch of a new customer service initiative) measurement, these extreme scores tend to get closer to the mean of the sample. This is known as the statistical regression effect. This can be attributed to a continuous change in consumer attitudes. Thus, subjects who display extreme attitudes may change their perception during the course of the experiment. This will affect experimental results as the change in scores is due to statistical regression and not due to the treatment (a pilot launch of a new customer service initiative)

3.10.1.7 Mortality

Mortality effect refers to the loss of subjects or test units in experiments, thus affecting experimental results. Suppose an educational researcher is conducting an experiment on the impact of television viewing on IQ scores on 100 students. In the course of the experiment, 15 students have dropped out from the experiment. Such a reduction in subjects or test units may impact experimental results.

3.10.2 External Validity

External validity refers to the 'the approximate validity with which we can infer that the presumed causal relationship can be generalized to and across alternate measures of the cause and effect and across different types of persons, settings and times'.[6] External validity examines to what extent the experimental findings can be generalized to the population from which test units are drawn. We can infer from the definition that experiments that are conducted in natural settings offer a greater external validity compared with those conducted in controlled environment. So a field experiment provides greater external validity compared with a laboratory experiment.

Experiments are conducted either in a laboratory environment or a field environment. The former means the experiment is conducted under artificial conditions. Field environment refers to conducting an experiment in real conditions. Both these environments have their advantages and disadvantages. The researcher has to analyse which environment will suit his requirements.

---

[6] See Ref. Cook and Campbell (1979).

3.10.2.1 Laboratory Environment

Laboratory experiments refer to experiments conducted in controlled conditions. Examples include showing advertisements or products to select consumers in controlled conditions and blind taste tests.

Conducting experiments in laboratory settings have many advantages over field experiments. The primary advantage is that the conditions can be controlled. Thereby, the effect of extraneous variables on dependent variables can be minimized. A controlled environment is also effective in eliminating the history effect.

The isolation achieved in laboratory settings will also help researchers achieve similar results, if the experiments are repeated number of times with the same test units in similar conditions. Laboratory experiments, therefore, provide more internal validity.

As the test units and resources required for laboratory experiments are less, it also helps researchers conduct the experiment in shorter time and cost effectively. This is why companies conduct laboratory experiments during the initial stages of product development, as costs and risks associated with experiments can be minimized. Apart from cost-effectiveness, laboratory experiments also help a company to lessen the risk of information about products or ideas being passed on to competitors. The risk is more in field experiments.

However, there are some drawbacks in laboratory experiments. One is that laboratory experiments are conducted in artificial conditions, and the results may not hold up well in actual conditions (in the market). So these experiments provide less external validity.

Also, the results of laboratory experiments are influenced by the testing effect, where the test units are aware that they are being tested, and so may not respond naturally.

3.10.2.2 Field Environment

Field experiments refer to experiments conducted in natural settings. These include launching products in select regions, observing consumer behaviour regarding a POP display in supermarkets and analysing customer response to trial offers. As field experiments are conducted in natural settings, they have a high degree of external validity. The disadvantages in field experiments are that as the researcher has no control over external variables, these experiments will have a low degree of internal validity. Field experiments also require greater time and effort and are expensive.

3.11 Type of Experimental Designs

With the basic understanding of experimentation concepts that we have gained, let us now examine the various types of experimental design. Experimental designs are classified into four key categories—pre-experimental designs, true experimental designs, quasi-experimental designs and statistical experimental designs.

In pre-experimental designs, there is no proper control mechanism to deal with threats to internal and external validity. True experimental designs allow researchers to randomly select test units for experimental groups and also assign treatments randomly to the experimental groups. Quasi-experimental designs do not allow researchers to fully manipulate the independent variable but provide a limited flexibility in assigning the treatments randomly to experimental groups. Statistical experimental designs have statistical control mechanisms to control extraneous variables. Exhibit 3.3 describes the notations used in explaining experimental designs.

Let us examine each type of experimental design in detail in the following section.

3.11.1 Pre-experimental Designs

Pre-experimental designs lack proper control mechanisms to deal with the influence of extraneous variables on experimental results. There are three prominent pre-experimental designs used by business researchers. They are

- One-shot design (after only design)
- One-group pre-test–post-test design
- Static group design.

Exhibit 3.3: Notations used in Experimentation

Following are the common symbols used in the experimental research

X = exposure of a group to an experimental treatment or independent variable

O = observation or measurement of the dependent variable on the test units. O_1, O_2, O_3 ... are the various observations or measurements of the dependent variable taken during the course of the experiment

R = random assignment of test units to experimental groups

EG = experimental group, which is exposed to the experimental treatment

CG = control group of test units involved in the experiment. However, this group is not exposed to experimental treatment

You need to note that the notation used in experimental designs assumes a time flow from left to right

---

3.11.1.1 One-Shot Design (After Only Design)

One-shot design involves exposing the experimental group to treatment X after which the measurement (O_1) of the dependent variable is taken. This can be shown symbolically as follows:

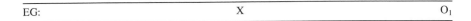

EG:	X	O_1

For example, a company may launch a sales promotion initiative in select supermarkets in a city for a month to ascertain the impact of sales promotion on sales. Then, it might measure the sales registered in that particular month. The higher sales may prompt the company to extend the sales promotion offers to other cities where it has a presence.

There are some drawbacks associated with this study. The test units are not selected randomly. Instead, their selection is based on the researcher's judgment.

The results might not reflect the experimental treatment's impact completely as various extraneous variables influence the dependent variable including history, maturation and mortality. As this study lacks proper control mechanisms to deal with extraneous variables, the internal validity of the experiment is affected. Moreover, we cannot infer results based on the measurement O_1, as there is no other measurement against which O_1 can be compared with.

Due to these limitations, one-shot design is not used for conclusive research. It is used more for exploratory research.

3.11.1.2 One-Group Pre-test/Post-test Design

This type of design involves exposing an experimental group of test units to experimental treatment (X). Measurements are taken before and after experimental treatment. This can be symbolically expressed as:

EG:	O_1	X	O_2

O_1 represents the measurement of the dependent variable before the experimental group is exposed to the treatment. O_2 represents the measurement of the dependent variable after the experimental group is exposed to the treatment. So the difference between O_1 and O_2 will be the impact of treatment on the dependent variable. For example, an HR manager may plan a training programme for employees and measure the productivity change. First, he may measure the productivity of employees. Then, the training programme will be conducted. After the training, employee productivity is again measured.

However, just like the one-shot design, this experimental design too lacks proper control mechanisms to limit the influence of extraneous variables. These include history, maturation, testing effect, statistical regression effect, selection bias and mortality effect.

3.11.1.3 Static Group Design

In static group design, two groups of test units, the experimental group and the control group, are involved in the experiment. The experimental group is exposed to the experimental treatment. The control group is not exposed to the experimental treatment.

The measurements are taken for both groups after the experiment. This can be symbolically expressed as follows:

EG:	X	O_1
CG:		O_2

We may note that O_1 is the measurement of the dependent variable of the experimental group after exposing it to the treatment and O_2 is the measurement of the dependent variable of the control group, which is not exposed to the treatment. The difference between these two measurements, that is, $O_1 - O_2$ will be the effect of treatment.

Various extraneous variables do influence experimental results—primary being selection bias. The non-random selection of test units may result in differences between the units assigned to the experimental group and the control group. Another extraneous variable that will influence the results is the mortality effect. Some test units may drop out from the experiment. This is more so for the experimental group if the treatment is strenuous.

3.11.2 True Experimental Designs

As discussed earlier, true experimental designs use randomization to control the influence of extraneous variables. Randomization refers to the assignment of test units to either experimental groups or control groups at random. Such selection of test units will reduce the differences between the groups on whom the experiment is being conducted. Apart from the use of the randomization technique, true experimental designs also use one or more than one control groups to reduce the effect of extraneous variables.

Following are prominent true experimental designs widely used in business research:

- Pre-test/post-test control group design
- Post-test only control group design
- Solomon four group design.

3.11.2.1 Pre-test/Post-test Control Group Design

In this design, two groups of test units, that is, experimental group and control group are considered for the experiment. The test units are assigned to these two groups randomly. Pre-test measurements of dependent variable are taken for the two groups. Then, the experimental group is exposed to the treatment. The post-test measurements of the dependent variable are taken for the two groups. It can be shown symbolically as below:

EG:	R	O_1	X	O_2
CG:	R	O_3		O_4

O_1 and O_2 are the pre-test measurement and post-test measurement of dependent variable of the experimental group. R represents that the assignment of testing units to each group is done on a random basis.

O_3 and O_4 are the pre-test and post-test measurement of dependent variable of the control group. We know that the control group is not exposed to experimental treatment.

The treatment effect (TE) can be calculated as follows:

$$TE = (O_2 - O_1) - (O_4 - O_3)$$

For example, a fertilizer company is launching a new fertilizer. To test its efficacy, the company has decided to conduct an experiment. For this, it has divided an agricultural field into a few parts. These parts are randomly assigned to the experimental group and the control group. Then, the pre-test measurements (productivity) of the fields are taken. The parts in the experimental group are treated with fertilizer and the parts in the control group are not exposed to the fertilizer treatment. The post-test measurements are taken. The differences between the pre-test and post-test measurements are analysed.

This design addresses most of the extraneous variables. Hence, it provides accurate results. However, this design may not control the testing effect. This is because pre-test measurements are taken, and such measurements will sensitise test units. This may have an impact on post-test measurements.

3.11.2.2 Post-test-Only Control Group Design

In this design, both the experimental and control groups participate in the experiment. The first is exposed to the experimental treatment and the second is kept unexposed. The post-test measurement of the dependent variables is taken for both groups. This can be shown symbolically:

EG:	R	X	O_1
CG:	R		O_2

The treatment effect (TE) can be obtained as follows:

$$TE = (O_2 - O_1)$$

To illustrate, a personal product company has claimed that the use of its new hair oil formulation will reduce hair fall by 50 % compared with other hair oils. To support this claim, the company has conducted an experiment by randomly assigning consumers who use a competing coconut oil brand to both the experimental group and the control group. The experimental group consumers are provided with the company's hair-oil formulation for 6 months, while the control group continues to use the competing hair-oil brand. Measurements are taken after 6 months.

This type of design will address most of the extraneous variables.

3.11.2.3 Solomon Four-Group Design

This type of design involves conducting an experiment with four groups, two experimental groups and two control groups. Six measurements are taken, two pre-test and four post-test. This study is also known as the four-group, six-study design. The design can be symbolically represented as follows:

EG:	R	O_1	X	O_2
CG:	R	O_3		O_4
EG:	R		X	O_5
CG:	R			O_6

Though the design addresses all extraneous variables, it is expensive and consumes time and effort. The design provides various measures, which can be analysed

They are:

$O_2 - O_1$
$O_4 - O_3$
$O_2 - O_4$
$O_6 - O_5$

3.11.3 Quasi-Experimental Designs

Quasi-experimental designs are used when it is not possible to assign test units randomly to experimental treatments or assign experimental treatment randomly to test units. In such cases, quasi-experimental designs help control extraneous variables, though not as effectively as true-experimental designs. It is better than pre-experimental designs. Prominent quasi-experimental design used by researchers is time-series design.

3.11.3.1 Time-Series Designs

In time-series designs, a series of measurements are taken before and after the test unit is exposed to the experimental treatment. This can be symbolically represented as follows:

EG:	O_1	O_2	O_3	X	O_4	O_5	O_6

Time-series designs are used for experiments performed over a longer period. For example, if a company wants to determine the impact of price changes on the sales of a product, the company takes a series of observations before the price is changed and trends are identified. Then, another series of observations are taken after changing the price. The trends after the treatment (post-price change) are compared with trends before the treatment (pre-price change) to determine whether they are similar or not. If there is an increase in sales levels after the price change, the researcher can conclude that the treatment had a positive effect on the dependent variable.

However, these experiments may not give absolutely accurate results. This is because of threats to internal validity. The history and instrumentation effects are key threats to internal validity. The simultaneous occurrence of events like boom or bust in global economy, or any calamity might affect experimental results. Another threat is the instrumentation effect, where there can be change in measurement units or the process followed by researcher to make measurements.

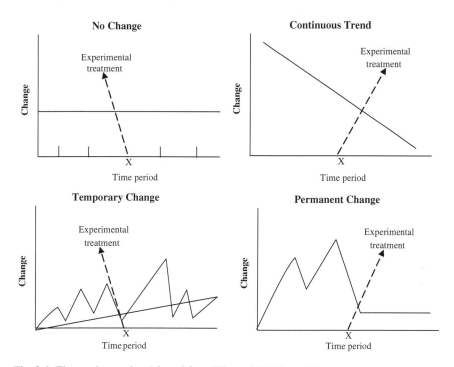

Fig. 3.6 Time series results. Adapted from Zikmund (2003), p. 281

The advantage of time-series design is that it aids in identifying permanent trends and temporary trends. This helps to design long-term and short-term business strategies. Various patterns that emerge from time-series experiments are shown in Fig. 3.6.

3.11.4 Statistical Designs

Unlike pre-experimental and true experimental designs, statistical designs aid in measuring the effect of more than one independent variable. Using these designs will help researchers to conduct a single experiment to analyse the effect of more than one independent variable, instead of conducting a series of experiments for each independent variable. It is also helpful in isolating the effects of most extraneous variables, thereby providing better experimental results. Four prominent experimental designs in this category are

- Completely randomized design
- Randomized block design
- Latin square design
- Factorial design.

Let us discuss each of these in detail.

3.11.4.1 Completely Randomized Design

Completely randomized design is used when the researcher has to evaluate the effect of a single variable. The effects of extraneous variables are controlled using the randomization technique. The key difference between completely randomized design and other statistical experimental designs is that the latter use the 'blocking' principle, which completely randomized design does not.

This design involves randomly assigning test units to treatments. For example, there are 'n' test units and 'k' experimental treatments. Then, the 'n' test units are assigned to 'k' treatments randomly. Later, the post-test measurements are evaluated.

This can be shown symbolically:

EG_1:	R	X_1	O_1
EG_2:	R	X_2	O_2
EG_3:	R	X_3	O_3

EG_1, EG_2 and EG_3 are three experimental groups, which are exposed to various experimental treatments.

X_1, X_2 and X_3 are three experimental treatments assigned to experimental groups.

For example, a researcher at a pharmaceutical company plans to evaluate the efficacy of a weight loss drug made by a particular company. For this, the researcher has selected a sample of 40 consumers. These consumers are assigned randomly to two treatment levels, 25 consumers to treatment 1 and 15 to treatment 2. Consumers under treatment 1 are asked to take the drug for 1 month. Consumers with treatment 2 are not given any drug. After the experiment, measurements are taken for both groups. Differences, if any, are analysed to see whether the drug is effective in weight control.

CBD has some drawbacks. The design is applicable only when test units are homogeneous. It can be used only in situations when a single variable is being evaluated. Another drawback is that this design can be used only when extraneous variables can be controlled.

3.11.4.2 Randomized Block Design

Randomized block design is used when the researcher feels that there is one major extraneous variable that will influence experimental results. In this design, the test units are blocked or grouped based on the extraneous variable, which is also called the blocking variable. For example, a company is testing the effect of price change on the sales of a product, and it has identified that advertising is a major influencing variable. In such cases, advertising is considered an extraneous variable. The

Table 3.2 Example for randomized block design

Price change	Store type		
	Drug stores	Supermarkets	Hypermarkets
Rs 10	Store 1	Store 6	Store 7
Rs 12	Store 3	Store 2	Store 8
Rs 14	Store 4	Store 5	Store 9

experimental group and the control group are matched according to the extraneous variable (advertising, in this case), ensuring that the effect of the extraneous variable is distributed equally to both groups. To illustrate further, a consumer products company wants to examine the impact of price change on the sales for its newly developed health drink. The company has decided to conduct the experiment using three different price levels Rs 10, Rs 12 and Rs 14, in nine retail outlets, namely Store 1, Store 2, Store 3, Store 4, Store 5, Store 6, Store 7, Store 8 and Store 9. The company has identified that the store type will also influence the product sales. For instance, drug stores may register higher sales compared with supermarkets and hypermarkets. Therefore, we can apply RDB in such situations. The retail outlets are segregated according to store type. Store 1, Store 3 and Store 4 are drug stores, Store 6, Store 2 and Store 5 are supermarkets and Store 7, Store 8 and Store 9 are hypermarkets. Then, treatment levels (price) are assigned randomly to each test unit (retail outlets).

This is shown in Table 3.2.

Using this design, two effects can be determined, the *main effect* and the *interaction*. The main effect refers to the average effect of a particular treatment on the dependent variable, regardless of extraneous variables. The interaction effect refers to the influence of the extraneous variable on the effect of treatment. In this example, the main effect is the direct effect of price change on the product sales. This can be achieved by determining the average impact of each treatment on each block. The interaction effect is the influence of the store type on the effect of price change. This can be obtained by determining the customer response to each price change for each store type.

3.11.4.3 Latin Square Design

Latin square design is used in situations where the researcher has to control the effect of two non-interactive external variables, other than the independent variable. It is done through the blocking technique as used in random block design. For example, a researcher wants to examine the impact of three different ads on sales. However, the researcher feels that pricing and income levels of consumers will also impact sales. So researcher wants to isolate the effect of the two extraneous variables—pricing and consumer income levels.

In this design, the blocking or extraneous variables (pricing and income levels) are divided into an equal number of levels and so is the independent variable (advertising programs). The table is then developed with levels of one extraneous variable representing the rows and levels of the other variable representing the

Table 3.3 Example for Latin square design

Pricing levels	Income levels		
	Low income	Middle income	HIGH income
Rs 10,000	Ad-B	Ad-A	Ad-C
Rs 12,000	Ad-C	Ad-B	Ad-A
Rs 14,000	Ad-A	Ad-C	Ad-B

columns. The levels of the independent variable (or treatments) are exposed to each cell on a random basis so that there should be only one treatment in each row and column. Then, the treatment effect is determined. Based on the results, it can be analysed which treatment level influences the dependent variable more.

In the advertising program example, we have created a 3 × 3 table where each extraneous variable has three blocks and so does the independent variable. The advertisements programmes that are to be tested are Ad-A, Ad-B and Ad-C. The pricing levels are Rs 10,000, Rs 12,000 and Rs 14,000. The income levels are low-income, middle-income and high-income groups. In the table, income levels are represented in columns; the pricing levels are represented in rows. The advertising programmes Ad-A, Ad-B and Ad-C are assigned to each cell. Table 3.3 depicts this.

However, there are some assumptions in this design. It assumes that there is negligible or no interaction effect between the two extraneous variables. As a result, we cannot examine the interrelationships between pricing, income levels and the advertising programmes. Another assumption is that the number of levels of all three variables are equal.

The Latin square design has some drawbacks. The assumption that all variables should have the same number of levels (the two extraneous variables and the independent variable) is not possible in all cases. So, in situations, where any of the variables does not have the same number of levels as that of the other two variables, this design is not valid.

This design also assumes that there is no interaction effect between the extraneous variables. Interaction effect refers to the measurement of the amount of influence the level of one variable has on another variable. The interaction effect exists between two variables when the simultaneous effect of two variables is different from the sum of the individual effects of both the variables. In situations, where there are inter-relationships between the variables, this design cannot be applied.

3.11.4.4 Factorial Design

Factorial design overcomes the drawbacks of the Latin square design regarding the interaction effect. It can be used in cases where there is interrelationship between the variables. Factorial designs are used to examine the effect of two or more independent variables at various levels.

Table 3.4 Example for factorial design

In-store promotion variable	Pricing variable		
	Rs 50	Rs 60	Rs 70
POP-display	C	A	F
Trial packs	D	E	B

Factorial design can be depicted in tabular form. In a two-factor design, the level of one variable can be represented by rows and the level of another variable by columns. Each test unit is assigned to a particular cell. The cell is exposed to a particular treatment combination randomly. This design enables a researcher to determine the main effect of each independent variable as well as the interaction effect between them.

For example, a market researcher plans to study the effect of in-store promotions on the sales of a product and the impact of price change too. The researcher has decided to use two types of in-store promotions—POP display and trial packs, and three price levels—Rs 50, Rs 60 and Rs 70. Six stores, namely A, B, C, D, E and F, have been selected for the experiment.

Using factorial design, we can develop Table 3.4, with rows containing in-store promotions variable and columns containing pricing variable. We assign test units (supermarkets) to each cell randomly. The test unit (supermarket) in each cell is then exposed to a particular treatment combination (see Table 11.3). So supermarket A is exposed to POP-display and Rs 60 price level and supermarket B is exposed to trial packs and Rs 70 price level. Post-test measurements are taken. The outcome of this experiment can help the researcher to understand three key aspects:

- The impact of pricing on the sales of a product
- The impact of in-store promotions on the sales
- The sales-effect interrelations between in-store promotions and pricing.

3.12 Questions

1. In an experimental design, the primary goal is to isolate and identify the effects produced by the…

    a. Dependent variable
    b. **Extraneous variable**
    c. Independent variable
    d. Test unit

2. An experiment has high… if one has confidence that the experiential treatment has been the source of change in the dependent variable.

   a. **Internal validity**
   b. External validity
   c. Internal and external validity
   d. Internal and external reliability

3. Which of the following is a threat to internal validity of an experimental design

   a. Maturation
   b. Interaction of setting and treatment
   c. **Interaction effects of pre-testing**
   d. Reactive effects of experimental design

4. Which of the following effect in internal validity occurs when test units with extreme scores move closer to the average score during the course of the experiment

   a. **Statistical Regression**
   b. Selection bias
   c. Maturation
   d. Instrumentation

5. Which of the following statement is incorrect with respect to 'An experimental design is a set of procedures specifying

   a. **How to test units (subjects) are divided into homogeneous sub samples**
   b. What independent variables or treatments are to be measured
   c. What dependent variables are to be measured
   d. How the extraneous variables are to be controlled

6. Randomization of test units is a part of…

   a. Pre-test
   b. Post-test
   c. Matching
   d. **Experiment**

7. A characteristic that distinguishes true experiments from weaker experimental designs is that true experiments include

   a. **Random assignment**
   b. Matching
   c. Repeated measurements of the dependent variable
   d. Random sampling

References

ASQ Statistics Division Newsletter (2000), vol 19(issue 2)

Beri GC (1989) Marketing research, 1st edn. Tata McGraw-Hill, New Delhi

Cook T, Campbell D (1979) Quasi experimentation: design and analysis issues for field settings. Houghton Mifflin Company, Boston

Sudman S (1980) Improving the quality of shopping centre sampling. J Mark Res 17:423–431

Zikmund WG (2003) Business research methods, 7th edn. Thomson South-Western, Singapore, p 281

Part III
Sources and Methods of Data Collection: Qualitative and Quantitative Data

Chapter 4
Scales and Measurement

Once the research problem has been clearly established, the most important part of the research, namely data collection, begins. A proper measurement system has to be developed before actually venturing into the field to collect data. At this stage, a researcher has to address some fundamental issues relating to the variables that need to be measured, and the different measurement scales that have to be used for measuring the characteristic that are relevant to the research study.

The process of assigning numbers or labels to different objects under study to represent them quantitatively or qualitatively is called measurement. Measurement thus can be understood as a means to denote the amount of a particular attribute that a particular object possesses. An important aspect of measurement is that there are certain rules that will define the process of measurement; for instance, a rule might be developed which says that number 1 should be assigned to people who are from South India and number 2 should be assigned to people who are from North India. It is, however, important to note that measurement is done for the attributes of the units under study but not the units themselves. For example, the height, weight, age or other such attributes of a person are measured but not the person himself.

In this chapter, we discuss some of these issues involved in measurement, such as determining the variables that have to be measured in a business research process, the different types of measurement scales available and their uses. The criteria for good measurement are also covered, and finally, the chapter concludes with a discussion on the different errors that arise during the process of Measurement.

4.1 Identifying and Deciding on the Variables to be Measured

The primary step in the measurement process is to identify the area or the concept that is of interest for the study. A *concept* can be understood as a general idea derived or inferred from specific instances or occurrences. Once a concept has

S. Sreejesh et al., *Business Research Methods*,
DOI: 10.1007/978-3-319-00539-3_4,
© Springer International Publishing Switzerland 2014

been identified, for example, studying the motivational levels of employees in an organization, the researcher can focus on developing a construct. A *construct* is a general idea or an abstract inferred or derived from specific instances. Constructs can also be considered as certain types of concepts which exist at different levels of thought that are developed to simplify complex situations concerning the area of study. They are developed for theoretical usage as well as for explaining the concepts themselves.

After developing a construct the subsequent process in the research is to define the concept constitutively and then operationally. A constitutive definition of the concept will specify the research boundaries and also will define the central theme of the study. The most important use of defining the concept (under study) constitutively is to clearly demarcate it from other concepts. The primary purpose of defining the concept constitutively is that it will help the researchers in framing and addressing the research question in an appropriate manner. For instance, if we just say that we want to study the education system in India, this will not help at all in developing a research question, since it has to be clearly defined as to what education system needs to be studied—is it primary education or secondary or higher education, or is it related to an adult education programme and so on. So the constitutive definition in this example would be, say, 'Primary education covering state government aided schools (classes I to V)'.

Exhibit 4.1: Studying Role Ambiguity

The constitutive definition of role ambiguity can be framed in the following manner. Role ambiguity is a direct function of the discrepancy between the information available to the person and that which is required for adequate performance of his role. Subjectively, it is the difference between his actual state of knowledge and that which provides adequate satisfaction of his personal needs and values.

On the other hand, the operational definition can be framed as the state of uncertainty (measured on a five point scale ranging from highly uncertain to highly certain) an employee feels regarding the duties and responsibilities of his job relating to his co-employees and customers.

The measurement scale that has been developed consists of a 45-item scale. Each of these 45 items is analysed on a five-point scale. The five points in the scale represent

1 = highly   certain,   2 = certain,   3 = neither   certain   nor   uncertain,
4 = uncertain, 5 = highly uncertain.

Some of the items that have been measured are given below:

- What is the amount of work that I am expected to do?
- What should I do to improve my chances of getting a promotion?

- How vulnerable is my position in the organization?
- How far will my boss go to back me?
- What methods would my boss use to evaluate my performance?
- What is the level of service that I should provide to my customers?
- Which specific company strengths should I present to the customers?
- How the top management expects me to handle ethical situations in my job?
- How much information should I provide to managers from other departments?
- About how much time does my family feel I should spend on the job?

Adapted from Singh and Rhoads (1991)

Once the constitutive definition is clearly defined, it becomes easier to develop an operational definition. The operational definition defines precisely what attributes and features of the concept are to be measured. It also specifies the process of assigning a value to the concept. Although operational definitions can be developed for defining the characteristics that need to be measured, it is sometimes impossible to measure certain features that may nevertheless be crucial for the study. For instance, if we want to study the behaviour of employees towards the senior management, then it is very difficult to measure the behaviour of these employees; however, by defining behaviour as the action or reaction of an individual in response to external stimuli, we can develop some scales for measuring behaviour, for example, by asking respondents some indirect questions about how they would react to certain decisions of the top management and so on. An operational definition, therefore, acts as an interface between the theoretical concepts and the live environment. We can analyse the constitutive and operational definitions along with the measurement scales in Exhibit 4.1. In this Exhibit, the operational definition of role ambiguity has been developed for studying salespeople and customer service people, on the assumption that role ambiguity increases the stress factor leading to job dissatisfaction.

Determining the variables that need to be measured is very important in business research. In normal measurement applications, scales are usually comparable; for instance, if we want to measure the height of a person, we measure it in centimetres or in inches, where both scales are comparable. But in business research, we rarely find such comparable scales of measurement. While conducting research regarding business issues, a researcher has to initially define what is to be measured, how it will be measured and also the concept that needs to be measured. The concept can be measured using several factors, but the appropriateness of the variable that has to be measured is very important. For example, if we want to measure the profitability of a particular product, then measuring the sales of the product would be more appropriate than measuring the productivity of the organization. A research study has even been conducted to measure the materialism aspect in human beings. It is discussed in Exhibit 4.2.

Exhibit 4.2: Measurement Scales for Measuring Materialism

A research study has been conducted to study a fundamental attribute affecting consumer behavior—namely the materialism of people. Three scales have been developed to test materialistic traits. These are the following: possessiveness, non-generosity and envy. Possessiveness has been defined as the inclination and tendency to retain control or ownership of one's possessions. Generosity is the willingness to share with others, and therefore, in the context of materialism, we can understand non-generosity is the unwillingness to share with others. Envy has been defined as an interpersonal attitude involving displeasure and ill-will at the superiority of another person in happiness, success, reputation or the possession of anything desirable. The primary reason for studying the materialism aspects of people is to understand people's behaviour as consumers, their affinity towards possessions (possessiveness), their willingness to share the possessions with others (non-generosity) and their feelings about objects in others' possession (envy).

A sample of 338 members comprising people from different walks of life like students pursuing business education, employees in an insurance firm, students at a religious institute, shop floor workers and so on was selected. The sample was tested for reliability, validity and their relationships to measures of happiness. The study found that possessiveness and non-generosity were very similar between male and female members in the sample, but it was found that men were more envious than women.

Adapted from Belk (1984)

While developing measurement variables, researchers often face the problem of construct equivalence. This refers to the perceptions and beliefs of the measurement variables of different people that are related to the study. Different perceptions based on the customs, religious aspects, culture and socio-economic factors of different societies will affect the development of constructs for the research study. For instance, consuming beef is not accepted in Hindu dominant India, but in the western countries, it is a common phenomenon. As a result, common questionnaires cannot be developed for both these areas if a study on beef consumption patterns is carried out across the world.

4.2 Development of Measurement Scales

Developing measurement scales is a critical dimension of business research. A scale can be defined as a set of numbers or symbols developed in a manner so as to facilitate the assigning of these numbers or symbols to the units under research following certain rules. Generally, it is very easy to measure certain parameters such as sales of a particular product or the profitability of a firm, or the productivity of the employees in an organization and so on. These are relatively easier because they can be measured quantitatively by applying different scales for measurement. On the other hand, it is relatively difficult to measure some aspects like the motivational levels of employees in an organization, the attitude of customers towards a particular product, or the customer acceptance levels of a new design of a product and so on. Measurement of such concepts is very difficult because the respondents may be unable to put their feelings across exactly in words, and sometimes, the scales may not be capable of drawing the right response from the respondent.

Exhibit 4.3: Measuring Customer Retention

Customer retention has become a vital ingredient in business success. Researchers adopt different approaches for measuring the customer retention rates. One such method is the crude retention rate, which represents the absolute percentage of customers retained. For instance, if 80 out of 100 customers are retained then the retained percentage is 80. However, researchers try to adopt better methods of measuring the customer retention rate such as weighted retention rates, where the customers are weighted according to the volume of purchases made by them. Another useful approach in measuring customer retention rate is the 'lifetime value' (LTV). Here, the net present value of the customer is analysed by the seller. In LTV analysis, costs such as the selling and servicing costs are considered, while costs involved in developing new customers are recorded as a sunk cost. The LTV of a customer is calculated by considering the net value of cash flows assuming a sustainable relationship with the customer in the future.

Although it is a better approach, LTV has some inherent disadvantages. Researchers are unsure about which attribute to consider for measuring the LTV should it be the age of the customer, the working life of the product, product life cycle or some other factor. Moreover, calculating the LTV for each and every individual customer is a very difficult process, and therefore, LTV of customers is normally carried out at an aggregate group level.

Adapted from K. Ramakrishan, (Strategic Marketing Research Team), 'Customer Retention: The Key to Business Performance', http://www.etstrategic-marketing.com/smNov-Dec2/art11.html

At times, the respondents might not be willing to reveal their opinions to the researcher. To overcome such difficulties, a researcher's primary objective is to seek the cooperation of the respondent and create an environment of trust and mutual understanding. The interviewer should try to reduce all the negative feelings of the respondent and develop a situation wherein the respondent feels free to share all his feelings relevant to the research with the interviewer. It is also important for the researcher to clearly specify what information he needs and why, if the research design permits. Companies generally develop scaling techniques to measure certain critical aspects of business, such as measuring customer retention, as discussed in Exhibit 4.3.

4.3 Types of Measurement Scales

The design of a measurement scale depends on the objective of the research study, and the mathematical or statistical calculations that a researcher expects to perform on the data collected using the scales. The objective of the research study may be as simple as classifying the population into various categories, or as complex as ranking the units under study and comparing them to predict some trends. Different types of measurement scales are given below.

- Nominal scale
- Ordinal scale
- Interval scale
- Ratio scale.

4.3.1 Nominal Scale

A nominal scale uses numbers or letters so as to identify different objects. The scale helps segregate data into categories that are mutually exclusive and collectively exhaustive. This scale assigns numbers to each of these categories and these numbers do not stand for any quantitative value, and hence, they cannot be added subtracted or divided. For example, a nominal scale designed to measure the nature of occupation (employment status) may be given as below:

Occupation: [1] Public sector [2] Private sector [3] Self-employed [4] Unemployed [5] Others.

In the above example, the numbers 1, 2, 3, 4 and 5 only serve as labels to the various categories of employment status, and hence, a researcher cannot use those numbers to perform any type of mathematical or statistical operations on those numbers. A nominal scale does not give any relationship between the variables, and the only quantitative measure is the frequency of items appearing under each category, that is, the number of people in public sector jobs, etc. One can only calculate the mode for the data collected using nominal scale.

4.3.2 Ordinal Scale

An ordinal scale is used to arrange objects according to some particular order. Thus, the variables in the ordinal scale can be ranked. For instance, if someone says that a person came second in the exam, then we can understand that there was another person who came first and some others were there who were ranked after him. This type of scale that gives ranks is called an ordinal measurement scale. Ordinal variables can only give us the information regarding relative position of the participants in the observation, but they do not give any information regarding the absolute magnitude of the difference between the first and the second position, or second and third position and so on.

For example, an ordinal scale used to measure the preference of customers (in Andhra Pradesh) for various mobile telephone service providers would ask a question like please rank the following mobile telephone service providers from 1 to 5 with 1 representing the most preferred and 5 the least preferred.

Airtel ____
Hutch ____
Idea ____
BSNL ____
Reliance ____

A respondent may rank these players depending on his experience/perception of them. If a respondent ranks Airtel as 1 and Idea as 2, a researcher can know that the respondent prefers Airtel. However, the limitation is that the researcher cannot be sure as to how strong the respondents' liking is for Airtel when compared to Idea.

4.3.3 Interval Scale

Interval scales are similar to ordinal scales to the extent that they also arrange objects in a particular order. However, in an interval scale, the intervals between the points on the scale are equal. This is the scale where there is equal distance between the two points on the scale. Examples of interval scales are Fahrenheit and Celsius scales used to measure temperature. In these scale, the difference between the intervals is the same, that is, the difference between 40° and 60° is the same as the difference between 25° and 45°. But the base point, freezing of water is represented by 32 °F and 0 °C. Thus, there is no natural zero (base) for these scales.

Similarly, we can design an interval scale with points placed at an interval of 1 point [10] ——— [9] ——— [8] ——— [7] ——— [6] ——— [5] ——— [4] ——— [3] ——— [2] ——— [1] and ask the respondents to place the mobile telephone service providers on this scale of 10–1. If Idea is assigned 8 and BSNL 4 we can say that the value of difference in preference is 4. But we cannot say that the liking for Idea is twice that for BSNL because we did not define a point of no liking, that is 0. The only statement we can make about a respondents preference for Idea and BSNL is 'he likes Idea more than BSNL' but we cannot give a ratio of the likings as there is no base zero.

Interval scales are suitable for the calculation of an arithmetic mean, standard deviation and correlation coefficient.

4.3.4 Ratio Scale

Ratio scales have a fixed zero point and also have equal intervals. Unlike the ordinal scale, the ratio scale allows for the comparison of two variables measured on the scale. This is possible because the numbers or units on the scale are equal at all levels of the scale. A very good example of ratio scale is distance; for instance, not only can we say that the difference between four miles and six miles is the same as the difference between six miles and eight miles but we can also say that eight miles is twice as long as four miles. In other words, a ratio scale can be defined as a scale that measures in terms of equal intervals and an absolute zero point of origin exists. This zero is common to a distance scale using yards, meters, etc. Age, height, weight, money scales are other common examples of ratio scales. Since their exist an absolute zero on the ratio scale, the data collected can be subjected to any type of mathematical operation say, addition, subtraction, multiplication and division.

4.4 Criteria for Good Measurement

Researchers normally develop their own scales for measuring variables for different attributes as it is very difficult to find readily available scales. It is in this process of developing scales that researchers have to be very careful, since the scales that they develop should primarily stand the tests of reliability, validity, sensitivity and so on. In the following sections, we will discuss the criteria for good measurement. There are five major criteria for analysing the goodness of a measurement, namely reliability, validity, sensitivity, generalizability and relevance.

4.4.1 Reliability

It is considered that if the outcome of a measuring process is reproducible, then the measuring instrument is reliable. Reliable measuring scales provide stable measures at different times under different conditions. For example, if a coffee vending machine gives the same quantity of coffee every time, then it can be concluded that the measurement of the coffee vending machine is reliable. Thus, reliability can be defined as the degree to which the measurements of a particular instrument are free from errors and as a result produce consistent results. However, in certain situations, poor data collection methods give rise to low reliability. The quality of the data collected can become poor if the respondents do not understand the questions properly and give irrelevant answers to them. There are three methods that can be used to evaluate the reliability of a measure. They are test–retest reliability, equivalent forms and internal consistency.

4.4.2 Test–Retest Reliability

If the result of a research is the same, even when it is conducted for the second or third time, it confirms the repeatability aspect. For example, if 40 % of a sample say that they do not watch movies, and when the research is repeated after sometime and the result is same (or almost the same) again, then the measurement process is said to be reliable. However, there are certain problems regarding the test–retest method of testing reliability, the first and foremost issue is that it is very difficult to obtain the cooperation and locate all the respondents for a second round of research. Apart from this, the responses of these people may have changed on the second occasion, and sometimes environmental factors may also influence the responses.

4.4.3 Equivalent Form Reliability

Some of the shortcomings of test–retest reliability can be overcome in this method. In equivalent form reliability, two measurement scales of a similar nature are to be developed. For instance, if the researcher is interested in finding out the perceptions of consumers on recent technologically advanced products, then he can develop two questionnaires. Each questionnaire contains different questions to measure their perceptions, but both the questionnaires should have an approximately equal number of questions. The two questionnaires can be administered with a time gap of about 2 weeks. The reliability in this method is tested by measuring the correlation of the scores generated by the two instruments. The major problem with equivalent form reliability is that it is almost impossible to frame two totally equivalent questionnaires.

4.4.4 Internal Consistency

Internal consistency of data can be established when the data give the same results even after some manipulation. For example, after a research result is obtained for a particular study, the result can be split into two parts and the result of one part can be tested against the result of the other; if they are consistent, then the measure is said to be reliable. The problem with internal consistency is that the reliability of this method is completely dependent on the way the data are divided up or manipulated. Sometimes, it so happens that different splits give different results. To overcome such problems with split halves, many researchers adopt a technique called as Cronbach's Alpha that needs the scale items to be at equal intervals. In case of difficulty in obtaining the data at equal intervals of time, then an alternate method called KR-20 (Kuder Richardson Formula 20) is used to calculate how consistent subject responses are among the questions on an instrument. Items on the instrument must be dichotomously scored (0 for incorrect and 1 for correct). All items are compared with each other, rather than half of the items with the other half of the items. It can be shown mathematically that the Kuder–Richardson reliability coefficient is actually the mean of all split-half coefficients.

4.4.5 Validity

The ability of a scale or a measuring instrument to measure what it is intended to measure can be termed as the validity of the measurement. For instance, students may complain about the validity of an exam, stating that it did not measure their understanding of the topic, but only their memorizing ability. Another example may be of a researcher who tries to measure the morale of employees based on their absenteeism alone; in this case too, the validity of the research may be questioned, as absenteeism cannot be purely attributed to low morale, but also to other conditions like prolonged illness, family reasons and so on. Validity can be measured through several methods like face validity, content validity, criterion-related validity and construct validity.

4.4.6 Face Validity

Face validity refers to the collective agreement of the experts and researchers on the validity of the measurement scale. However, this form of validity is considered the weakest form of validity. Here, experts determine whether the scale is measuring what it is expected to measure or not.

4.4.7 Content Validity

Content validity refers to the adequacy in the selection of relevant variables for measurement. The scale that is selected should have the required number of variables for measurement. For instance, if the state education department wants to measure whether all the schools in the city have adequate facilities, and for measuring this, it develops a scale to measure the attributes like the attractiveness of schools names, the frequency of old students meets, the different varieties of eatables that are prepared in the school canteen and so on. Here, it is clear that these variables considered for measurement do not possess any content validity as they will not serve the purpose of the research. The scale should instead be developed to measure aspects such as the number of classrooms, the number of qualified teachers on roll, the capacity of the playground and so on. It is often difficult to identify and include all the relevant variables that need to be studied for any research process.

4.4.8 Criterion-Related Validity

The criterion-related validity refers to the degree to which a measurement instrument can analyse a variable that is said to have a criterion. If a new measure is developed, one has to ensure that it correlates with other measures of the same construct. For instance, length of an object can be measured with the help of tape measure, calipers, odometers and also with a ruler and if a new technique of measure is developed then one has to ensure that this new measure correlates with other measures of length. If a researcher wants to establish criterion validity for a new measure for the payment of wages, then he may want to ensure that this measure correlates with other traditional measures of wage payment such as total number of days worked.

Criterion validity may be categorized as predictive validity and concurrent validity. *Predictive validity* is the extent to which a future level of a criterion variable can be predicted by a current measurement on a scale. A scale for measuring the future occupancy of an apartment complex for example may use this scale. A builder may give preference to only those repairs that may attract new tenants in the future rather than focusing on all the areas that need repair. *Concurrent validity* is related with the relationship between the predictor variable and the criterion variable. Both the predictor variable and the criterion variable are evaluated at the same point in time.

4.4.9 Construct Validity

Construct validity refers to the degree to which a measurement instrument represents and logically connects through the underlying theory. Construct validity, although it is not directly addressed by the researcher, is extremely important. It assesses the underlying aspects relating to behaviour; it measures why a person behaved in a certain way rather than how he has behaved. For instance, whether a particular product was purchased by a consumer is not the consideration, but why he has/has not purchased the product is taken into account to judge construct validity. This helps to remove any extraneous factors that may lead to incorrect research conclusions. For example, for a particular product, price may not be the factor that affects a person deciding whether to buy it. If this product is used in the measurement of a general relationship of price and quantity demanded, it does not have construct validity, as it does not connect with the underlying theory.

There are two statistical methods for analysing construct validity—convergent validity and discriminant validity. Convergent validity is the extent of correlation among different measures that are intended to measure the same concept. Discriminant validity denotes the lack of or low correlation among the constructs that are supposed to be different. Consider a multi-item scale that is being developed to measure the tendency to stay in low-cost hotels. This tendency has four personality variables; high level of self-confidence, low need for status, low need for distinctiveness and high level of adaptability. Additionally, this tendency to stay in low-cost hotels is not related to brand loyalty or high-level aggressiveness. The scale can be said to have construct, if it correlates highly with other measures of tendency to stay in low-cost hotels such as reported hotels patronized and social class (convergent validity). Has a low correlation with the unrelated constructs of brand loyalty and a high level of aggressiveness (discriminant validity).

4.4.10 Sensitivity

Sensitivity refers to an instrument's ability to accurately measure variability in stimuli or responses. Sensitivity is not high in instrument's involving 'agree' or 'disagree' types of response. When there is a need to be more sensitive to subtle changes, the instrument is altered appropriately. For example, strongly agree, mildly agree, mildly disagree, strongly disagree, none of the above are categories whose inclusion increases the scale's sensitivity.

4.4.11 Generalizability

Generalizability refers to the amount of flexibility in interpreting the data in different research designs. The generalizability of a multiple item scale can be analysed by its ability to collect data from a wide variety of respondents and with a reasonable flexibility to interpret such data.

4.4.12 Relevance

Relevance, as the name itself suggests, refers to the appropriateness of using a particular scale for measuring a variable. It can be represented as,

Relevance = reliability × validity.

If correlation coefficient is used to analyse both reliability and validity, then the scale can have relevance from 0 to 1, where 0 is the low or no relevance level to 1 which is the high relevance level. Here, if either of reliability or validity is low, then the scale will have little relevance.

4.5 Sources of Measurement Problems

When conducting a study, a researcher has to analyse the accuracy of the information that has been obtained, as several types of research errors can come in during a study. Some of the major research errors are discussed below.

4.5.1 Respondent-Associated Errors

A majority of research studies rely on eliciting information from respondents. If the researchers are able to obtain the cooperation of respondents and elicit truthful responses from them, the survey can easily achieve its targets. However, two respondent-associated errors arise when researchers do not obtain the information as stated above. These respondent errors are non-response error and response bias.

4.5.2 Non-response Errors

Non-response errors arise when the survey does not include one or more pieces of information from a unit that has to be part of the study. The research results will have some bias to the extent that those not responding are different from those who respond. Non-response errors include failure to respond completely or even failure to respond to one or more questions of the surveyor. Unit non-response occurs when a person or a household that exists in the data set does not respond. Item non-response is one where a person selectively responds to only certain questions of the survey and will not respond to one or more questions of the survey. The reasons for not responding to some questions may be: lack of knowledge or it may be that the respondent does not want to answer. Non-respondent error may become an important source of bias in the result of the survey if a large number of the potential respondents do not respond and if the non-respondents are significantly different from the respondents on some of the characteristics that are important for the study.

4.5.3 Response Bias

If the respondents consciously or unconsciously misrepresent the truth, then it amounts to response bias. Sometimes respondents deliberately mislead researchers by giving false answers so as not to reveal their ignorance or to avoid embarrassment and so on.

4.5.4 Instrument-Associated Errors

Instrument-associated errors can surface due to poor questionnaire design, improper selection of samples, etc. Even a simple thing like lack of adequate space in the questionnaire for registering the answers of the respondent can result in errors of this sort. Another type of instrument errors occurs if the questionnaire is complex or ambiguous as this can result in a lot of confusion for the respondent. If the questions in the questionnaire use complicated words and sentences, they will inadvertently lead to errors due to the misinterpretation of such questions by the respondents.

4.5.5 Situational Errors

Plenty of errors arise due to the situational factors. The respondent may not provide proper responses if a third person is present during the interview, or sometimes the third person might himself participate in the interview process without any invitation leading to inappropriate responses. Other factors such as the location of the interview also play a crucial part; for instance, if the researcher is conducting intercept interviews in public places, then the respondents may not respond as properly as they would if they were interviewed in their homes. If the researcher does not assure the respondent that the data provided will be kept confidential, the respondent may not part with certain information that may be crucial for the research.

4.5.6 Measurer as Error Source

The measurer may be a source of error because of some of the common mistakes committed by interviewers. During the process of the interview, the interviewer might encourage or discourage the respondent while giving responses to certain questions, through body language and gestures—smiles to encourage certain responses, frowning to discourage certain responses and so on. After the collection of the data, the interviewer might reword or rephrase the responses that may lead to errors. Failing to record the full response of the respondent, inappropriate coding and tabulations and application of irrelevant statistical tools for measurement will also lead to errors.

4.6 Attitude Measurement

Attitudes have been understood as learned predispositions that project a positive or negative behaviour consistently towards various objects of the world. Attitudes are generally formed on a permanent basis and they develop as a combination of several interrelated beliefs. People in society have different attitudes towards different aspects of the world. Attitudes play a major role in a person's good or bad behaviour, based on the standards set by society. A person may have a negative attitude towards society and go against its customs and beliefs. On the other hand, a person with a positive attitude will not go against standards set by the society. There will be some people, who take the mid-path, conforming in some things and rebelling in others. Further, attitudes are not just confined to one aspect but a predisposition towards several features, a world-view as such. To give a small example, a person may have a positive attitude towards a particular hotel, based on its clean and hygienic environment and the tasty food it serves.

In any company or industry, it is crucial to measure customer attitudes to understand their behaviour towards products and services. Although it is difficult to measure attitudes qualitatively, attempts have been made to do this with a certain degree of accuracy. Having an accurate measure of consumer attitudes towards various business situations and marketing mix variables saves companies from committing huge sums to business activities that do not add value to customers or stakeholders.

In this chapter, we will discuss the components of attitude, the definition of scaling and different types of single item scales and multi-item scales. The chapter concludes with a discussion on considerations for selecting an appropriate scale.

4.7 Components of Attitude

Attitude has three components—the cognitive, the affective and the behavioural components. If a person says that he loves Britannia biscuits because they are tastier and will always eat them, the statement comprises all these three components of an attitude. Firms usually study components of attitudes in consumers to improve their marketing communications to attract customers and to develop a competitive advantage. Let us now elaborate these components.

4.7.1 Cognitive Component

The knowledge and perceptions acquired by a combination of direct experience with the attitude object and related information from various sources are based on cognition of an individual. This is termed cognitive component. Such knowledge in a person commonly leads to a belief that a particular type of behaviour leads to a particular outcome. The cognitive component of attitude consists of beliefs, opinions, knowledge and information held by a person regarding an object or an issue. The knowledge comprises awareness about the existence of the object, belief about its different characteristics and features of the product, apart from the relative importance the person gives to each characteristic.

Let us give an illustration. Anand, a businessman, is planning to travel to Delhi from Hyderabad by air. He remembers the names of several carriers, which he can use, such as Indian Airlines, Jet Airways, Air Deccan and so on. This is his knowledge about the existence of an object. This knowledge is not just confined to awareness. Anand will have certain beliefs about each airline based on his personal experience or through experiences of relatives and friends, knowledge gained through advertisements, books, magazines etc. This constitutes beliefs about different features of the object. Anand may also feel that the service in Indian Airlines is superior to Air Deccan. This is called placing relative importance. Anand's beliefs may not be entirely accurate, but to him, they are facts. Once these positive beliefs increase, they give rise to a favourable cognitive component towards an object. Marketers use various marketing mix variables to attract the customer and overtime try to nurture positive beliefs about their products and services in the minds of customers.

4.7.2 Affective Component

A person's emotions or feelings towards an object comprise the affective component of an attitude. Researchers treat such feelings of individuals as their favourable or unfavourable assessment of an object. Such feelings, which are called the affective component of attitude, may transform themselves into emotionally charged states such as anger, happiness, shame, distress, guilt and so on. These types of experiences will influence one's perception of an object and that person's later behaviour. For instance, a woman might say that she loves shopping at Lifestyle and that Shoppers' Stop does not have as wide a range of apparel as Lifestyle does. The woman's overall emotional feelings form the affective component. It is important to note that two persons may share a cognitive component, but when it comes to the affective component, one may have a positive affective component and the other a negative affective component towards the same object.

4.7.3 Behavioural Component

The behavioural component comprises a person's future actions and intentions. It is concerned with the likelihood or tendency that an individual will behave in a particular fashion with regard to an attitude object. Going back to our previous example, if Anand wants to fly Indian Airlines in the future too or the lady wants to buy clothes from Lifestyle in her next shopping excursion too, these are the behavioural components of attitude. These intentions, however, have limited timeframes. Sometimes suggestions become a behavioural component. For instance, when an individual suggests that a friend travel by Indian Airlines, it is a behavioural component of that individuals' attitude.

4.8 Relationship Between Attitudes and Behaviour

It is difficult to analyse the relationship between attitudes and behaviour. Analysing the future behaviour of a group of people is relatively easier than analysis for a single individual. Researchers have discovered that there are certain critical aspects governing the attitudes and behaviour of consumers. They are:

1. A product or service usage will be maximum if the person develops a positive attitude towards it. The converse is also true.
2. Attitudes of consumers towards products that they have never tried will be neutral.
3. When attitudes are developed based on actual trial and experience of a product, attitudes predict behaviour effectively. On the other hand, when attitudes are based on advertising, consistency in attitude and behaviour is considerably reduced.

4.9 Changing Attitudes

Changing customer attitudes, and changing them positively towards a company and its products, is the most important activity of businesses across the world today. Whenever sales of a product fall or market share declines, it becomes imperative for marketers to identify ways and means to overcome the downturn. Changing attitudes of stakeholders becomes the top priority in company's development efforts. Companies can attempt to change the attitudes of customers (an important stakeholder) towards a product in three ways:

- Altering existing beliefs about a product
- Changing attitudes by changing the importance of beliefs
- Adding new beliefs.

4.9.1 Altering Existing Beliefs About a Product

A marketer's fundamental responsibility here is to convert the neutral or negative belief that a customer holds about the product into a positive belief. For this, the marketer may attempt to change consumer perceptions about the product or service. Several tactics can be used. For instance, petrol stations have long been viewed as dusty, poorly lit places where weary petrol pump service personnel dressed shabbily serve. This perception or belief has been entirely changed by BPCL, which, by branding petroleum products and developing petrol stations into shopping malls (like in Western countries) has changed existing beliefs about petrol stations. BPCL's strategy is discussed in Exhibit 4.4.

However, marketers need to understand that customer beliefs cannot be changed by advertising alone. Any change achieved cannot be sustained if there is no tangible quality in the product to support advertising claims. Second, marketers trying to change consumer beliefs should ensure that the change is incremental rather than drastic. For example, an aggressive advertising campaign aimed at changing traditional beliefs of a community may meet with customer resistance. Therefore, the change process should be slow and preferably take the customer through all the stages in the learning process.

Exhibit 4.4: Bharat Petroleum's Efforts to Change Face

Petrol pumps in India have come a long way from being dusty, poorly lit places manned by shabbily clothed and indifferent personnel, to the shopping malls of the early twenty-first century. Bharat Petroleum Corporation Ltd. (BPCL), a leading player in the Indian petroleum industry, has got wide acclaim for having brought about this change in the fuel retailing business.

With the deregulation of the oil industry in April 2002, Indian players realized the need to become more customer focussed. BPCL's pioneering efforts to create brand awareness for its products were thus welcomed. BPCL's first foray into petrol pump retailing was through Bharat Shell Ltd. (Shell). The store, offering eatables, soft drinks, stationery, newspapers, magazines, frozen foods, light bulbs, audio cassettes and CDs, came as a pleasant surprise to Indian consumers.

By July 1999, 35 of BPCL's retail outlets across the country had 'Bazaar' stores running successfully. In October 2000, BPCL introduced another revolutionary concept by launching a McDonald's fast food outlet at a petrol pump near Mathura (UP) on the Delhi–Agra highway. The 4,000 sq.ft., 180-seat outlet was set up at a cost of Rs 40 million. McDonald's paid a fixed rent, besides a percentage of its sales to BPCL for using the facility. The outlet was expected to pull in foreign and domestic tourists headed to and from Agra, besides residents of surrounding areas.

In January 2001, BPCL further upgraded the 'Bazaar' stores and, a month later, launched the 'In and Out' stores at around 40 outlets in Bangalore, Mumbai, Delhi, Kolkata and Chennai. To offer enhanced customer service, BPCL tied up with various companies from different industries. These included fast food, photography, music, financial services, ISPs, e-commerce portals, document centers, ticketing, greeting cards, ATMs and courier services. All these efforts have helped BPCL significantly in changing customer beliefs.

4.9.2   Changing Attitudes by Changing the Importance of Beliefs

Another strategy is to change customer attitudes by changing the importance of beliefs that a customer holds about a particular product feature. For example, when Kelloggs entered India, it faced a lot of problems initially to sell its products, as a consequence of which it tried to change the people's attitude towards its products. This resulted in significantly improving its sales. Exhibit 4.5 discusses the repositioning strategy of Kelloggs' for changing customers' attitude towards the product.

4.9.3   Adding New Beliefs

An altogether different strategy adopted by marketers for changing customer attitudes is to develop new beliefs in customers about products. Adding new beliefs is an important job for marketers. Once such new beliefs are clearly communicated to consumers, there is a likelihood of higher sales since customers who previously did not bother to buy a product may now choose to buy it. For instance, traditionally, salt has been promoted on the taste attribute. Tata promoted salt with iodine content as essential for health (Iodine helps the growth, development and functioning of the thyroid gland), thus completely changing common beliefs about salt.

Exhibit 4.5: Kellogg's Repositioning Strategy

Kellogg's started its India operations in September 1995. Its initial offerings were cornflakes, wheat flakes and Basmati rice flakes. Later, it introduced the breakfast cereals Chocos and Frosties. Despite good quality products and support from the parent company's technical, managerial and financial resources, Kellogg's products failed in the Indian market. Kellogg realized that it was a tough task to get Indian consumers to accept its products. Kellogg banked heavily on the quality of its crispy flakes. But pouring hot milk on the flakes made them soggy. As Indians boil their milk before drinking, unlike in the West, the milk was usually warm or lukewarm. Americans often use cold milk for cereals, retaining their crispness. Indians also like to add sugar to their milk. When Kellogg flakes were put in hot milk, they became soggy and did not taste good. In cold milk, it was not sweet enough for Indian tastes because the sugar did not dissolve easily in cold milk. The rice and wheat versions too did not do well. In fact, some consumers even referred to the rice flakes as rice corn flakes.

Kellogg's began working towards better positioning for its products. The company's research showed that the average Indian consumer did not give much importance to the level of iron and vitamin intake and looked at quantity, rather than quality, of food consumed. Kellogg's worked towards changing the positioning of Chocos and Frosties—which had not been placed on the health platform but had been projected instead as 'fun-filled' brands.

In 1995, Kellogg had a 53 % share of the Rs 150 million breakfast cereal market, which had been growing at 4-5 % per annum till then. By 2000, the market size was Rs 600 million, and Kellogg's share increased to 65 %. Analysts claimed that Kellogg' entry was responsible for this growth. The company's improved prospects were clearly attributed to the shift in positioning, increased promotion and an enhanced media budget. The effort to develop products specifically for the Indian market helped Kellogg make significant inroads into the Indian market.

4.10 Association Between Measurement of Beliefs and Situation

It is generally found that there is a lesser relationship between researchers' measurements and the actual prevailing situation. In other words, the match between what the researcher finds and what actually happens is low owing to a number of reasons. For projecting a favourable attitude towards a product, a respondent should first have a felt need for the product. For instance, a respondent should need a car;

only then might he or she display a positive or negative attitude towards a particular brand of car. A person may have a favourable attitude towards a car, but this is not sufficient and has to be backed with the ability to purchase the product. Often, certain parameters of the purchase process are neglected while measuring attitudes. For example, a person might have decided to buy a product and may have decided on a particular brand, but on the day of purchase, the person may be lured away by a competitor's better promotional campaign. Or the person may decide to buy a brand that is cheaper and use the money saved for some other purpose. Sometimes the person's attitude may change or be influenced by other family members while making a purchase. These are some issues that will reduce the intensity of association between measurement of beliefs and the actual situation.

4.11 Attitude Scales

We have understood how important it is for marketers to measure attitudes. Marketers try to understand these attitudes and influence them to gain an advantage in the market. Measuring attitudes is a highly difficult process and unlike measurement scales in the physical sciences like measuring height, weight etc., measurement scales for attitude are less precise. In the following sections, we will discuss the different attitude scales that can be used to measure attitudes as precisely as possible.

Exhibit 4.6: Types of Attitude Scales

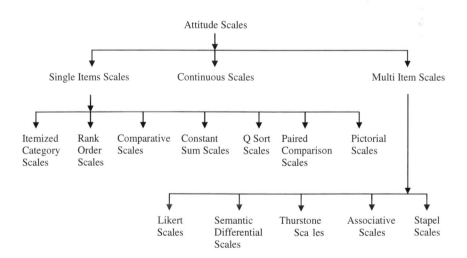

Source ICMR Centre for Management Research

4.12 Definition of Attitude Scale and Scaling

An Attitude Scale is a set of items (questions or statements) that probe a single aspect of human behaviour, attitudes, or feelings. Scaling is the process of measuring quantitative aspects of subjective or abstract concepts. It is a method to assign numbers or symbols to some attributes of an object. Scaling involves developing a continuum, based on which measured objects are located. For instance, if we want to measure the satisfaction levels of customers using a product, we might develop a six-point scale where respondents can choose one if they are least satisfied, three if they are moderately satisfied and six if they are highly satisfied. Scales are uni-dimensional or multi-dimensional. The former, as the name suggests, is used to measure one particular attribute of an object. For instance, while using a scale for measuring customer satisfaction levels, although several items will contribute to the measurement, these will be combined to give the final rating on customer satisfaction. A multi-dimensional scale is used to measure several attributes of an object, for example work environment, interpersonal relations, and behaviour of top management and compensation procedures. These will all be measured to determine the motivational levels of employees in an organization.

4.13 Types of Attitude Scales

There are two major types of scales used to measure the attitudes of respondents. They are single item scales and multi-item scales. The different types are shown in Exhibit 4.6

4.13.1 Single-Item Scales

Single-item scales are those with only one item to measure. Itemized category scales are most commonly used under single-item scales. Besides, itemized category scales, there are several other scales such as comparative scales, rank order scales and so on, which are used for attitude measurement. We will discuss each of these in the following sections.

4.13.2 Itemized Category Scales

Itemized category scales are those in which respondents have to select an answer from a limited number of ordered categories. Respondents are given the scale that contains a number or a brief description about a particular category. These categories are ordered in terms of position of the scale and respondents have to select one category that they feel best describes the object. It is easy to develop itemized category scales. Exhibit 4.7 gives an itemized category scale where a hotel customer is asked to indicate the level of satisfaction for service provided.

Exhibit 4.7: Itemized Category Scale

Given below is a itemized category scale ranging from highly satisfied to highly unsatisfied. Please select one of the following options based on your satisfaction levels of the hotel service.

Highly Satisfied   Considerably Satisfied Reasonably Satisfied   Unsatisfied Highly Unsatisfied

---

Adapted from Tull and Hawkins (1998), p. 380.

4.13.3 Rank: Order Scales

Rank order scales are comparative scales, where the respondent is asked to rate an item in comparison with another item or a group of items against each other based on a common criterion. For instance, a respondent may be asked to rank three motorcycle brands on attributes such as cost, mileage, style, pick-up and so on. Although it is easy to develop a rank-order scale, it has some disadvantages. It is very difficult to include every possible brand or attribute on a scale. Therefore, a respondent may rate a brand as number one, but it might not be his first choice as the brand he prefers may not have been included in the list at all. Sometimes, respondents may feel that the attributes used to construct the scale are not relevant to judging the subject under research. One major shortcoming is that the researcher will not have any clue about why the respondent has given a particular rating for items listed on the scale. Exhibit 4.8 shows a rank order scale for ranking different brands on motorcycle on specified attributes.

Exhibit 4.8: Rank Order Scale used for Analysing Motorcycles

Please rank the following brands of motorcycles with 1 being the brand that best meets the characteristic being evaluated and 7 being the worst on the characteristic being evaluated. Let us now start rating these brands basing on their affordability, first. Which brand has the highest affordability? Which is second? (Record the answers below).

Brand of motorcycle	Affordable cost	High mileage	Stylish	Great pickup
Hero Honda				
TVS				
Bajaj				

Adapted from Tull and Hawkins (1998), p. 384.

4.13.4 Q-Sort Scales

When the number of objects or characteristics to be rated is very large in number, it becomes difficult and tedious for respondents to rank order. In such cases, Q-sort scaling is used. Here, respondents are asked to sort out various characteristics or objects that are being compared into various groups so that the distribution of the number of objects or characteristics in each group follows a normal pattern. For instance, let us consider that the designing team of a toy manufacturing company has come out with hundreds of new product ideas with slight variations. The research team's task is to find out from customers which combination of features is the best and will generate maximum sales. To accomplish this, Q-sort scaling is the best method. The procedure followed is:

Respondents are given a set of cards, usually varying from 80 to 120 cards, containing different categories of items to be selected from. For instance, if respondents have to rate 100 different products according to their tastes and preferences, each respondent will be given about 100 cards containing a product and its features. Respondents are then asked to segregate the cards into 10 stacks so that the first stack contains a set of cards that are highly preferred by respondents. The 10th stack will contain a set of cards that are least preferred by them. The individual stacks in between (2nd and 9th) should be prepared by the respondent in such a way that they range from higher preference to lower preference. Once the stacks are ready, the cards in each stack should be arranged in the respondents' order of preference, based on criteria like features of a product, communication processes and customer service. This gives the best and the worst product in each stack. The disadvantage of this process is that it asks a lot of time and effort on the part of respondents.

4.13.5 Comparative Scales

In the itemized category scale, respondents select a category that they feel best describes a product. The problem here is that respondents may select a category based on their own perceptions. For instance, respondent A might select a category based on his or her view of an ideal brand, respondent B may pick a brand based on knowledge of an existing brand and respondent C might choose based on some other criteria. Ultimately, the selection process lacks uniformity. To overcome this, comparative scales have been developed, where the researcher provides a point of comparison for respondents to provide answers. Therefore, all respondents will have a uniform point of comparison for selecting answers. For instance, rather than asking a person to evaluate the quality of sweets in one sweet shop in Hyderabad, the respondents will be asked to evaluate the quality of that sweet shop in comparison with another sweet shop in Hyderabad. Exhibit 4.9 gives a comparative rating scale.

Exhibit 4.9: Comparative Scales

Given below is the scale ranging from excellent to very poor. If you were asked to rate the sweet shop 'X' in comparison to sweet shop 'Y' in Hyderabad. Which one will you choose. If you choose excellent then select the first option.

☐   ☐   ☐   ☐   ☐   ☐

Excellent   Very Good   Good   Both are same   Poor   Very poor

---

4.13.6 Paired Comparison Scales

In paired comparison scales, respondents are asked to select one of two items in a pair based on preset criteria. As each item is compared with all other items, the number of times an item is selected from a pair gives its rank. The higher the number, the better is the rank. In this method, the shortcoming of rank order scaling is overcome, as it is easy for respondents to select one item from two rather than ranking a long list of items. Another advantage is that the problem of order bias is eliminated as no set pattern is followed while providing respondents the pairs. A typical paired comparison scale for toothpaste is shown in Exhibit 4.10.

Exhibit 4.10: Paired Comparison Scale for a Toothpaste

Please select one item each from the following pairs that is most important to you for selecting a toothpaste.

a. Fights decay   b. Affordable
a. Affordable   b. Longer germ protection
a. Longer germ protection   b. Fights decay

4.13.7 Constant Sum Scales

In constant sum scales, respondents are asked to divide a given number of points, usually 100, among two or more attributes based on the importance they attach to each attribute. These scales are often used in place of paired comparison scales to eliminate the long lists in paired comparisons. Here, respondents have to rate an item in relation with all other items. Ranking for each item is based on the points assigned by the respondent to the items. The disadvantage of this approach is that the researcher is limited to giving 10 items for the respondent as a higher number of items will confuse the respondent. Exhibit 4.11 shows the constant sum scale where respondents are asked to rate 10 characteristics of a supermarket for a total sum of 100 points.

Exhibit 4.11: Constant Sum Scale Used for a Supermarket

Given below are the ten characteristics of a supermarket. Please give each characteristic some point(s) based on your assessment, so that the total points add up to 100. The higher number of points allocated to a particular characteristic, the higher its importance to you. However, if any particular characteristic is unimportant to you, then you need not assign any points to it. However, it is essential that all points given add up to 100.

Characteristics of a supermarket	Number of points
The supermarket is conveniently located	_____
The supermarket has enough range of products	_____
All the items in the store are conveniently located	_____
Sales persons are cooperative	_____
Aisle space is comfortable	_____
Prices are very much affordable	_____
The ambiance in the store is pleasing	_____
Soft music played in the store is entertaining	_____
Billing counters are sufficient	_____
Parking facility is adequate	_____
	_____
	100 points

4.13.8 Pictorial Scales

Here, the different types of scales are represented pictorially. The respondents are asked to rate a concept or statement based on their intensity of agreement or disagreement, on a pictorial scale. Pictorial scales have to be developed carefully so that respondents will not have problems selecting appropriate responses. These scales are generally used for respondents who cannot analyse complex scales, such as young children or illiterates. Typical pictorial scales are a thermometer scale or a scale depicting a smiling face. Exhibit 4.12 shows the smiling face scale for measuring the effectiveness of an advertisement campaign for a chocolate.

Exhibit 4.12: Smiling Face Scale

(Verbal Instructions)

Face 1 should be selected, if you did not like the chocolate ad at all and face 5 should be selected if you liked it very much, now how did you like it?

Adapted from Neelankavil et al. (1985)

4.13.9 Continuous Scales

Continuous scales are those where respondents are asked to rate items being studied by marking at an appropriate place on a line drawn from one extreme of the scale to the other. These scales are rarely used in marketing research as they do not give accurate results and the scoring process is complicated. This scale's only advantage is that it is very easy to develop. For instance, if a fast food outlet such as Pizza Hut wants to find out whether customers are satisfied with its overall service, then a continuous scale can be developed as shown in Exhibit 4.13

Exhibit 4.13: Continuous Rating Scale

Given below is a continuous scale ranging from 0 to 100 points. You have to indicate a point that best describes how you rate the overall service. If you rate it the best then it would be 100.

How would you rate the overall service of Pizza hut?

Best ------------------I--- Worst

    100   90   80   70   60   50   40   30   20   0

4.13.10 Multi-Item Scales

Let us move now to multi-item scales. These scales are used when it is difficult to measure people's attitudes based only on one attribute. For instance, to measure respondents' attitudes towards the Indian Railways, if you ask them only whether they are satisfied with Indian Railways or not, it will not suffice. People may say that they are satisfied on an overall basis, but there might be number of factors that they find unsatisfactory. Thus, it is impossible to capture the complete picture with one overall attitude-scale question. To measure individual attributes, a number of scales have been developed that can measure a respondent's attitude on several issues on a scale ranging from most favourable to least favourable. The Semantic, Likert, Thurstone and differential scales are some examples that follow such measurement techniques. Developing multi-item scale involves certain crucial steps that have been discussed in Exhibit 4.14.

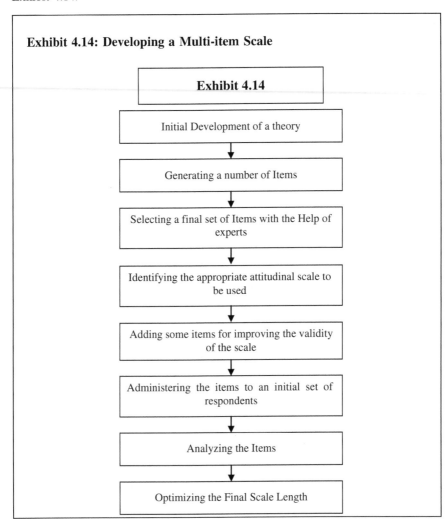

Exhibit 4.14: Developing a Multi-item Scale

Exhibit 4.14

Initial Development of a theory

Generating a number of Items

Selecting a final set of Items with the Help of experts

Identifying the appropriate attitudinal scale to be used

Adding some items for improving the validity of the scale

Administering the items to an initial set of respondents

Analyzing the Items

Optimizing the Final Scale Length

4.13.11 Semantic Differential Scales

Semantic differential scales are used to describe a set of beliefs that underline a person's attitude towards an organization, product or brand. This scale is based on the principle that individuals think dichotomously or in terms of polar opposites such as reliable/unreliable, modern/old fashioned, cold/warm.

The respondents are asked to rate an attitude object on a set of itemized, seven-point rating scale, bounded by bipolar phrases or adjectives. The initial process of developing a semantic differential scale starts with determining the object to be rated. Once this object is determined, respondents are asked to express their attitudes towards the object, using the dichotomous pair on a scale. Such points are

---

Exhibit 4.15: A Semantic Differential Scale for Measuring the Attitudes of Respondents for a Newspaper

Given below is a semantic differential scale, where a respondent has chosen his options on a 7 point scale based on 9 bi-polar categories.

1 2 3 4 5 6 7

Contemporary	Old Fashioned
Comprehensive News Coverage	News coverage is very limited
Interesting Supplements	Uninteresting Supplements
Balanced coverage of news	Unbalanced coverage of news
Quality of language is high	Quality of language is poor
Too much international coverage	Too less international coverage
Excellent Editorial Articles	Worst Editorial Articles
Appealing to youth	Not at all appealing to youth
Not inclined towards any political party	Inclined towards a political party

then plotted on a graph. This is the most efficient technique for determining the strengths and shortcomings of a product/service or a company in the market.

While designing the scale, care should be taken that all negative or positive adjectives or phrases do not appear on one side. This avoids a person from picking either only positive or negative phrases.

Another problem that should be addressed while developing a seven-point semantic scale is the response of four. If the respondent selects four for all items, then it becomes neutral without indicating any specific direction. Exhibit 4.15 represents the semantic differential scale administered for measuring the attitudes of respondents towards a newspaper. It can also be used for comparing the products with that of the competition. Consider four brands of cars being rated on the same scales, as shown in the Exhibit 4.16.

Exhibit 4.16: Semantic Differential Scale for Comparing Four Brands of Cars

Below given is the semantic differential scale rated by a responding by comparing 4 brands of cars.

| | Mitsubishi (L) Lancer | Skoda Octavia (O) |
| | Hyundai (E) Elantra | Honda (C) City |

Fast	EL	___	O	___	C	___	___	Slow
Large	___	L	E	O	C	___	___	Small
Plain	___	___	E	L	O	C	___	Stylish
Inexpensive	___	___	C	L	E	O	___	Expensive

Adapted from Tull and Hawkins (1998), p 390.

4.13.12 Stapel Scales

A Stapel scale is an attitude measure that places a single adjective or an attribute describing an object in the centre of an even number of numerical values. In general, staple scales are constructed on a scale of 10 ranging from −5 to +5, without a neutral point (zero). The respondent is asked to rate attributes on this scale.

Stapel scales are similar to semantic differential scales, but here there is only one pole (single adjective) rather than bipolar adjectives. This scale is useful for researchers to understand the positive and negative intensity of attitudes of respondents. The numeric value assigned to an adjective shows how well it describes the object. The higher the positive value, the better it describes the object.

One big disadvantage is that the respondent might select all attributes on a positive or negative range. A Stapel scale that is designed to measure the attitude of passengers towards an airline is shown in Exhibit 4.17.

Exhibit 4.17: Stapel Scale for Measuring the Attitudes of Flight Passengers

Below given is a staple scale designed to measure your attitude on three attributes. Please circle one number from the following three columns that best describes your attitude towards them.

+5	+5	+5
+4	+4	+4
+3	+3	+3
+2	+2	+2
+1	+1	+1
Friendly cabin crew	Comfortable interiors	Accurate timings
-1	-1	-1
-2	-2	-2
-3	-3	-3
-4	-4	-4
-5	-5	-5

4.13.13 Likert Scales

Likert scales consist of a series of statements where the respondent provides answers in the form of degree of agreement or disagreement. This expresses attitude towards the concept under study. The respondent selects a numerical score for each statement to indicate the degree of agreement or otherwise. Each such score is finally added up to measure the respondent's attitude. The various steps involved in developing a Likert scale are given below.

- Identify the concept that needs to be measured
- Develop a series of statements (say, 100) that articulate respondents' feelings towards the concept
- Every test item is categorized by the respondent as generally favourable or unfavourable based on the attitude that needs to be measured

- A pre-test is conducted to measure the intensity of the favourable or unfavourable attitude of respondents towards each test item. The scale would have intensity descriptors like, highly favourable, favourable, neutral, unfavourable and highly unfavourable. These responses are given a numerical weight.

The total attitude score is represented by the algebraic sum of the weights of the items. To make the measuring process uniform, the weights are consistently assigned. For instance, if 5 were assigned to reflect strong agreement with a favourable situation, then 5 should be assigned to show strong disagreement with an unfavourable situation too.

After the results have been obtained, the researcher selects items that reveal a clear discrimination between high and low total scorers by identifying the highest and lowest quartiles based on total scores. Subsequently, mean differences are computed for these high and low groups.

Finally, a set of items is chosen that represent the greatest difference between the highest and the lowest mean values.

Likert scales are very popular among researchers for measuring the attitudes of people. But, in practical situations, commercial researchers are more concerned with finding the respondents attitudes towards individual components, rather than overall positive or negative attitudes of respondents. For instance, the manufacturer of a brand of shoes will be more interested in finding out why people are not buying the brand rather than respondents' attitudes towards shoes in general. A typical Likert scale is discussed in the Exhibit 4.18.

Exhibit 4.18: Likert Scale

A Likert scale for evaluating the attitudes of customers, who have not used a vacuum cleaner, but are aware of its existence, is given below.

Here are some statements that describe how customers might feel about vacuum cleaners.

Please indicate your agreement or disagreement. For each statement given below, please circle the appropriate number to indicate whether you: 1-strongly agree, 2-agree, 3-neutral, 4-disagree and 5-strongly disagree.

	Strongly agree	Agree	Neutral	Disagree	Strongly disagree
The product is costlier	1	2	3	4	5
I do not find time to use a vacuum cleaner	1	2	3	4	5
Advertising of the product is not convincing enough	1	2	3	4	5

(continued)

(continued)

	Strongly agree	Agree	Neutral	Disagree	Strongly disagree
I have never used a vacuum cleaner	1	2	3	4	5
I am satisfied with the way I am cleaning my house right now	1	2	3	4	5
Using a vacuum cleaner is cumbersome	1	2	3	4	5
Competitor's vacuum cleaner has better features	1	2	3	4	5
The initial enthusiasm to use a vacuum cleaner dies down at a later stage and it is permanently kept in the store room	1	2	3	4	5
The demonstration of the product given by the salesperson is not effective	1	2	3	4	5

4.13.14 Thurstone Scales

In Thurstone scales, researchers select a group of 80 to 100 items indicating the different degrees of favourable attitude towards a concept under study. Once items are selected, they are given to a group of judges, who are asked to categorize them according to how much they favour or disfavour them. The judges are asked to treat intervals between categories as equal and analyse each item without expressing their own attitudes. Once the results are obtained, all those items that have a consensus from the judges are selected and items where there was no consensus are eliminated. These results are then distributed uniformly on a scale of favourability. This scale is then administered to a set of respondents for measuring their attitude towards a particular concept. Although the thurstone method is time-consuming as it involves a two-stage procedure, it is easy to administer. This method comes under criticism because the scale values are developed based on the attitudes of the judges.

4.13.15 Profile Analysis

Profile analysis is a process where two or more objects are rated by respondents on a scale. Profile analysis can be considered as an application of the semantic differential scale. Comparing different objects visually, based on different attributes, is possible in this approach. The major disadvantage is that it is very difficult to interpret the profiles as the number of objects increases. The profile analysis is used in Exhibit 4.19 to compare the three jeans brands.

4.14 Considerations in Selecting a Scale

Researchers tend to use those scales that are easy to administer and develop. For instance, a rank order scale can be quickly developed, while a semantic differential scale takes longer time and is cumbersome. It is also important to consider the client's requirements before selecting a scale. The type of data that are needed also plays an important role in selection. Some other factors that have to be considered while selecting a scale are: balanced versus unbalanced, the numbers of categories to be used, whether the categories should be odd or even and whether the choice be forced or unforced. Let us give some details.

Exhibit 4.19: A Profile Analysis Profile Analysis for Measuring the Attitudes of Respondents towards Jeans Brands

Given below is a profile analysis of three jeans brands where a respondent has indicated his attitude towards them on a five point scale based on five bi-polar categories.

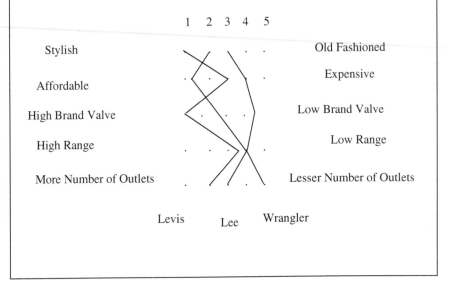

4.14.1 Balanced Versus Unbalanced Scales

A balanced scale is one, which has the same number of positive and negative categories, while an unbalanced scale is weighted towards one or the other end. A balanced scale is used in situations where a broad range of responses are expected. An unbalanced scale is used where the results of preliminary research lean more towards one side of the scale than the other. For instance, if preliminary research conducted to measure the performance of a new solar powered car indicates that it is generally liked by the people, then a scale with categories such as (1) excellent, (2) very good (3) good, (4) fair and (5) poor is developed.

4.14.2 Number of Categories

The number of categories that have to be included in the scale should be decided based on the research concept. If a scale is developed with very few categories (say, 2. good/bad), then it does not reveal the respondents' true attitudes. At the same time, if a scale contains 10 or more categories, the respondent might get confused and will not be able to accurately assign items to the different categories. Therefore, it is always better to develop a scale that contains between five and nine categories.

4.14.3 Odd or Even Number of Scale Categories

If a scale has an even number of categories, it means that it does not have a neutral point. This restricts the respondents and forces them to choose a negative or a positive aspect of a scale. So respondents who are actually neutral cannot express this feeling. Adding a neutral point in the scale helps respondents. Some feel that respondents can take the easy way out by saying that they are neutral and need not concentrate on their inner and real feelings. Deciding whether to have an odd number or an even number of categories on the scale is dependent on the nature of research to be conducted. For instance, if a company has recently changed the design and is attempting to study whether the customers have liked it, it cannot expect the respondents to be highly emotional towards the package design, and therefore, it needs to have neutral category (odd number). While if a company only wants to know how strongly the consumers like or dislike a product, then adding a neutral category will not serve the purpose.

4.14.4 Forced Versus Unforced Choice

If respondents are given adequate choice for selecting a response, it becomes an unforced choice. If they are not given any choice for selecting a response, then it becomes a forced choice. An unforced decision can be either in the form of 'Neutral' (which a respondent chooses if he is not inclined towards either object) or 'Do not know' (which a respondent can choose if he lacks the knowledge to answer the question). When these two categories are included in the scale, it becomes an unforced choice, as the respondents do not have to select a positive or negative opinion when they do not have any opinion. When a neutral or do not know category is not included in the scale, it obviously becomes a forced choice. Restricting the choice of respondents, although essential in some research studies, should be avoided as a rule.

References

Belk RW (1984) Three scales to measure constructs related to materialism: reliability, validity and relationships to measures of happiness. Adv Consumer Res 11(1):291 (6 pp)
Neelankavil JP, O'Brien JV, Tashjian R (1985) Techniques to obtain market-related information from very young children. J Advert Res
Singh J, Rhoads GK (1991) Boundary role ambiguity in marketing-oriented positions: a multidimensional multifaceted operationalization. J Mark Res 28(3):328 (10 pp)
Tull DS, Hawkins DI (1998) Marketing research—measurement and method, 6th edn. Prentice Hall of India, New Delhi

Chapter 5
Questionnaire Design

A questionnaire is a set of questions to be asked from respondents in an interview, with appropriate instructions indicating which questions are to be asked, and in what order. Questionnaires are used in various fields of research like survey research and experimental design. A questionnaire serves four functions—enables data collection from respondents, lends a structure to interviews, provides a standard means for writing down answers and help in processing collected data.

A questionnaire will be ineffective if it is not designed in a manner easily understood by both the interviewer and the interviewee. If there is a single, fundamental principle for developing a sound questionnaire design (Labaw 1980) it is that the respondent defines what you can do: the types of questions you can reasonably ask; the types of words you can reasonably use; the concepts you can explore; the methodology you can employ. The design is dependent on the researcher's decision to collect qualitative data for better understanding and generation of hypotheses on a subject (exploratory research), or quantitative data to test specific hypotheses.

This chapter discusses the various steps in questionnaire design like:

- Preliminary decisions
- Question content
- Response format
- Question wording
- Questionnaire sequence
- Questionnaire pre-test, revision and final draft

Let us elaborate each of these aspects.

5.1 Preliminary Decisions

A researcher has to take many decisions before framing the actual questionnaire. These decisions relate to the information required, the target respondents and the choice of interviewing techniques.

S. Sreejesh et al., *Business Research Methods*,
DOI: 10.1007/978-3-319-00539-3_5,
© Springer International Publishing Switzerland 2014

5.1.1 Required Information

The researcher is expected to know and understand the survey's objectives before he or she can take further steps. In framing a questionnaire, the researcher must ensure that the questions are designed to draw information that will fulfil research objectives. Sometimes researchers end up designing questionnaires that study the peripheral issues related to a problem or an opportunity but fail to give insight into the actual problem. Such questionnaires will act as a drain on a company's resources and the data so collected may mislead the top management while making decisions.

To avoid such situations, a researcher should go through the secondary data and research studies that are similar to the current research. This helps in planning current research based on existing research findings related to the topic under study. The researcher can also conduct informal interviews with the prospective target audience to understand the nature of the problem and the information that would help managers in solving a problem.

5.1.2 Target Respondents

Before conducting the actual survey, the researcher must make sure of the target population for the survey. For example, in case of market research, a researcher has to decide whether to include both users and non-users of a product or service. This is a crucial step, as the sampling frame would be drawn after the target respondents are defined.

Defining the target respondents becomes vital as the task of developing a questionnaire that will be suitable to all cross-sectional groups of a diversified population.

5.1.3 Interviewing Technique

In developing a questionnaire, a lot depends on the choice of interviewing technique. The format and type of questions will be different for personal interviews, focus groups, telephonic interviews and mailed questionnaires. A questionnaire designed for direct interviewing cannot be used for a survey through mail. In personal interviews, the respondent should be clearly told the details and the form of answers the questions require. It is prudent for questionnaires to be brief and to the point in telephonic interviews. Mail survey questionnaires should give clear instructions about the type of details that are desired, as an interviewer does not mediate these interviews.

5.2 Question Content

A clear definition of the problem and the objectives framed thereafter, play a major role in deciding the content of the questions. In other words, the general nature of the questions and the information they are supposed to elicit decide the question content. In this process, things become easier because there are some set standards that can be followed.

Irrespective of the type of research, a researcher has to find answers to five major questions while deciding the question content. They are

I. What is the utility of the data collected?
II. How effective is a question in producing the required data?
III. Can the respondent answer the question accurately?
IV. Is the respondent willing to answer the question accurately?
V. What is the chance of the responses being influenced by external events?

5.2.1 The Utility of Data

A researcher should ensure that each question in the questionnaire contributes to the survey. For this, every question needs to be screened before it is added to the questionnaire. This screening test analyses the usefulness of the data that will be gathered by that particular question. Questions like, 'Does it significantly contribute towards answering the research question?' 'Will its omission affect the analysis of any other data?' and 'Can the same information be gathered through any other question?' have to be asked. If the question does not answer any of these questions positively, or generates just 'interesting or good to know information', then it should be dropped. However, in special cases, it becomes necessary to ask unnecessary and disguised questions to avoid any response bias.

5.2.2 Effectiveness in Producing Data

After it is decided to include the question in the questionnaire, it should be assessed whether the question will be able to generate the required information or if it needs to be broken down into two specific questions (double-barrelled questions) to elicit better and accurate answers from respondents. In simple words, the question should be effective enough to extract the required information from the interviewee.

5.2.3 The Participant's Ability to Answer Accurately

It is necessary that respondents understand the question in a way that the researcher wants. This will eliminate the probability of potentially incorrect responses. This can be tackled by using simple words to frame the questions. A respondent's inability to answer a question may arise from three sources—genuine ignorance about the topic, inability to recollect the answer and inability to verbalize the response.

Ignorance: This refers to respondents being unaware or uninformed about the subject of the question. This can lead to respondent bias as respondents will rarely admit to lack of knowledge on a topic. These respondents will participate at the expense of accuracy. To cover up their ignorance, they provide some answers or the other, assuming that the interviewer will be impressed with their knowledge level.

Inability to recollect: This happens when respondents forget an answer because of recall and memory decay. This happens when questions overtax the respondents recall ability. For example, questions like 'What was your expenditure on grocery items in the last week?' requires respondents to bank on their memory to answer it. It is a fact that many of us cannot exactly keep track of factual details relating to recent activities. But while responding to questions on the same, we tend to give the best answer that we can recollect. Some aspects of forgetfulness in a respondent that are of concern to researchers are:

Omission—when the interviewee is unable to remember if an incident actually occurred. For instance, while answering the above question, the respondent might not recollect the purchases made in the last week and hence might fail to give the actual data.

Telescoping—when the interviewee thinks that an event that occurred sometime in past occurred more recently. In other words, the respondent may report purchases made a fortnight ago as done in the last week.

Creation—when the interviewee feels that the incident or event did not occur at all. In other words, total forgetfulness.

The above three aspects of forgetting increase with the length of the recall period. The telescoping and creation aspects can be minimized by using short recall periods. This means that the interviewee should be asked questions, which need only recall of incidents and events from the near past. Omission can be dealt with only by aided or unaided recall measures.

Inability to verbalize: This refers to the respondents' inability to verbalize factors influencing their buying motives. It is not quite possible to answer questions like, 'Why did you buy that car?', 'What made you buy that brand of shoes?' This is because many times people buy things for reasons other than what they admit to themselves. There might be definite reasons behind the purchase like habit, vanity, taste, etc. but when asked 'Why?' people are generally unable to articulate reasons, as they are not conscious of what is in their sub-conscious. Researchers can awaken the sub-conscious minds of the respondents through effective projective techniques.

5.2.4 The Respondent's Willingness to Answer Accurately

This refers to the researcher assessing the likelihood of the respondent answering a particular question accurately. A respondent's unwillingness to answer a specific question can result in item non-response (where the respondent completes the rest of the questions other than those he or she is uncomfortable with), refusal to complete the rest of the questionnaire or in deliberate falsification. Questions such as, 'Were you involved in any extra-marital relationship in the 10 years of your marriage?' 'Would you resort to stealing things in a supermarket if you knew there were no hidden cameras?' are virtually sure to attract stereotyped responses or refusals from participants.

This refusal can be because of the question being offending, too personal and embarrassing, reflecting on prestige, or when the respondents decide the topic is irrelevant to their interests. Hence, researchers should carefully look into the inclusion of such questions. If the information from such questions is essential, the questions can be framed subtly so that the respondent's attention is not attracted. Very often, questions of a personal nature will be answered by respondents in an anonymous survey that is if they do not have to give their real names or identities.

5.2.5 Effect of External Events

Sometimes the respondent's answer to a particular question is exaggerated or understated due to the interference of external events. Example of external events is weather or time. For example, a questionnaire designed to find the potential footfalls for a big apparel showroom that is to come up in a business district investigated the shopping patterns of women by asking them 'how many times did you go shopping in the past 1 week?' The survey was conducted just after a week of heavy rain in the particular city. The shopping frequency reported by respondents was dismaying as most of them had naturally preferred to stay indoors without going shopping in the rains. Though the answers were right for the particular question, it was not truly representative of the shopping frequency of the respondents. Hence, questions should be framed after considering external events. A better way to frame the question would have been to keep it 'situation free' and frame it in a general manner to avoid linkage with external events. The question in the above example could have been, 'how many times do you shop in a week?'

5.3 Response Format

The response format required by a question depends on the nature of the research. The format usually deals with issues relating to the degree of freedom that should be given to respondents while answering a question. Two popular response formats are

- Open-ended questions
- Close-ended questions.

5.3.1 Open-Ended Questions

A type of question that requires participants to respond in his/her own words without being restricted to pre-defined response choices is known as an open-ended question. They are also called infinite response or unsaturated type questions. Open-ended questions are structured in themselves. Although they probe for unstructured responses, there is a definite structure in the arrangement of questions in the questionnaire. They help establish rapport, gather information and increase understanding. Open-ended questions act as memory prompts, as they at times require the respondent to recollect past experiences. Therefore, the interviewer should refrain from making suggestions. He should rather invite the participant to use his/her own choice of words to answer. The interviewer should get the respondent to talk as much as possible and record answers in the same words used by the interviewee.

Open-ended questions are useful when the respondent is able to provide a narrative answer, when the researcher is uncertain what answers are needed or wants to conduct exploratory research. Such questions can be sub-divided into three sub-types—free response, probing and projective.

5.3.2 Free Response

Free-response questions typically fluctuate in the degree of freedom they give to the interviewee. Look at the following questions.

Q What do you think of the performance of the Indian hockey team in the recent Athens Olympics?
Q How would you evaluate Dhanraj Pillay's performance in the Athens Olympics?

The second question seeks a more directive response about a particular member of the Indian hockey team rather than asking about the whole team.

5.3.3 Probing

Probing open-ended questions are those where the actual open-ended questions are reached a little later in the process. Consider the following example.

Q Which brand of soft drink do you like? Coke or Pepsi?
A Pepsi.
Q Why do you prefer Pepsi to Coke?
A I like the taste.
Q What aspect of its taste do you like? (Probe)

This is where the interviewer starts probing to get to the specific product attributes linked to the interviewee's liking of Pepsi and the role that the sub-conscious mind of the interviewee plays in influencing the buying decisions.

5.3.4 Projective

A vague question or stimulus used by the researcher to project a person's attitudes from the responses is known as a projective open-ended question. Such questions are primarily used in projective techniques and have been extensively covered in the chapter 'Qualitative and Observation Studies'.

For the advantages and disadvantages of open-ended questions, refer Exhibit 5.1

5.3.5 Close-Ended Questions

Questions, which restrict the interviewee's answers to pre-defined response options, are called close-ended questions. Close-ended questions give respondents a finite set of specified responses to choose from. Such questions are deemed appropriate when the respondent has a specific answer to give (for example, gender), when the researcher has a pre-defined set of answers in mind, when detailed narrative information is not needed or when there is a finite number of ways to answer a question. These questions are common in survey researches. Four major structures exist for close-ended questions. They are:

- Binary
- Ranking questions
- Multiple choice
- Checklist

5.3.6 Binary Questions

These are also known as dichotomous questions as they permit only two possible answers. The respondent has to choose one of the two permissible answers. Binary questions are helpful in collecting simple, factual data, and they should be used to record classification data about the interviewee (demographic data). These questions have the response options '"Yes" or "No"' or '"True" or "False"' or '"Agree" or "Disagree"'. Such questions should generally not be included in a questionnaire because these choices may not cover the whole range of possible responses. The respondent might be compelled to give answers whether or not they represent their true feelings. This tends to affect the survey's accuracy.

Exhibit 5.1 Advantages and disadvantages of open-ended and close-ended questions

	Advantages	Disadvantages
OPEN-ENDED	• Open-ended questions can discover uncommon but intelligent opinions of which the surveyor would otherwise have remained unaware	• Coding open-ended questions is difficult and time consuming
	• The respondent has greater freedom of expression	• As the questions require more thought and time on the part of the interviewee, it reduces the number of questions that can be asked within a specified time span
	• There is no bias due to limited response ranges	• There are chances that a researcher/interviewer might misinterpret a response as it becomes difficult pooling an opinion across the sample
	• Respondents have freedom to qualify their answers	
CLOSE-ENDED	• Close-ended questions are more specific and easy to answer	• The options might not reveal the true feelings of the participants
	• They provide a high level of control to the interviewer by obliging the interviewee to answer questions using a particular set of options	• Misleading conclusions can be drawn because of poor questionnaire design and limited range of options
	• The uniformity of the questions makes them easier to code, record and analyse results quantitatively	• Requires pre-testing and prior open-ended research to ensure that choices offered are the relevant ones
	• No difference between articulate and inarticulate respondents	
	• Higher response rate	
	• Less expensive and time consuming	

5.3.7 Ranking Questions

These questions require the participant to rank the response options listed on a continuum basis in order of preference. Ranking questions are used to get information that reveals participants' attitudes and opinions. These questions list several alternatives that might influence an individual's decision-making. The participant assigns a rank to each option listed as per the scale mentioned. Consider the following example:

The factors that influence your decision to buy from a particular supermarket are listed below. Please rank them from the most important (1) to the least important (7).

Conveniently located	——
Helpful sales staff	——
Owner is a known person	——
Recommended by a friend or relative	——
Regular discounts offered	——
Instant home delivery	——
Availability of everything I need	——

Such questions make it easy to compare different alternatives at the same time.

5.3.8 Multiple-Choice Questions

These questions cover all significant degrees of response. The respondent has to select an option that best describes their feelings. These are mostly a variation of binary questions with more responses provided. These are also known as 'cafeteria' questions. Three issues that should be considered while framing such questions are—the response options should be collectively exhaustive to qualify it as a valid question; the position of the responses should be varied to avoid the selection of any particular response due to position bias and the response options offered should be distinct from one another. The reasons behind the popularity of multiple-choice questions are their simplicity and applicability.

5.3.9 Checklist Questions

These are questions where the participant has the freedom to choose one or more of the response options available. This is different from multiple-choice questions in that it gives freedom to the respondents to choose one or more of the options available. Consider the following question.

Q Which premium brand of shirts do you possess? (Tick as many of the following as apply)

- Allen Solly
- Louis Phillippe
- Van Heusen
- Color Plus
- Zodiac

It should be ensured that options are placed in a random sequence rather than in any preferential order. Apart from the options selected by the researcher, an option called 'others' should be provided so that the respondent can fill it in if he wants to. With all significant categories present, this method facilitates replies from the respondent and subsequent tabulations. For the advantages and disadvantages of close-ended questions, refer Exhibit 5.1

Exhibit 5.2 Examples of common problems with question wording

Avoid objectionable and sensitive questions	*Objectionable:* How often do you travel in a bus without a ticket?
	Unobjectionable: How often do you forget to take a ticket while travelling by bus? (Disguised)
Avoid biased questions	*Biased:* Do you think that TV has a negative effect on children?
	Unbiased: What are your views about the effects of TV on children?
Avoid vague questions	*Vague:* How satisfied are you with Celebrity Resorts?
	Better: How would you describe the hospitality in Celebrity Resorts in your own words?
Avoid unwarranted Presumptions	*Presumptive:* How satisfied are you with the speed of response for on-site technical support? (assumes that customers are satisfied)
	Better: How satisfied or dissatisfied are you with the speed of response for on-site technical support?
Avoid the use of leading questions that prompt the respondent to a particular answer	*Leading:* Would you prefer a supermarket nearer your home?
	Better: How often would you shop from a supermarket based on its distance from your house?
Avoid asking negative Questions	*Negative:* Sales persons should not be allowed to make visits in the evening. Agree/Disagree
	Positive: Sales persons should be allowed to make visits at any time. Agree/Disagree

(continued)

(continued)	
Ensure that the wording is completely unambiguous	*Ambiguous:* How seldom, occasionally and frequently do you purchase stock? *Unambiguous:* How often do you purchase stock?a) Seldom b) Occasionally c) Frequently
Avoid double-barrelled questions	*Double-barrelled:* Do you drive or take the bus everyday to office? Yes/No *Better:* How do you go to your office everyday? Drive or take a bus?
Have as narrow a reference range as possible	*Too broad a time perio*d: How many times have sales promotions influenced you to switch brands over the last 1 year? *Better:* How many times in the last month have sales promotions influenced you to switch brands?

5.4 Question Wording

Designing questionnaires can be an exercise in effective cross-communication, as it tests the communication abilities of the person framing them. The effective translation of the desired question content into appropriate words does the trick in gathering responses. Questions tend to get longer to be explicit, present alternatives and explain meanings. In such cases, lack of appropriate words can result in the respondent misunderstanding the question and giving inappropriate answers or even refusing to answer. A slight mistake in questionnaire wording can be annoying and cause potential problems in data analysis, resulting in incorrect results. Although the importance of wording has been recognized, the search for a set of basic rules for questionnaire wording still remains elusive. However, guidelines developed from previous research experiences tell us that the following factors should be looked into while framing a questionnaire.

I. Shared vocabulary
II. Unsupported assumptions
III. Frame of reference
IV. Biased wording
V. Adequate alternatives
VI. Double-barrelled questions
VII. Generalizations and Estimates

Refer Exhibit 5.2 for common problems with question wording.

5.4.1 Shared Vocabulary

An interview of any kind is mostly an exchange of ideas between the interviewer and the interviewee. This exchange takes place mostly through words. This makes it imperative for the interactive language to be kept simple and easily understood by both parties. A couple of things are worth ensuring in this respect. First, the involvement and usage of technical language has to be dealt with carefully. This is necessary as using highly technical language in the questions may create understanding problems for both the interviewer and the interviewee. The second issue is the appropriate choice of words. It is not enough to ensure that the words are simple. It also has to be seen that the words are not ambiguous or vague.

5.4.2 Unsupported Assumptions

Questionnaires should avoid the use of implicit assumptions for better response rates. A questionnaire should not contain questions framed on assumptions that are not explained in the questions. A question should not leave anything for the respondents and the audience to interpret. The question should be supported with valid assumptions that would make it clearer to the audience. Unsupported, implied assumptions tend to produce exaggerated estimates from respondents. Consider the following question to a lady. 'How often does your man accompany you to...?' This will elicit varied responses and may even be misinterpreted. The question assumes that every lady has a spouse or a boyfriend, which is obviously not the case. Consider another question. 'Would you favour a ban on overcrowding of buses?' This is sure to provide an inflated estimate of the public's demand, unless the assumption 'even if it means an increase in bus fares?' is added. When the assumption is explicit in the question itself, it tends to produce the right estimates of the demand for products.

5.4.3 Frame of Reference

A single word can have several connotations under different situations. Words such as 'often' and 'regularly' can mean different time frames for different individuals. The word 'capacity', for example, can mean very different things to an industrialist and an educator. But the framework of social desirability makes the interviewer extend a common frame of reference to the participants. The interviewer assumes that the interviewee has understood the question in its denotative terms and qualifies the answer as valid. This is a mistake as the respondent might have answered the question using an individual frame of reference rather than from the interviewer's point of view.

5.4.4 Biased Wording

Questionnaires should avoid the use of biased wording. This tends to influence the responses of the participants in predetermined ways. Biased and loaded words tend to be emotionally coloured, eliciting automatic feelings of approval or disapproval. They make participants aware of the desired response, thereby taking the focus away from the actual response.

For example, a question to a factory employee, 'Would you favour the replacement of manual labour by machinery?' is sure to receive a negative response. A way of asking the question to read the sub-conscious mind of the employee would be, 'How do you think the introduction of machines would affect labourers in a factory?'

Similarly, a question in a customer feedback form, 'How satisfied are you with the service provided at our restaurant?' is biased as the question implies that the customer is already satisfied and asks them to grade the service.

The question should rather be phrased, 'How satisfied or dissatisfied are you with the service provided at our restaurant?', thereby avoiding bias.

5.4.5 Adequate Alternatives

Questionnaires should give an ample number of alternative answers to each question. This too helps avoiding bias in responses. Alternatives should be explicit rather than implicit. This gives respondents the freedom to choose among alternatives rather than delve into their own mind to recollect responses. It is a faster way to gather responses. For example, consider the following question:

How often do you purchase stock?

(a) Seldom
(b) Occasionally
(c) Frequently

5.4.6 Double-Barrelled Questions

Questionnaires should avoid asking double-barrelled questions like, 'Do you like fuel-efficient cars with comfortable seats?' This is actually a combination of two questions. It does not distinguish between people who prefer cars due to their fuel-efficiency and people who prefer a car for its comfortable seats or other competing reasons. Such questions can be easily divided into two different questions. Answers to double-barrelled questions will be ambiguous because two or more ideas are included.

5.4.7 Generalizations and Estimates

Questionnaires should be structured to avoid generalizations and estimates. It is seen that when respondents are asked for the frequency of a particular activity over a longer period, they tend to provide generalizations and estimates rather than the actual figures. This trend can be reduced by changing the time reference point to a more specific base. Answers that require calculations by the respondent should also be avoided. Minimal necessary information can be gathered and then the calculations should be done by the interviewer.

5.5 Questionnaire Sequence

The structure of a questionnaire is an important aspect in questionnaire design. The questionnaire structure is framed depending upon whether it is self-administered or the administration is facilitated by an interviewer. Questionnaire structure pertains to the proper sequencing for better and effective responses. The sequencing tends to drive the interview through a 'funnel-shaped' process, starting with general questions and progressing to more specific ones. The interviewer, before moving to sequential steps, gives a brief introduction about the survey's basic purpose survey and client confidentiality. This sequencing is explained through the following steps:

- Lead-in questions
- Qualifying questions
- Warm-up questions
- Specifics questions
- Demographics questions

5.5.1 Lead-in Questions

This is the introductory phase of the interview and consists of tactfully designed ice-breakers. These can prove crucial in gaining the participant's confidence and cooperation. The questions should be simple, non-threatening and not too personal at this stage. A good way to start the session is by asking a 'ringer or throw away' question or a dichotomous question with two responses. These questions measure the respondent's interest and willingness to respond. The questions can be about hot topics of the day, where responses are of little importance to the survey. A typical lead-in question is given below.

Q It is often said that the economic condition in India is a by-product of the political situation. Do you agree with this?

A YES/NO

5.5.2 Qualifying Questions

These are questions that slowly lead to the survey's objective. This stage is characterized by questions that evaluate the respondent and qualify him/her for further questioning. Depending on the responses, the interviewer directs the interview towards a relevant set of questions. Prior to this, it should be ensured that the interviewees are related to the survey in some meaningful terms. A survey for estimating market potential for a new fluoride-based toothpaste brand should ask qualifying questions like the following.

Q Which type of toothpaste do you like?
A Fluoride Herbal Calcium

Depending upon the interviewee's response, the interviewer can further give directions to the next questions.

5.5.3 Warm-Up Questions

This stage plays on the respondent's mind by making him/her think of certain facts related to the survey questions. Questions like, 'When was the last time you bought toothpaste?'; 'Was it fluoride content or herbal?'; 'Looking back, can you recollect how many times you might have used fluoride toothpastes over the last 1 year?' tend to make the respondent think and recollect past experiences. A person who is straightaway asked such questions may not be interested in answering or providing details, but after a series of lead-in and qualifying questions, the resistance slowly decreases and gives way to cooperation.

5.5.4 Specific Questions

This stage consists of questions that are specific to the research objectives. As such, they are asked of participants who show a favourable response or are end users of the product, in this case, fluoride toothpastes. These questions tend to estimate the usage pattern and influential factors in using fluoride content toothpaste. These specific questions play a major role in data collection and analysis. After ensuring that enough rapport has been established, this section can probe to gain insight into sensitive issues.

5.5.5 Demographic Questions

These are a necessary part of every survey. Responses to survey questions cannot be analysed until they are sorted out according to the different characteristics pertaining to the study. This is especially true for surveys that analyse responses based on the demographic characteristics of respondents. These usually consist of a set of questions related to age, sex, location, occupation, etc. These questions are kept to the end to avoid interviewee resistance and to prevent the interviewee's attention from being diverted.

5.6 Questionnaire Pre-testing, Revision and Final Draft

Pre-testing refers to testing the questionnaire on a small sample of respondents selected on a convenient basis that is not too divergent from the actual respondents. The aim is to identify and eliminate flaws and problems. Pre-testing includes testing all aspects of the questionnaire starting from the question content to question sequence. This helps reveal incomprehensible meanings, wrong order of questions, leading questions and awkward responses. No matter what the final mode of administration is, pre-testing should be done by personal interviews. This will facilitate interviewers to observe respondents' reactions and attitudes, giving them a first-hand experience of the potential problems and the data that can be expected from a questionnaire.

The responses gathered from pre-testing are coded to facilitate analysis. Pre-testing enables the researcher to revise the questionnaire by identifying flaws and eliminating any ambiguous questions. It also helps researchers to verify if interviewers resort to proper sample selection procedures.

After the revision, the research instrument is ready for its final draft, which is to be used for the actual survey.

5.7 Summary

A good questionnaire is imperative for good survey results. A questionnaire can be judged based on its relevance (no collection of unnecessary information) and accuracy (information should be reliable and valid). This chapter discussed the proper designing of a questionnaire for better results. As no established rules exist for such designing, the steps outlined in this chapter are taken from experiences accumulated through various studies. The first step in questionnaire designing is arriving at preliminary decisions regarding the issues of required information, the target respondents and the interview techniques to be adopted. This is necessary as the content, format, wording and sequencing of the questionnaire will depend on these basic factors. The next step is to determine the questionnaire content, so that it deals with identifying the need for data, the question's ability to yield data, the participant's ability to answer without generalizations and estimates and willingness to answer sensitive questions.

Knowing how each question should be phrased requires familiarity with the different types of questions. This leads to the next step of the questionnaire designing, that is questionnaire response format. This deals with issues of using open-ended or close-ended questions. Open-ended questions require the respondent to do most of the talking while close-ended questions restrict the respondent's responses to the available options. Each has its own advantages and disadvantages and is suited to different interviewing techniques.

Experiences from previous researches have helped establish general guidelines regarding questionnaire wording and sequence. It should be ensured that questions resort to shared vocabulary and adequate alternatives for better understanding and response rates. The questions should be free of implicit assumptions, biased and loaded words. It should also be free of questions that are double-barrelled and that would provoke the respondent to provide generalizations and estimated answers. Questionnaire sequencing is very important to elicit required information from the participant. The opening questions should arouse the respondent's interest in the survey. The specific and general questions should be followed in order. This means that the questions are sequenced in the following manner: lead-in, qualifying, warm-up, specific and demographic.

Last, the questionnaire should be pre-tested before administration for detecting flaws and revised with necessary corrections and deletions. This would lead to the final draft to be used in the actual survey.

Reference

Labaw, Philip Gendall (1980) A framework for questionnaire design: Labaw Revisited, Mark Bull 1998, 9, 29–39

Part IV
Multivariate Data Analysis Using IBM SPSS 20.0

Chapter 6
Data Preparation and Preliminary Analysis

After data collection is over and all completed questionnaires are in hand, a researcher has to analyse the data collected through the research. Data analysis plays an important role in transforming a lot of data into verifiable sets of conclusions and reports. Proper analysis helps the researcher to gain insights from the data and to arrive at informed judgments and conclusions. However, if the purpose of research is not defined properly or if research questions are irrelevant, even the best analytical techniques cannot produce good results. Data analysis may give faulty results even when research is done properly. This is because of the application of inappropriate methods to analyse data.

In this chapter, we will start with preliminary data preparation techniques like validation, editing and coding, followed by data entry and data cleaning. The penultimate section discusses various types of survey tabulations. This is followed by the final section of the chapter, which provides insight into data mining and its applications. The various steps in data preparation and preliminary data analysis are shown in Fig. 6.1.

6.1 Validating and Editing

Validation is the preliminary step in data preparation. It refers to the process of ascertaining whether the interviews conducted complied with specified norms. The essence of this process lies in detecting any fraud or failure by the interviewer to follow specified instructions (Beegle 1981). In many questionnaires, we find there is a separate place to record the respondent's name, address and telephone number and other demographic details. Though no apparent analysis can be done on such data, it is the basis for what is called 'validation'. Validation helps to confirm if the interview was really conducted.

Editing is the process of checking for mistakes by the interviewer or respondent in filling the questionnaire. Editing is usually done twice before the data are submitted for data entry.

S. Sreejesh et al., *Business Research Methods*,
DOI: 10.1007/978-3-319-00539-3_6,
© Springer International Publishing Switzerland 2014

Fig. 6.1 Stages of data
analysis

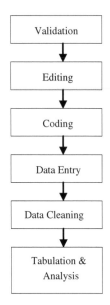

The first editing is done by the service firm, which conducted the interviews. The second editing is done by the market research firm that outsourced the interviews. Editing is a manual process that checks for problems cited below:

Finding out whether the interviewer followed the 'skip pattern'. The questionnaire is designed so that depending on the respondent's response, the interviewer skips to the next relevant question. This is called the 'skip pattern'. Sometimes it might happen that interviewers skip questions when they should not and vice versa. In the sample questionnaire shown in Fig. 12.2, the interviewer should skip to question 7 if the response to the first question is either (A) or (E) or (F).

Responses to open-ended questions are vital for business researchers and their clients. Eliciting the correct responses to open-ended questions shows the interviewer's competence. Hence, interviewers are instructed to probe initial responses and are asked not to distort the actual wordings or interpret the response of an open-ended question.

For instance, different possible responses for the second question are shown Fig. 6.2.

Question: Why do you eat chocolates?
Respondent 1: Because I like chocolates
Respondent 2: I like chocolates. I like their taste and softness. (Indicates interviewer probed further into the response.)
Respondent 3: I like chocolates because they give me energy

In the first response, the interviewer failed to extract the correct response. The objective of probing is to extract the reason behind eating chocolates. In the second

Date: --------
Respondent's telephone number   ------------
Respondent's address   ---------------
Respondent's age:
1. How many chocolates do you eat in a typical week?
A. Less than 5
B. Between 5 and 10
C. Between 11 and 20
D. More than 20
E. Don't know
F. None
(INTERVIEWER- IF RESPONSE IS "A", "E" OR "F", GO TO
QUESTION 7)
2. Why do you eat chocolates?
    Respondent's answer --
3. Which brand of chocolates do you prefer most?
a) Cadbury's
b) Nutrine
c) Nestle
d) Amul
e) Others (specify) ------------------------
4. When do you like to eat chocolates?
Response ------------------------------
5. Do you prefer chocolates to sweets? (Y/N)
6. Do you have any negative associations with chocolates?
      ----
7. What is your age group?
a) Under 10
b) Between 10 and 20
c) Between 21 and 30
d) Above 30
e) Refused to answer, no answer or don't know
May I know your name? My office calls about 10% of the people I
visit to verify if I have conducted the interviews.
 Gave name -------------
 Refused to give name: ---------
Thank you for your time. Have a good day.

Fig. 6.2 Sample questionnaire consumer survey on chocolate consumption pattern

response, the interviewer might have asked further questions like, 'Do you like ABC brand of chocolates?' On a positive reply, the interviewer might have probed more by asking, 'What do you like about it?' This is the correct way to elicit responses for open-ended questions. The interviewer can even go further and probe how a specific product characteristic is attached to the individual's sub-conscious.

Though editing is time-consuming, it has to be done with care and patience because it is important to data processing.

6.1.1 Treatment of Unsatisfactory Responses

During editing, the researcher may find some illegible, incomplete, inconsistent or ambiguous responses. These are called unsatisfactory responses. The responses are commonly handled by assigning missing values, returning to the field or discarding unsatisfactory respondents.

Assigning missing values—Though revisiting the respondent is logical, it is not always possible to re-visit the field every time the researcher gets an unsatisfactory response from participants. In this situation, a researcher may resort to assigning missing values to unsatisfactory responses. This method can be used when the number of unsatisfactory responses is proportionately small or variables with unsatisfactory responses are not the key variables.

Returning to the field—Sometimes the interviewer has to re-contact respondents if the responses provided by them are unsatisfactory. This is feasible especially for industrial or business surveys, where the sample size is small and respondents are easily traceable. The responses, however, may be different from those originally given.

Discarding unsatisfactory responses—In this approach, unsatisfactory responses from participants are totally discarded. This method is well suited when:

- Proportion of unsatisfactory respondents is very small compared with the sample size
- Respondents with unsatisfactory responses do not differ from other respondents with respect to important, demographic and user characteristics
- Unsatisfactory responses for each respondent are proportionately more in each questionnaire
- Responses on key variables are missing
- To reiterate, editing has to be done with patience and care because it is an important step in the processing of questionnaires.

6.2 Coding

The process of assigning numbers or other symbols to answers in order to group the responses into limited categories is known as coding. For example, instead of using the word 'landlord' or 'tenant' in response to a question that asks for identification of one's residential status, one can use the codes 'LLD' or 'TNT'. This variable can also be coded as 1 for landlord and 2 for tenant, which is then known as numeric coding. This type of categorization and coding sacrifices some detail but is necessary for efficient data analysis. It helps researchers to pack several replies into a few categories that contain critical information required for analysis.

6.2.1 Categorization Rules

A researcher should follow four rules while categorizing replies obtained from a questionnaire. The categories are—appropriate, exhaustive, mutually exclusive and derived from one classification principle.

Appropriate. Categorization should help to validate the hypotheses of the research study. If a hypothesis aims to establish a relationship between key variables, then appropriate categories should be designed to facilitate comparison between those variables. Categorization provides for better screening of data for testing and establishing links among key variables. For example, if specific income is critical for a testing relationship, then wider income classifications may not yield the best results upon analysis.

Exhaustive. When multiple-choice questions are used, an adequate list of alternatives should be provided to tap the full range of information from respondents. The absence of any response from the set of response options given will prove detrimental as that specific response will be underrepresented in the analysis. For example, a questionnaire designed to capture the age group of respondents should list all possible alternatives that a respondent may fall into.

Mutually exclusive. Complying with this rule requires that a specific alternative is placed in one and only one cell of a category set. For example, in a survey, the classification may be (1) Professional (2) Self-employed (3) Government service (4) Agriculture (5) Unemployed. Some self-employed respondents may consider themselves as professionals, and these respondents will fit into more than one category. A researcher should avoid having categories that are not mutually exclusive.

Single Dimension. This means every class in the category set is defined in terms of one concept. If more than one dimension is used, it may not be mutually exclusive unless there is a combination of dimensions like (1) Engineering student (2) Managerial student and the like in the response options.

6.2.2 Code Book

To make data entry less erroneous and more efficient, a rule book called a 'code book' or 'coding scheme' is used, which guides research staff. A code book gives coding rules for each variable that appears in a survey. It is also the basic source for locating the positions of variables in the data file during the analysis process. Most code books generally contain the question number, variable number, location of the variable's code on the input medium, descriptors for the response options and variable name. A code book for the questionnaire in Fig. 6.2 above is shown in Fig. 6.3 below.

6.2.3 Coding Close-Ended Questions

It is easy to assign codes for responses that would be generated by close-ended questions. This is because the number of answers is fixed. Assigning appropriate codes in the initial stages of research makes it possible to pre-code a questionnaire. This avoids the tiresome, intermediate step of framing the coding sheet prior to data entry. Coding makes it easier for data to be accessed directly from the questionnaire. The interviewer assigns appropriate numerical responses to each item (question) in the questionnaire. This code is later transferred to an input medium for analysis.

6.2.4 Coding Open-Ended Questions

Questionnaire data obtained from close-ended questions are relatively easy to code as there are a definite number of predetermined responses. But a researcher cannot always use close-ended questions as it is impossible to prepare an exhaustive list of responses for a question aimed at probing a person's perception or attitude to a particular product or issue. Thus, use of open-ended questions becomes inevitable in business research.

However, coding the data collected from open-ended questions is much more difficult as the responses are unlimited and varied.

In the questionnaire shown in Fig. 6.2, questions 2, 4 and 6 are open-ended questions. After preliminary evaluation and coding, response categories for the second question are shown in Fig. 6.3. The response categories also include the 'other' category to satisfy the coding rule of exhaustiveness.

Content analysis for open-ended questions. A qualitative method known as content analysis can be used to analyse the text provided in the response category of open-ended questions. The purpose is twofold. First, content analysis systematically and objectively derives categories of responses that represent homogenous

Fig. 6.3 Code book
(Adapted from Donald and
Pamela (1999)

Question number	Variable number	Code description	Variable name
1	1	Number of chocolates 1 = Less than 5 2 = Between 5 and 10 3 = Between 10 and 20 4 = Above 20 5 = Don't know 9 = Missing	NO-OF-CHOCOLATES
2	2	Reason(s) 0 = Not mentioned 1 = Mentioned	REASON
2	3	Taste Soft Size Low price Sweet smell Others	TASTE SOFT SIZE COST SMELL OTHERS
3	4	Brand 1 = Cadbury's 2 = Nutrine 3 = Nestle 4 = Amul 5 = others 9 = missing	BRAND
4	5	Occasion 0 = not mentioned 1 = mentioned	OCCASION
4	6	Festival Marriage Friends Time pass Happy occasion Bought new goods Gift Others	FESTIVAL MARRIAGE FRIENDS TIMEPASS HAPPY-OCC BOUGHT-NEW GIFT OTHERS
5	7	Preference 1 = yes 0 = no	PREF
6	8	Negative Association 0 = mentioned 1 = not mentioned	ASSOCIATION
6	9	Tooth decay Worms Expiry date Heart disease Others	TOOTH DECAY WORMS EXPIRY-DATE HEART DISEASE OTHERS
7	10	Age group 1 = below 10 2 = between 10 and 20 3 = between 21 and 30 4 = above 30 9 = missing	AGE
		Name	NAME

thoughts or opinions. This facilitates interpretation of large volumes of lengthy and detailed responses.

Second, content analysis identifies responses particularly relevant to the survey. This form of content analysis is known as open coding or context-sensitive scheme coding. It requires the researcher to name categories through a detailed examination of data. Thus, rather than a pre-determined framework of possible responses, the researcher works using actual responses provided by respondents to generate the categories used to summarize data. This involves an iterative interpretation process of first reading the responses and then rereading them again to establish meaningful categories, and finally, re-reading select responses to refine the number and meaning of categories in a manner that is most representative of the respondents' text. Each response is then coded into as many categories as necessary to capture the 'full picture' of the respondent's thoughts or opinions. To reduce potential coding errors, responses out of context of the question are not coded.

Let us look at the example questionnaire and do content analysis for the second open question in Fig. 6.2.

Q 'Why do you eat chocolates?' (Sample responses are as follows)

- I can afford to buy them.
- It's shape and size are nice.
- No other confectionery can match the taste of chocolates.
- It's very sweet.
- I enjoy the taste.

1. I love the taste and softness.

The first step in analysis requires that the categories selected should reflect the objectives for which the data have been collected. The research question is concerned with the reason behind the respondents' interest in eating chocolates. The categories selected are keywords. The first pass through the data produces a few general categories as shown in Fig. 6.4. These categories should contain one dimension of reason and be mutually exclusive. The use of 'other' makes the

Fig. 6.4 Example of coding for an open-ended question

Categories	
1.Taste	-

2.Soft	-

3.Size	-

4.Low price	-

5.Sweet smell	-

6.Others	-
------	

category set exhaustive so that any dimension, which cannot be captured in the listed categories, can be assigned to the 'other' category.

In general, a second evaluation of responses and categories is made so that some sub-categories can be found which remain undiscovered in the first evaluation.

Q 'Why do you like chocolates?' (Tick as many of the following as applicable) (Presume answers will be given)

6.2.5 Coding 'Do not Knows'

Although researchers include the option of 'do not know' in the possible answers to a question to ensure exhaustiveness, at times it poses problems while analysing. This is particularly so if a considerable number of respondents choose the 'do not know' option. Respondents may choose this response either because they really do not have an answer or because they do not want to answer the question because of personal reasons.

Though the 'do not know' (DK) option is inserted in the questionnaire to assess the actual number of respondents who do not know the answer, the number of evasive respondents choosing that option often negates this purpose.

There are two kinds of DK responses, that is, the 'legitimate DK' and the 'disguised DK'. Responses of the first kind are acceptable. Respondents give such answers when they are unaware of the answer may be due to recall problems or memory decay. The second type of response is mainly because of poor preparation of the questionnaire or the questioning process. At times, the respondent may be reluctant to answer the question or may feel that the question is inconsequential.

Researchers and the interviewers in the field play a major role in decreasing the proportion of 'disguised DK'. A carefully designed questionnaire can decrease the number of 'disguised DK' responses. The rest can be handled by interviewers in the field. An interviewer must identify in advance possible questions that entail key variables, for which DK responses would make things difficult. The researcher can use various probing techniques to get definite answers or find out why the respondent has selected a DK response.

There is always a possibility that a considerable number of DK responses might be generated for some questions despite efforts to check the occurrence of such responses. In such cases, the researcher can either ignore that response or allocate the frequency to all other responses in the ratio that they occur. For example, in Table 6.1, 21 % of the respondents below 10 years select the DK response. Here, the researcher can either ignore the last column or allocate the DK responses to other two responses (<5 and >20) proportionally.

Table 6.1 Handling DK responses

Question: How many chocolates do you eat in a typical week?
Answers:

Age	Less than 5 (%)	Above 20 (%)	"Don't know" responses (%)
Below 10	29	56	21
10–20	44	24	55
21–30	21	15	17
Above 30	6	5	7
Total n	312 (100)	142 (100)	46 (100)

6.3 Data Entry

Technological innovations in computer and multimedia have changed the way researchers enter data. Data entry helps convert information gathered by secondary or primary methods to a medium that facilitates viewing and manipulation. The different means available for data entry are discussed below.

Optical Scanning. These are data processing devices that can 'read' responses on questionnaires. These instruments examine darkened small circles and ellipses. Optical scanners help process marked answers in a questionnaire and store answers in a data file. This technology is generally used for routine data collection. It reduces the number of times the data are handled, thereby reducing the number of errors possible. A common application of optical scanning is scanning of answer sheets to evaluate examination papers of competitive exams that have huge number of participants.

Barcode Reader. This technology can be used to simplify the interviewer's role as a data recorder. Instead of writing the respondent's answers by hand or typing them, the interviewer can pass a bar code wand over the appropriate codes. This technique, however, requires codes for all possible answers.

Voice Recognition. This technology, still in its nascent stage, provides interesting alternatives for the telephone interviewer. This pre-programmed system, upon getting a voice response, automatically branches to the logically next question in the questionnaire. Currently, systems are just recording voice responses. These are rapidly developing to translate voice data into data files.

6.4 Data Cleaning

Data cleaning includes consistency checks and treatment of missing responses. Compared with the preliminary consistency checks during editing, checking at this stage is more thorough and extensive, as it uses computers. This is done in two ways: error checking routines and marginal reports.

Error checking routines are computer programs that check for various conditions that could lead to potential errors. For example, if a particular field on the data records should only have a code in the range 1–4, then a logical statement can be programmed to check for the occurrence of an invalid code in that field. Technological advancements have also made it possible to generate reports, which specify the number of times a particular condition was not met and the list of data records on which the condition was not met.

Another approach to error checking is the marginal report or one-way frequency table. The rows of this report are fields of the data record. The columns depict the frequency with which each possible value was encountered in each field. The report assists in determining the use of inappropriate codes and detecting whether skip patterns were properly followed. If all the numbers are consistent and comply with the coding, there is no need for further cleaning. However, in case logic errors are detected, necessary corrections can be made on the computer data file.

This is the final error check in the process, after which the computer data file is deemed 'clean' and ready for tabulation and statistical analysis.

6.5 Tabulation of Survey Results

Once data are cleansed off all errors and are stored in a database, it should be tabulated to facilitate further analysis.

A researcher can tabulate data in two ways—one-way frequency tabulation and cross tabulation.

6.5.1 One-Way Frequency Tabulation

The most commonly used tabulation technique is the one-way frequency table, as shown in Table 6.2. The one-way frequency table shows the number of respondents who gave each possible answer to each question. Table 6.2 shows that 225 respondents (45 %) like Cadbury's chocolate, 155 respondents (31 %) prefer Nestle chocolates and 83 respondents (16.6 %) prefer Amul chocolates. For every question, the responses are tabulated in this manner to get the first summary report of the survey. The following table shows a computer generated one-way frequency table for Question 3 in the questionnaire shown in Fig. 6.2, when a survey is administered for 500 respondents. In addition to frequencies, one-way frequency tables indicate the percentage of those responding to a question that gave each possible response.

Table 6.2 One-way frequency

Q-3. Which brand of chocolates do you prefer most?

Brand	Total 500 (100 %)
Cadbury's	225 (45 %)
Nestle	155 (31 %)
Amul	83 (16.6 %)
Nutrine	31 (6.2 %)
Do not know/other	6 (1.2 %)

6.5.2 Cross Tabulation

Frequency tables and percentage distributions, averages provide a glimpse into the survey responses, response data can be further organized in a variety of ways. For example, each question can be categorized on gender basis, like how male, female respondents answered the same question. These are known as cross tabulations. This simple yet powerful tool is the most often used tool in the next stage, that is, analysis. Many researchers would not need to go any further than cross tabulation in doing analysis. The idea is to look at responses to one question in relation to responses to other questions. Here, data are organized into groups, categories or classes to facilitate comparisons. Table 6.3 shows simple cross tabulation. This cross tabulation table shows frequencies and percentages of respondents according to their preferences and their consumption.

The most common way of designing cross tables is to create a table where the columns represent various demographic factors such as age and lifestyle characteristics like working people, retired personnel, etc. These are indicators of state of mind. The behaviour of these indicators is captured in the rows. This approach permits easy comparison of the relationship between the state of mind and behaviour. The question might be directed at probing how people in different age groups differ with regard to the particular factor under examination. An example of this type of table is shown in Table 6.4. Here, we took demographic factor age as the data given in the columns. Behaviour towards different brands is the factor under consideration. Behaviour towards each brand is captured in the rows

Table 6.3 Simple cross tabulation

	Ages of respondents				Total
Brand	<10	10–20	21–30	More than 30	
Cadbury's	93	73	39	20	225 (45 %)
Nestle	69	44	22	20	155 (31 %)
Amul	39	20	12	12	83 (16.6 %)
Nutrine	11	9	6	5	31 (6.2 %)
Others	3	3	0	0	6 (1.2 %)
TOTAL	215 (43 %)	149 (29.8 %)	79 (15.8 %)	57 (11.4 %)	500(100 %)

Table 6.4 Cross tabulation

Brand	Number of chocolates	Ages of respondents				Subtotal	Total
		<10	10–20	21–30	More than 30		
Cadbury's	<5	42	34	20	11	107	225 (45 %)
	5–10	31	21	12	5	69	
	10–20	15	12	5	2	34	
	More than 20	5	6	2	2	15	
Nestle	<5	36	26	13	12	87	155 (31 %)
	5–10	21	12	6	5	44	
	10–20	8	4	2	2	16	
	More than 20	4	2	1	1	8	
Amul	<5	21	11	6	5	43	83 (16.6 %)
	5–10	12	5	3	4	24	
	10–20	4	3	2	2	11	
	More than 20	2	1	1	1	5	
Nutrine	<5	5	4	2	3	14	31 (6.2 %)
	5–10	3	3	2	1	9	
	10–20	2	1	1	1	5	
	More than 20	1	1	1	0	3	
Others	<5	2	1	0	0	3	6 (1.2 %)
	5–10	1	2	0	0	3	
	10–20	0	0	0	0	0	
	More than 20	0	0	0	0	0	
Total		215 (43 %)	149 (29.8 %)	79 (15.8 %)	57 (11.4 %)		500 100 %

(number of chocolates of a particular brand, say Nestle, by respondents in the age group 10–20 is 44).

Cross tables can be produced on almost all parameters for given survey data. A careful exercise should be undertaken before any cross table is prepared, to ensure that the cross tables are true in delivering information that is synchronous with research objectives.

Apart from cross tables and frequency tables, there are many different ways of representing survey data. Graphical representation of data includes line charts, pie charts and bar charts.

6.6 Data Mining

Data mining involves discovering knowledge by analysing data from various perspectives and refining it into useful information. It is a powerful new technology having great potential to help companies increase revenue and cuts costs based on information derived from huge databases. Data mining techniques are used to identify valid, novel, useful and understandable patterns in data. Data mining tools can counter business questions that were traditionally too time-consuming to resolve. They search databases for hidden patterns and predictive information that experts may miss. Unlike traditional database queries, which can answer a query, data mining attempts to discover patterns and trends in data and infers rules from these patterns.

For instance, a simple database query can be 'How many units of 100 gm *Rin Shakti* was sold in the month of August in Kolkata?' On the other hand, data mining may discover that *Chik* shampoo is often purchased together with *Rin Shakti*, although the products appear unrelated. With the patterns discovered from data mining, a manager can support, review and examine decisions.

6.6.1 Data Mining in Management Research

Data mining is a new concept but is being used by various companies in retail, finance, logistics and civil aviation industries. These companies use data mining

---

Exhibit 6.1
  What can Data Mining do for you?

- **Identify your best prospects and retain them as customers**
  By concentrating your marketing efforts only on your best prospects, you will save time and money, increasing effectiveness of your marketing operation.

- **Predict cross-sell opportunities and make recommendations**
  Whether you have a traditional or web-based operation, you can help your customers quickly locate products of interest to them—and simultaneously increase the value of each communication with your customers.
- **Learn parameters influencing trends in sales and margins**
  Can this be done with OLAP (on-line analytical processing) tools? While OLAP can help prove a hypothesis—this is possible only if you know what questions to ask in the first place. Mostly, you have no clue on what combination of parameters influences your operation. In these situations, data mining is the only real option.

Segment markets and personalize communications

There might be distinct groups of customers, patients or natural phenomena that require different approaches in their handling. If you have a broad customer range, you would need to address teenagers in California and married homeowners in Minnesota with different products and messages optimize your marketing campaign.[1]

techniques to make sense of huge historic data available with them and to improve their operations and marketing strategies. Data mining uses various pattern recognition, statistical and mathematical techniques to crunch through huge volumes of data and help analysts identify important facts, relationships, trends, patterns, exceptions and discrepancies that might escape researchers' attention. To understand the various ways in which data mining can be useful, refer Exhibit 6.1.

In businesses, data mining is used to discover patterns and establish relationships in the data to help managers formulate better business strategies. Data mining can help reveal sales trends, develop better marketing campaigns and precisely estimate customer loyalty. For the specific uses of data mining, refer Exhibit 6.2

Data mining technology can generate new business opportunities by:

Automated Prediction of Trends and Behaviour. Data mining helps to find predictive data from huge databases that can be used for making predictive decisions. Questions that usually require extensive analysis by managers can now be answered from data generated through data mining.

Data mining helps to identify prospects for target marketing. It uses historic data related to promotional mailing and selects prospects that can be targeted to maximize returns from a mail. Data mining also helps researchers to forecast financial well-being of the company and sounds an alert about forthcoming problems.

---

[1] *Source* http://www.asicb.com/portal/modules.php?name=Content&pa=showpage&pid=26.

Exhibit 6.2

Uses of data mining

Data Mining can be used for:

Market segmentation—Identify the characteristics of customers of each product line and product category of a company.

Customer defection—dentify customers who are most likely to shift loyalties to competitors.

Fraud detection—Identify fraudulent transactions and those which leave loopholes for committing fraud.

Direct marketing—Identify prospects for mailer promotions.

Interactive marketing—Predict the tastes and preferences of visitors to a web site.

Market basket analysis—Determine product categories that are purchased together. Example tea powder and sugar; bread and jam; soaps, shampoos, hair oils etc.

Trend analysis—To reveal the difference between typical customers this month and last month.[2]

Automated Discovery of Hidden Patterns in Data. Huge data stored in company databases have enormous information regarding the company's functioning. It is useful to the management only if they can find the hidden patterns in the data. Data mining helps establish patterns that are followed by sales data, financial data, etc. Researchers working in financial institutions can use data mining to find out if there is any misappropriation of accounts etc.

Exhibit 6.3

Data mining applications

Banking: The Bank of America has used data mining to sculpt detailed demographic views of the banking habits and financial assets of select groups of customers. Querying their data warehouse averages at 30 s. The system draws data from the entire bank and its 30 business units, making it a truly enterprise-wide database able to serve 1,200 users, making over 2,500 complex queries daily.

Finance: Gilman Securities uses data mining to differentiate how the financial markets react to the volatility of different business sectors. Example: finding the relationship(s) between rate of changes between the Japanese Yen and the Government bond market.

Retail: One of the larger retailing operations in America, the Army and Air Force Exchange Service (known to military personnel as 'the PX') has

---

[2] *Adapted from* http://www.eco.utexas.edu/~norman/BUS.FOR/course.mat/Alex/.

used automated data mining to predict how much a particular woman will spend annually, given her age, her dependents and her annual wage level, to target advertising and sales to reach the appropriate customer base.

Insurance: Winterthur Insurance has more than 1 million customers in Spain—given the higher cost of underwriting new customers compared to working with current ones, reducing churn is an ongoing challenge. Winterthur must predict which customers may leave and why. After implementing data mining applications, Winterthur was able to focus more easily on reducing customer churn and retaining profitable customers.[3]

Companies can link their computer networks from across branches to work through data and establish patterns in product sales and customer profiles. AT and T, A.C. Nielsen and American Express are some well known companies that are implementing data mining techniques for sales and marketing. These systems analyse huge databases and provide insights into customer buying behaviour. This helps marketers to frame-winning strategies. For more examples of data mining applications in different industrial sectors, refer Exhibit 6.3.

6.6.2 The Data Mining Process

Data mining is a 5-step process, which includes sampling, exploring, modifying, modelling and assessing as described below.

Sampling. The first step in data mining is to decide whether one should tune the system to work on sample data or analyse the entire data existing in the database. This decision becomes vital when the processing power of systems available with the organization is less. If the data are very huge and the processing power is limited or speed is more important than complete analysis, it is better to draw samples than processing the entire data. However, if data are not very large and the processing power is high or if it is important to understand patterns for every record in the database, a researcher should not go for sampling.

Exploring. This stage starts with data preparation, which may involve cleaning data, selecting sub-sets of records and in case of data sets with large numbers of variables ('fields'), performing preliminary feature selection operations to make the number of variables manageable (depending on the statistical methods considered).

Modifying. This stage pertains to data modification if errors are detected in the exploration stage. This phase is a host to clustering, fractal-based transformation, application of fuzzy logic, data reduction programs like factor analysis,

---

[3] *Source* http://www.morebusiness.com/running_your_business/technology/d935705338.brc.

correspondence analysis and clustering. This stage helps to categorize newly discovered key variables separately.

Modelling. Different modelling techniques used in data mining consist of neural networks, decision tree models, sequence-based models, classification and estimation models and generic-based models. Any of these can be used in the construction of the model once the data are prepared.

Assessing. This final step helps evaluate the performance of the designed model. One way to test the model is to run it for known data. For example, if you know which segment of the given market is risky, you can check to see whether the model selected this segment or not.

6.7 Summary

Preparation of data in a presentable form is essential for good analysis. To make the data collected presentable, a researcher subjects it through various processes like validation and editing, coding, data entry and data cleaning. Each process screens the data in its own specific way before forwarding it to the next screening stage. The very essence of validating lies in detecting fraud or failure by the interviewer to follow specified instructions. After validation, data moves forward for editing. Editing is the process where the editor checks for mistakes on the part of the interviewer or the respondent in filling the questionnaire. It tries to probe if the interviewer has failed to record answers to certain questions or if he or she has failed to follow the prescribed skip pattern. Any shortcomings are rectified and the data are updated for the next processing stage, that is coding.

Coding is the process of assigning numbers or other symbols to answers to group the responses into distinct categories. It assists researchers to bunch several responses into a few key categories that contain critical information required for analysis. For convenience, researchers maintain a codebook that spells out guidelines for coding each of the variables that appear in the questionnaire. This makes it easier to code the data collected in a systematic way. After proper coding, this data are fed into a computer where the process of data cleaning takes place. Data cleaning is more thorough and extensive, as it makes use of the computer and is done in two ways, that is, error checking routines and marginal reports. After data cleaning, the data are ready for analysis. Analysis means that the data are tabulated for facilitating further calculations. Tabulation can be done in various ways, prominent among which are one-way frequency tabulation and cross tabulation. An emerging concept in data analysis is data mining. This has a great future for its multi-faceted applicability. This involves discovering knowledge by analysing data from various perspectives and refining it into useful information. As such, it has a wide variety of applications in management research because it predicts trends and behaviours and discovers hidden patterns in data that can help companies cut costs and improve profitability.

References

Beegle RH (1981) 'How Does the Field Rate?' Advertising age. Oct. 20, 1980. Need honesty, better quality from research suppliers, field services'. Marketing News. 18 Sept 1981

Donald RC, Pamela SS (1999) Business research methods sixth edition. Tata McGraw-Hill, New Delhi, p 458)

Chapter 7
Experimental Analysis of Variance (ANOVA)

7.1 Launching Fruit Flavoured Soft Drinks at Fresh Cola[1] (A)

India's market for soft drinks is expected to expand to $7.2 billion by 2015 from $ 3.1 billion in 2010, according to Euromonitor International.[2] The soft drink market has witnessed a steady growth in India. The market growth rates since 1990 were observed to be as below:

Period	Growth rate (%)
1990–1991 to 1996–1997	9.4
1996–1997 to 2001–2002	7.8
2001–2002 to 2006–2007	6.5
2004–2005 to 2009–2010	5.4
2009–2010 to 2014–2015	3.5

Source Ministry of Food Processing Industries, Government of India

The market shares of different regions/segment are as below:

Region/segment	Share (%)
North	24
East	18
West	32
South	6
Rural	30
Urban	70

Source Ministry of Food Processing Industries, Government of India

---

[1] This case was written by Prof. Serenest S and Prof. L. Shridharan. This is a fictitious case and is intended to be used as a basis for class discussion.
[2] As reported at the site http://www.bloomberg.com/news/2012-09-11/coca-cola-masala-gets-5-billion-to-catch-pepsi-in-india-retail.html.

S. Sreejesh et al., *Business Research Methods*,
DOI: 10.1007/978-3-319-00539-3_7,
© Springer International Publishing Switzerland 2014

Coke and Pepsi together have a combined market share of around 95 %. In physical terms, the demand for aerated soft drinks has grown from 105 million cases in 1990–1991 to 403 million cases in 2009–2010 and is expected to touch 479 million cases in 2014–2015. The annual per capita consumption of soft drinks at around 5–6 l in India is considered far below the global standards. Even neighbouring countries like Sri Lanka, Pakistan and Thailand averaged at 21, 17 and 73 l, respectively.[3]

The low consumption rate and the large population in India leave room for local players as well in the soft drinks market, despite Coke and Pepsi together sharing 95 % of the market. Fresh Cola, a regional player from south India, exists in this space, headquartered at Kochi. The company has been in existence for over two decades, with its presence mainly in southern India. As a third-tier non-alcoholic carbonated Beverage Company, Fresh Cola produces and sells carbonated soft drink and bottled water. Its products come from its five bottling plants, located in the four southern states in the country.

In the meeting of the Board of Governors of the company held on 15 April 2012, Mr. Narayanan Kutty, the Chairman of the company, suggested that with a growing market in the country for non-alcoholic fruit flavoured drinks, Fresh Cola must consider entering this market segment. He asked Mr. Phillip Varghese, Director (Marketing), to look into the feasibility of introducing these drinks and present a report in the next board meeting scheduled to be held in October 2012. The Board also suggested that the company should go for independent and stand alone brand names appealing to consumers.

After the meeting, Varghese returned to his chamber and pondered over the board room discussion. He too felt that Fresh Cola must enter the fruit flavoured drinks segment. The main concern was to understand consumer preferences towards different fruit flavoured drinks. However, he realized that considerable groundwork is needed even to zero down on the idea of launching the fruit drinks and if decided in favour, the question would be 'which all fruit flavour drinks should be launched'. Some focused thinking led to the following questions:

a. How to measure consumer preference when the products are not yet in the market?
b. Can Varghese expect all flavours to be equally popular?
c. Can extraneous variables like gender or age have a bearing on consumer preferences of different brands?
d. If so, how to nullify their effects in understanding consumer preferences for different brands?
e. Can the nature of store outlets have a bearing on the likelihood of purchase of different brands?

---

[3] Source: Ministry of Food Processing Industries, Government of India (http://mofpi.nic.in/ContentPage.aspx?CategoryId=548).

f. Could there be some additional effect due to a combination of some of these variables on brand purchase likelihood, besides the effects of the individual variables?

After considerable introspection and interaction with industry peers, Varghese realized that he would require the assistance of a professional market research firm to deal with the variety of queries listed above and the likes. Accordingly, after consulting his CEO, Mr. John Mathai, he invited Mr. Sreejesh Menon, Vice President (Research), *India International Research Inc. (IIRI),* a leading market research firm and posed his concerns to him. Menon discussed the concerns with his research team and came out with a plan of study, which was approved by Varghese. In the first leg, a series of focus group discussions were proposed to identify the different flavours consumers like in fruit flavoured soft drinks and the preferred brand name for each flavour. Subsequent to resolving this issue, a series of experimental studies were proposed to address the other issues using a taste test of the proposed drinks. The consumer preference was to be measured through respondent's rating of likelihood of purchase based on tasting the drink on 0–100 scale, with 0 representing 'no possibility of purchase' and 100 representing 'certainty of purchase'.

IIRI got on to the job quickly. To identify the preferred flavour alternatives and brand names, IIRI conducted ten focus group interviews, with 8 respondents in each group. The groups were spread over the age group of 10–50 years, the major market segments. The analysis of the exploratory investigation showed the feasibility of introducing three different varieties of fruit flavoured drinks to their product line. These flavours were—apple, strawberry and grapes—with suggested brand names as Bravo, Delight and Cool, respectively. With these findings available within 10 days of study initiation, they were reported to Varghese. He appreciated the quick work and asked the R and D Department of the company to develop the three fruit flavoured soft drinks—Bravo (*apple flavour*), Delight (*strawberry flavour*) and Cool (*grapes flavour*). The R and D team assured him that they will have the test products ready within one month. As promised, the R and D Department delivered the three drinks within a month. This brought IIRI to its second leg of research—the taste tests under different experimental conditions.

7.1.1 Experiment-1

To answer the query 'whether all the flavours would be equally popular', Menon planned this experiment. A taste test was conducted with 100 randomly selected respondents, with each respondent exposed to only one brand assigned randomly and data on his/her purchase likelihood of that brand was recorded.

7.1.2 Experiment-2 (a)

The *second experimental study* mainly conducted to investigate whether the consumers' preferences significantly differ across brands (with three different flavours), coupled with a goal to analyse whether the response differs between males and females. This is mainly carried out with the gut feeling that the respondents' preferences for these three brands will be influenced by the gender of the respondents. In other words, gender is used as a blocking variable (classified into male and female), each block being a homogeneous group in itself. Respondents from each block are randomly assigned to the treatment groups (Bravo, Delight and Cool). Each respondent first tasted the respective brand and then rated the likelihood of purchase for that brand.

7.1.3 Experiment-2 (b)

This *experimental study* focused on whether the consumers' preferences significantly differ across brands (with three different flavours), coupled with a goal to analyse whether the response differs among different age-groups. Once again this was done with the gut feeling that respondents' preferences for these three brands will be influenced by the age-group of the respondents. In other words, age-group is used as a blocking variable (classified as school going, college going and adults), each block being a homogeneous group in itself. Respondents from each block are randomly assigned to the treatment groups (Bravo, Delight and Cool). Each respondent first tasted the respective brand and then rated the likelihood of purchase for that brand.

7.1.4 Experiment-3

Menon knew from his long experience that each customer mostly buys soft drinks usually from a preferred outlet/store. In this *experimental study*, in addition to controlling age-group of consumers, he wanted to control the type of stores (defined as drug stores, supermarkets and kirana stores) from where these three brands are likely to be purchased. To implement the design, age of the respondents and type of stores were blocked into three levels (same as the number of levels for the treatment variable, i.e. the brand), as shown in Table 7.1. In the Table, rows represent the age-group and columns represent the type of stores, both extraneous variables each of which are blocked into three levels. Each level of brand (the independent variable) is then assigned randomly to each cell in the table in such a way that each level of the independent variable would appear only once in each row and in each column.

Table 7.1 Experiment-3 (Age-group and type of stores as blocking variables)

Age of the consumer	Type of Stores		
	Drug store	Super market	Kirana Store
School going	B	A	C
College going	C	B	A
Adults	A	C	B

Note A, B and C denotes the three different brands, which have, respectively, apple, strawberry and grapes flavours

7.1.5 Experiment-4

In addition to examining the effect of different flavour, the research firm was also interested in simultaneously examining the effect of store type on the brand purchase likelihood. Under *Experiment-4*, the firm intended to analyse the simultaneous impact of flavour and store type on the likelihood of brand purchase. As part of this experiment, the research firm manipulated the store type into four levels (defined as drug stores, supermarkets, hypermarket and kirana stores) and flavour into three levels, as shown in Table 7.2. This combination has created $4 \times 3 = 12$ cells. Thus, twelve different product combinations were created, each having a specific level of store and flavour. Data on brand purchase likelihood were collected at store end from randomly selected purchasers visiting the stores by offering only one brand to a customer for taste test.

7.1.6 Questions for Discussion

1. What are experimentation, experimental research and experimental design?
2. Why do we need to conduct experimental studies?
3. What are the methods of control in an experimental study?
4. List out the characteristics of experimental research.
5. What are the steps involved in conducting an experimental study?
6. Suggest and discuss appropriate experimental designs for each of the experiments proposed under this case.

Table 7.2 Experiment-4

Store type	Flavour
Drug store	Bravo (apple) delight (strawberry) cool (grapes)
Super-market	
Hypermarket	
Kirana store	

7.2 Launching Fruit Flavoured Soft Drinks
at Fresh Cola (B)

After deciding on the experimental designs for each experiment, the research team at IIRI collected data under each of the experiment reported as below:

7.2.1 Experiment-1

The file *freshcola1.xls* reports data for each individual on purchase likelihood for the brand he/she was exposed to under the experiment. The data need to be analysed to answer the above query.

7.2.2 Experiment-2 (a)

The file *freshcola2.xls* reports data for each individual on purchase likelihood for the brand he/she was exposed to (reported as 1 for Bravo, 2 for Delight and 3 for Cool) under the experiment, along with gender information (reported as 1 for males and 2 for females). The data need to be analysed to answer the above query.

7.2.3 Experiment-2 (b)

The data in the file *freshcola2.xls* was explained earlier. The file also contains data on age-group of each respondent (reported as 1 for school children, 2 for college students and 3 for adults). The data need to be analysed to answer the above query.

7.2.4 Experiment-3

The file *freshcola3.xls* reports data for each individual on purchase likelihood for the brand he/she was exposed to (reported as 1 for Bravo, 2 for Delight and 3 for Cool) under the experiment, along with information on the age-group of each respondent (reported as 1 for school children, 2 for college students and 3 for adults) and the store type where interviewed (reported as 1 for drug store, 2 for supermarket and 3 for kirana store). The data need to be analysed to answer the above query.

7.2.5 Experiment-4

The file *freshcola4.xls* reports data for each individual on purchase likelihood for the brand he/she was exposed to (reported as 1 for Bravo, 2 for Delight and 3 for Cool) under the experiment, along with information on the store type where interviewed (reported as 1 for drug store, 2 for supermarket, 3 for hypermarket and 4 for kirana store). The data need to be analysed to answer the above query.

Analysis Results (Fresh Cola: Experiment-4)

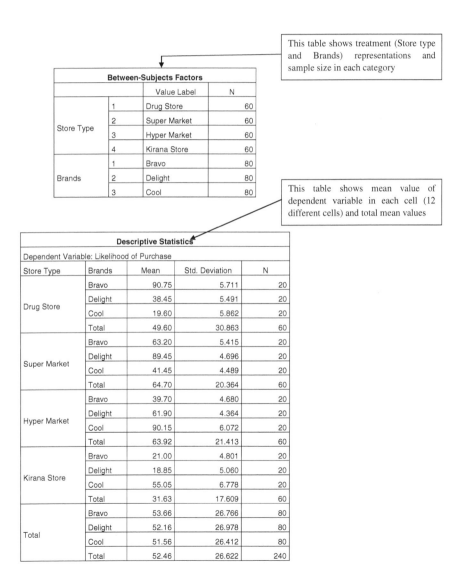

This table shows treatment (Store type and Brands) representations and sample size in each category

Between-Subjects Factors

		Value Label	N
Store Type	1	Drug Store	60
	2	Super Market	60
	3	Hyper Market	60
	4	Kirana Store	60
Brands	1	Bravo	80
	2	Delight	80
	3	Cool	80

This table shows mean value of dependent variable in each cell (12 different cells) and total mean values

Descriptive Statistics

Dependent Variable: Likelihood of Purchase

Store Type	Brands	Mean	Std. Deviation	N
Drug Store	Bravo	90.75	5.711	20
	Delight	38.45	5.491	20
	Cool	19.60	5.862	20
	Total	49.60	30.863	60
Super Market	Bravo	63.20	5.415	20
	Delight	89.45	4.696	20
	Cool	41.45	4.489	20
	Total	64.70	20.364	60
Hyper Market	Bravo	39.70	4.680	20
	Delight	61.90	4.364	20
	Cool	90.15	6.072	20
	Total	63.92	21.413	60
Kirana Store	Bravo	21.00	4.801	20
	Delight	18.85	5.060	20
	Cool	55.05	6.778	20
	Total	31.63	17.609	60
Total	Bravo	53.66	26.766	80
	Delight	52.16	26.978	80
	Cool	51.56	26.412	80
	Total	52.46	26.622	240

Levene's Test of Equality of Error Variances[a]

Dependent Variable: Likelihood of Purchase

F	df1	df2	Sig.
.801	11	228	.639

Tests the null hypothesis that the error variance of the dependent variable is equal across groups.

a. Design: Intercept + Treatment_1 + Treatment_2 + Treatment_1 * Treatment_2

This indicates that the assumption of homogeneity of variances is followed. Because Levene's test is insignificant, we know that the variances are significantly equal across groups. This test follows a regression approach to test the homogeneity across groups.

Tests of Between-Subjects Effects

Dependent Variable: Likelihood of Purchase

Source	Type III Sum of Squares	df	Mean Square	F	Sig.	Partial Eta Squared
Corrected Model	162911.012[a]	11	14810.092	521.044	.000	.962
Intercept	660555.337	1	660555.337	23239.431	.000	.990
Treatment_1	43380.146	3	14460.049	508.728	.000	.870
Treatment_2	187.200	2	93.600	3.293	.039	.028
Treatment_1 * Treatment_2	119343.667	6	19890.611	699.785	.000	.948
Error	6480.650	228	28.424			
Total	829947.000	240				
Corrected Total	169391.662	239				

a. R Squared = .962 (Adjusted R Squared = .960)

Partial Eta Squared indicates how much of the variance in Purchase likelihood can be Predicted from each independent variables

R Squared is the variance explained by all the independent variables to the dependent variable.

Rule of Thumb: by Cohen (1988)
For eta: small = .10, medium = .24, and large = .31;
for *R squared:* small = .10, medium =.36, and large = .51.

Shows the interaction effect is statistically significant. When the interaction is statistically significant, you should analyze the **"simple effects"** (differences between means for one variable at each particular level of the other variable). If interaction is significant, giving inferences using main effect (due to treatments) is somewhat misleading

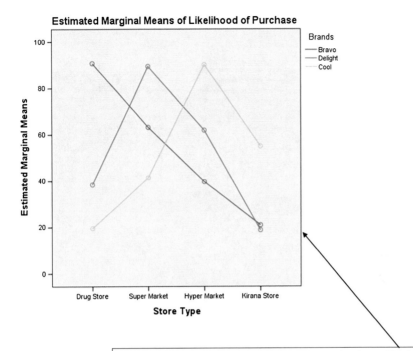

Estimated Marginal Means of Likelihood of Purchase

If you find a significant interaction, you should examine the **profile plots** of cell mean to visualize the differential effects. If there is a significant interaction, the lines on the profile plot will not be parallel. In this case, the plot indicates that brand Bravo's purchase likelihood is high in Drug store, compared to super market, hyper market and Kirana stores. Brand Delight's purchase likelihood is very high when it's there in Super market, compared to other three stores. Brand Cool's likelihood of purchase is high in Hyper market compared to other stores. In all these three brands are shown least likelihood preference when they are in Kirana stores This interpretation, based on a visual inspection of the plots, needs to be checked with inferential statistics.

How to Analyse Two Way Factorial ANOVA Results

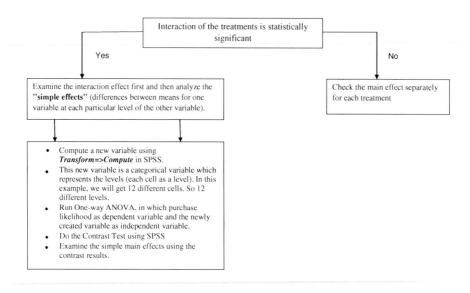

Interaction of the treatments is statistically significant

Yes

No

Examine the interaction effect first and then analyze the **"simple effects"** (differences between means for one variable at each particular level of the other variable).

Check the main effect separately for each treatment

- Compute a new variable using *Transform=>Compute* in SPSS.
- This new variable is a categorical variable which represents the levels (each cell as a level). In this example, we will get 12 different cells. So 12 different levels.
- Run One-way ANOVA, in which purchase likelihood as dependent variable and the newly created variable as independent variable.
- Do the Contrast Test using SPSS
- Examine the simple main effects using the contrast results.

One-Way ANOVA and Contrast Test Results

The overall F is significant at p<.001

ANOVA

Likelihood of Purchase

	Sum of Squares	df	Mean Square	F	Sig.
Between Groups	162911.013	11	14810.092	521.044	.000
Within Groups	6480.650	228	28.424		
Total	169391.663	239			

Contrast Coefficients

Contrast	Twelve new cell codes											
	1.00	2.00	3.00	4.00	5.00	6.00	7.00	8.00	9.00	10.00	11.00	12.00
1	1	-1	0	0	0	0	0	0	0	0	0	0
2	1	0	-1	0	0	0	0	0	0	0	0	0

Contrast Tests

		Contrast	Value of Contrast	Std. Error	t	df	Sig. (2-tailed)
Likelihood of Purchase	Assume equal variances	1	27.55	1.686	16.341	228	.000
		2	51.05	1.686	30.280	228	.000
	Does not assume equal variances	1	27.55	1.760	15.654	37.893	.000
		2	51.05	1.651	30.918	36.587	.000

Contrast 1 looks at the difference Between codes 1 and 2 (Brand Bravo in Drug store and Brand Bravo in Super Market)

7.2.6 Questions for Discussion

1. Suggest appropriate analysis tool for each of the experiments to draw meaningful conclusions on the queries. Recall that Varghese has to report to the Chairman, Mr. Kutty on these at the Board meeting scheduled for October 2012.

Chapter 8
Multiple Regression

8.1 Introduction

Multiple regression analysis is one of the dependence technique in which the researcher can analyze the relationship between a single-dependent (criterion) variable and several independent variables. In multiple regression analysis, we use independent variables whose values are known or fixed (non-stochastic) to predict the single-dependent variable whose values are random (stochastic). In multiple regression analysis, our dependent and independent variables are metric in nature; however, in some situations, it is possible to use non-metric data as independent variable (as dummy variable).

Gujarati and Sangeetha (2008) defined regression as:

'It is concerned with the study of the dependence of one variable, the *dependent variable*, on one or more other variables, the *explanatory variables*, with a view to estimating and/or predicting the (population) mean or average value of the former in terms of the known or fixed (in repeated sampling) value of the later'.

8.2 Important Assumptions of Multiple Regression

1. Linearity—the relationship between the predictors and the outcome variable should be linear
2. Normality—the errors should be normally distributed—technically normality is necessary only for the *t*-tests to be valid, estimation of the coefficients (errors are identically and independently distributed
3. Homogeneity of variance (homoscedasticity)—the error variance should be constant
4. Independence (no autocorrelation)—the errors associated with one observation are not correlated with errors of any other observation
5. There is no multicollinearity or perfect correlation between independent variables.

S. Sreejesh et al., *Business Research Methods*,
DOI: 10.1007/978-3-319-00539-3_8,
© Springer International Publishing Switzerland 2014

Additionally, there are issues that can arise during the analysis that, while strictly speaking, are not assumptions of regression, are none the less, of great concern to regression analysis. These are

1. Outliers; it is an observation whose dependent variable value is unusual given its values on the predictor variable (independent variable).
2. Leverage; an observation with an extreme value on a predictor variable is called a point with high leverage.
3. Influence; an observation is said to be influential if removing the observation substantially changes the estimate of coefficients. Influence can be thought of as the product of leverage and outliers.

8.3 Multiple Regression Model with Three Independent Variables

One of the well-known supermarket chains (ABC group) in the country has adopted an aggressive marketing decision particularly to increase the sales of its own private brands in the last 19 months. Recently, the company decided to investigate its product sales in the last 19 months. In the last 19 months, the company has invested lot of money in three strategic areas: Advertisement, marketing (excluding advertisement and distribution) and its distribution network. The company decided to do a multiple regression analysis to predict the impact of advertisement, marketing, and distribution expenses on its sales (Table 8.1a).

8.4 Multiple Regression Equation

A multiple regression equation with three independent variables is given below:

$$Y_t = \beta_1 + \beta_2 x_{2t} + \beta_3 x_{3t} + \beta_4 x_{4t} + u'_t \tag{1}$$

$$Sales_t = \beta_1(constant) + \beta_2(Advertisement\ Ex.)_t + \beta_3(Marketing\ Ex.)_t$$
$$+ \beta_4(Distribution\ Ex.)_t$$
$$+ u'_t \tag{2}$$

Here, Y_t is the value of the dependent variable (here it is sales) on time period t, β_1 is the intercept or average value of dependent variable when all the independent variables are absent. $\beta_2\beta_3$, and β_4, are the slope of sales (partial regression coefficients) with respect independent variables like advertisement expenses, marketing expenses, and distribution expenses holding other variables constant. For example, the coefficient value β_2 implies that one unit change (increase or

Table 8.1a Sales, advertising, marketing, and distribution expenses

Months	Sales (In lakhs)	Advertising expenses (In lakhs)	Marketing expenses (In lakhs)	Distribution expenses (In lakhs)
1	9324.6	9	129.8	139.9
2	11870.8	20.2	206.1	124.7
3	15118.6	9.8	105.1	169.9
4	19406.4	17.2	53	483.9
5	21715.4	11.5	65	495
6	28270.2	38.9	68.5	618.4
7	41960.1	41.9	81	850.3
8	64647.5	139.9	203	1273.2
9	77826.3	344.9	439.6	1624.6
10	83059.5	451.6	767.7	1538.3
11	78855.6	656.3	1680	1474.9
12	94407	882	1638	1732
13	90615	1051	1376	1594
14	92313	1170	2063	1588
15	92038	1676	2361	2041
16	111281	2518	354	1188
17	134859	2044	195	1133
18	151252	2257	234	1069
19	174580	3389	234	1376

decrease) of in advertisement will lead to β_2 unit time changes (increase or decrease) in sales holding other variables constant. u'_t is the random error in Y, for time period t.

8.5 Regression Analysis Using SPSS

How to Check Linearity Assumption.mp4

Step 1   Open the data file named **Supermarket.sav** (Fig. 8.1).

Step 2   Go to Analyze => Regression =>Linear to get the Linear Regression window as given in Fig. 8.2.

Step 3   Click the dependent variable **Sales** from the left panel of the Linear Regression window into dependent variable (right panel) and other three variables into Independent window (Fig. 8.3).

Step 4   Click the **Statistics** option and select **Estimates, Model fit,** and **Descriptives,** then click on **Continue** to get the main window of Linear Regression (Fig. 8.4).

Step 5   Go to the main window of linear regression and click **OK** (Fig. 8.5).

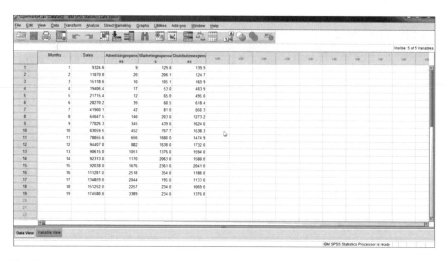

Fig. 8.1 SPSS data view window

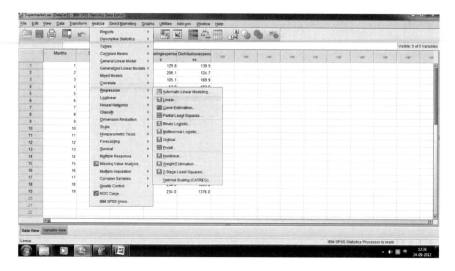

Fig. 8.2 SPSS linear regression window

8.6 Output Interpretation for Regression Analysis

Table 8.1b in SPSS regression output shows the model summary, which provides the value of R (Multiple Correlation), R^2 (Coefficient of Determination) and Adjusted R^2 (R^2 adjusted with Degrees of Freedom). In this model, R has a value of 0.970. This value represents the multiple correlation between dependent and independent variables. The value of R^2 shows all the three independent variables

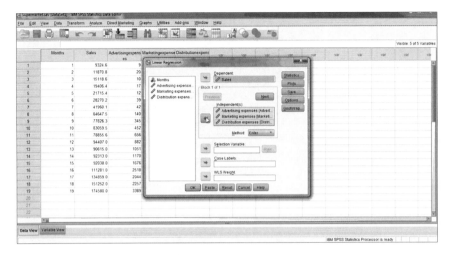

Fig. 8.3 SPSS linear regression window

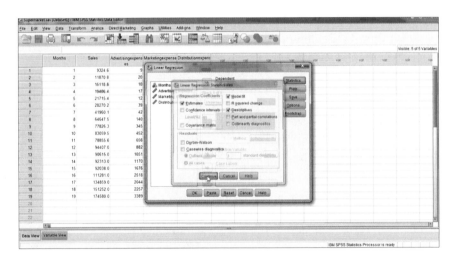

Fig. 8.4 Linear regression statistics window

can account for 94 % of the variation in sales. In other words, if the researcher would like to explain the contribution of all these three expenses on sales, looking at the R^2 it is possible. This means that around 6 % of the variation is sales cannot be explained by all these expenses. Therefore, it can be concluded that there must be other variables that have influence on sales.

Table 8.2 reports an analysis of variance (ANOVA). This table shows all the sums of squares associated with regression. The regression sum of square explains the sum of squares explained by the model or all the independent variables. Residual sum of squares explains the sum of squares for the residual or

Fig. 8.5 SPSS linear regression window

unexplained part. Total sum of squares explains the sum of squares of the dependent variable. The third column shows the associated degrees of freedom for each sum of squares. The mean sum of squares for the regression and residuals are calculated by dividing respective sum of squares by its degrees of freedom. The most important part in this table is F value, which is calculated by taking the ratio of mean square of regression and mean square of residual. For this model, the F value is 78.742, which is significant ($p < .01$). This result tells us that there is less than a 0.1 % chance that an F-ratio this large would happen if the null hypothesis were true. Therefore, looking at the ANOVA table, we can infer that our regression model results in significantly better prediction of sales.

Looking at the ANOVA explained in Table 8.2, we cannot make inference about the predictive ability of individual independent variables. Table 8.3 provides details about the model parameters. Looking at the beta vales and its significance, one can interpret the significance of each predictor on the dependent variable. The value 6908.926 is the constant term which is β_1 in Eqs. 1 and 2. This can be interpreted as when no money is spent on all these three areas (advertising, marketing, and distribution) or $X_2\, X_3\, X_4 = 0$, the model predicts that average sales would be 6908.92 (remember our unit of measurement is in lakhs). The coefficient value for advertising expenses is 33.56(β_2) is the partial regression coefficient for advertising expenses. This value represents the change in the outcome associated with the unit change in the predictor or independent variable, while other variables

Table 8.1b Model summary

Model	R	R^2	Adjusted R^2	Std. error of the estimate
1	0.970[a]	0.940	0.928	13093.8291

[a] Predictors: (constant), distribution expenses, advertising expenses, marketing expenses

Table 8.2 ANOVA[a]

Model		Sum of squares	df	Mean square	F	Sig.
1	Regression	40500692519.872	3	13500230839.957	78.742	0.000[b]
	Residual	2571725425.134	15	171448361.676		
	Total	43072417945.006	18			

[a] Dependent variable: sales
[b] Predictors: (constant), distribution expenses, advertising expenses, marketing expenses

Table 8.3 Coefficients[a]

Model	Unstandardized coefficients		Standardized coefficients	t	Sig.
	B	Std. error	Beta		
1 (Constant)	6908.926	6840.615		1.010	0.329
Advertising expenses	33.569	3.545	0.709	9.468	0.000
Marketing expenses	−15.625	6.203	−0.244	−2.519	0.024
Distribution expenses	43.485	9.002	0.524	4.831	0.000

[a] Dependent variable: sales

hold constant. Therefore, it can be interpreted that if our independent variable is increased by one unit (here advertising expenses), then our model predicts that 33.56 unit times change in depended variable (here sales) occurs while holding other variables like marketing expenses and distribution expenses constant. As our unit of measurement for the advertising expenses were in lakhs, it can be interpreted that an increase in advertising expenses of Rs. 1 lakhs will increase the sales 33,56000 lakhs (100000 * 33.569) holding other expenses constant. In the same fashion, one can also interpret the other coefficients. The negative sign of the coefficients indicates an inverse relationship between dependent and independent variables.

Standard Error Column explains the standard error associated with each estimate or coefficients. The standardized coefficients column shows the standardized coefficient values for each estimate in which the unit of measurement is common. These coefficients can be used for explaining the relative importance of each independent variable when the unit of measurement is different for different independent variables. Looking at the coefficients, one can infer that advertising expense is the most important predictor followed by distribution expenses.

The last two columns show t-value and associated probability. The t-value can be calculated as unstandardized coefficients divided by its respective standard error. The t-test tells us whether the β-value is different from 0 or not. The last column of the Table 8.3 shows the exact probability that the observed value of t would occur if the value of β in the population were 0. If the probability value is less than 0.05, then the researcher agree that result reflect a genuine effect or β is different from 0. From the table, it is evident that for all the three independent variables, the probability value is less than that the assumed 0.05 level, and so we can say that in all the three cases, the coefficient values are significantly different from zero or it significantly contributes to the model.

8.7 Examination of Major Assumptions of Multiple Regression Analysis

8.7.1 Examination of Residual

Examining the residual provide useful insights in examining the appropriateness of the underlying assumptions and regression model fitted A **residual** is the difference between the observed value of Y_i and the value predicted by the regression equation $\hat{Y}_i$. Residuals are used in the calculation of several statistics associated with regression. *Without verifying that your data have met the regression assumptions, the results may be misleading.*

8.7.2 Test of Linearity

When we do linear regression, we assume that the relationship between the response variable and the predictors is linear. This is the assumption of linearity. If this assumption is violated, the linear regression will try to fit a straight line to data that does not follow a straight line. Checking the linear assumption in the case of simple regression is straightforward, since we only have one predictor. All we have to do is a scatter plot between the each response variable (independent variable) and the predictor (dependent variable) to see if nonlinearity is present, such as a curved band or a big wave-shaped curve. The examination of linearity can be examined through the following video.

How to Check Normality Assumption.mp4

8.7.3 Test of Normality

The assumption of a normally distributed error term can be examined by constructing a histogram of the residuals. A visual check reveals whether the distribution is normal. It is also useful to examine the normal probability of plot of standardized residuals compared with expected standardized residuals from the normal distribution. If the observed residuals are normally distributed, they will fall on the 45-degree line. Additional evidence can be obtained by determining the percentages of residuals falling within $\pm 2\ SE$ or $\pm 2.5\ SE$. More formal assessment can be made by running the tests: Shapiro–Wilk, Kolmogorov–Smirnov, Cramer–von Mises and Anderson–Darling.[1]

How to Autocorrelation Assumption.mp4

8.7.4 Test of Homogeneity of Variance (Homoscedasticity)

The assumption of constant variance of the error term can be examined by plotting the residuals against the predicted values of the dependent variable, $\hat{Y}_i$. If the pattern is not random, the variance of the error term is not constant. See the video *How to check Normality Assumption*.

8.7.5 Test of Autocorrelation

How to Check No Multicollinearity Assumption.mp4

A plot of residuals against time, or the sequence of observations, will throw some light on the assumption that the error terms are uncorrelated or no autocorrelation. A random pattern should be seen if this assumption is true. A more formal procedure for examining the correlations between the error terms is the Durbin–Watson test (Applicable only for time series data).

8.7.6 Test of Multicollinearity

The presence of multicollinearity or perfect linear relationship between independent variables can be identified using different methods. These methods are:

1. VIF (Variance-Inflating factor): As a rule of thumb, If the VIF value exceeds 10, which will happen only if correlation between independent variables exceeds 0.90, that variable is said to be highly collinear (Gujarati and Sangeetha 2008).

---

[1] *Null hypothesis* the observations are normally distributed, *alternative hypothesis* not normally distributed.

2. TOL (Tolerance): The closer the TOL to zero, the greater the degree of collinearity of the variables (Gujarati and Sangeetha 2008).
3. Conditional Index (CI): If CI exceeds 30, there is severe multicollinearity (Gujarati and Sangeetha 2008).
4. Partial Correlations: High partial correlation between independent variables also shows the presence of multicollinearity.

How to Check No Multicollinearity Assumption.mp4

8.7.7 Questions

Examine the following fictitious data				
Model	R	R^2	Adjusted R square	Std. error of the estimate
1	0.863	0.849	0.850	13.8767

1. Which of the following statements can we *not* say?

   (a) The standard error is an estimate of the variance of y, for each value of x.
   (b) **In order to obtain a measure of explained variance, you need to square the correlation coefficient**.
   (c) The correlation between x and y is 86 %.
   d) The correlation is good here as the data points cluster around the line of fit quite well. So prediction will be good.
   (e) The correlation between x and y is 85 %.

2. The slope of the line is called:

   (a) **Which gives us a measure of how much y changes as x changes**.
   (b) Is the point where the regression line cuts the vertical axis.
   (c) A correlation coefficient indicates the variability of the points around the regression line in the scatter diagram.
   (d) None of the above.
   (e) The average value of the dependent variable.

3. Using some fictitious data, we wish to predict the musical ability for a person who scores 8 on a test for mathematical ability. We know the relationship is positive. We know that the slope is 1.63 and the intercept is 8.41. What is their predicted score on musical ability?

(a) 80.32
(b) −4.63
(c) **21.45**
(d) 68.91
(e) 54.55

4. We have a negative relationship between number of drinks consumed and number of marks in a driving test. One individual scores 3 on number of drinks consumed, another individual scores 5 on number of drinks consumed. What will be their respective scores on the driving test if the intercept is 18 and the slope 3?

(a) It is not possible to predict from negative relationships.
(b) Driving test scores (Y-axis) will be 51 and 87 [individual who scored 5 on drink consumption].
(c) Driving test scores (Y-axis) will be 27 [individual who scored 3 on drink consumption] and 33 [individual who scored 5 on drink consumption].
(d) **Driving test scores (Y-axis) will be 9 [individual who scored 3 on drink consumption] and 3 [individual who scored 5 on drink consumption]**.
(e) None of these.

5. You are still interested in whether problem-solving ability can predict the ability to cope well in difficult situations; whether motivation can predict coping and whether these two factors together predict coping even better. You produce some more results.

Dependent variable coping skills in difficult situations

	Unstandardized coefficients		Standardized coefficients	t	Sig.
	B	Std. error	Beta		
Constant	−0.466	0.241		1.036	0.302
Problem	0.200	0.048	0.140	2.082	0.030
Motivation	0.950	0.087	0.740	10.97	0.000

Which of the following statements is incorrect?

(a) As motivation increases by one standard deviation, coping skills increases by almost three quarters of a standard deviation (0.74). Thus, motivation appears to contribute more to coping skills than problem solving.
(b) As motivation increases by one unit coping skills increases by 0.95.

(c) **The *t*-value for problem solving is 2.082 and the associated probability is
    0.03. This tells us the likelihood of such a result arising by sampling error,
    assuming the null hypothesis is true, is 97 in 100.**

(d) Problem solving has a regression coefficient of 0.20. Therefore, as problem
    solving increases by one unit coping skills increases by 0.20.

(e) None of these.

Chapter 9
Exploratory Factor and Principal Component Analysis

Chapter Overview

This chapter provides an introduction to Factor Analysis (FA): A procedure to define the underlying structure among the variables in the analysis. The chapter provides general requirements, statistical assumptions and conceptual assumptions behind FA. This chapter explains the way to do FA with IBM SPSS 20.0. It shows how to determine the number of factors to retain, interpret the rotated solution, create factor scores and summarize the results. Fictitious data from two studies are analysed to illustrate these procedures. The present chapter deals only with the creation of orthogonal (uncorrelated) components.

9.1 What is Factor Analysis

According to Hair et al. (2010),[1] *'factor analysis is an interdependence technique whose primary purpose is to define the underlying structure among the variables in the analysis'*. Suppose a marketing researcher wants to identify the underlying dimensions of retail brand attractiveness. He begins by administering the retail brand attractiveness scale from the existing literature to a large sample of people ($N = 2000$) during their visit in a particular retail store. Assume that there are five different dimensions, which consist of 30 different items. What the researcher will end up with these 30 different observed variables, the mass number as such will say very little about the underlying dimension of this retail attractiveness. On average, some of the scores will be high, some will be low and some intermediate, but interpretation of these scores will be extremely difficult if not impossible. This is where the tool factor analysis (FA) comes in handy and it allows the researcher in 'data reduction' and 'data summarization' of this large pool of items to a few representative factors or dimensions, which could be used for further multivariate

---

[1] See Ref. Hair et al. (2010).

S. Sreejesh et al., *Business Research Methods,*
DOI: 10.1007/978-3-319-00539-3_9,
© Springer International Publishing Switzerland 2014

statistical analysis. The general purpose of FA is the orderly simplification of a large number of intercorrelated measures or condense the information contained in a number of original variables into a few representative constructs or factors with minimal loss of information. The application of FA is based on some of the following conditions: general requirement, statistical assumptions and conceptual assumptions (See Table 9.1).

FA is used in the following circumstances:

1. To identify underlying dimensions, or factors, that explains the correlations among a set of variables. For example, a set of personality trait statements may be used to measure the personality dimensions of people. These statements may then be factor analysed to identify the underlying dimensions of personality trait or factors.
2. To identify a new, smaller, set of uncorrelated variables to replace the original set of correlated variables in subsequent multivariate analysis (regression or discriminant analysis). For example, the psychographic factors identified may be used as independent variables in explaining the differences between loyal and non-loyal consumers.
3. To identify a smaller set of salient variables from a larger set for use in subsequent multivariate analysis. For example, a few of the original lifestyle

Table 9.1 Conditions for doing factor analysis

General Requirements

1. Type of scale: Observed variables should be measured in either interval or ration scales, or at least at the ordinary level
2. Number of Items: If the researcher has prior knowledge about the underlying factor structure and want to test the dimensionality, then at least five or more variables should be included to represent each factor structure
3. Sample size: The rule of thumb for sample size is to have at least five times as many cases as variables entered into factor analysis +10

Statistical Assumptions

1. Random sampling: Each participant will contribute one response for each observed variable. These sets of scores should represent a random sample drawn from the population of interest
2. Linearity: The relationship between all observed variables should be linear
3. Bivariate Normal Distribution: Each pair of observed variables should display a bivariate normal distribution (e.g. they should form an elliptical scattergram when plotted)

Conceptual Assumptions

1. Variable Selection: Factor analysis is based on the basic assumption that there exists an underlying structure for the selected set of variables. The presence of high correlation and subsequent interpretation of do not guarantee relevance, even if it meets statistical assumptions. Therefore, it is the responsibility of the researcher to select the set of variables or items that are conceptually valid and appropriate to represent the underlying dimension
2. Sample Homogeneity: Another important conceptual assumption with regard to the factor analysis is that the selected sample should be homogeneous with respect to the underlying factor structure. It is inappropriate to do factor analysis for a set of items once the researcher knows a priori that the sample of male and female is different because of gender. The ignorance of this heterogeneity, and subsequent mixing of two groups (males and females would results in getting a correlation matrix and factor structure, that will be a poor representation of the unique structure of each group

statements that correlate highly with the identified factors may be used as independent variables to explain the differences between the loyal and non-loyal users.

9.2 Factor Analysis Versus Principal Component Analysis

Most of us use both PCA and FA interchangeably and often confused with the usage. This is quite obvious because there are some important similarities between the two methods. Much of the literature in this field do not differentiated these two tools. The similarity is that both methods used generally to determine to identify groups of observed variables that tend to hang together empirically. However, the two methods are different in their goals and in their underlying models. Roughly speaking, you should use PCA when you simply need to summarize or approximate your data using fewer dimensions (to visualize it), and you should use FA when you need an explanatory model for the correlations among your data. Perhaps the most important thing that deals with the differentiating aspect is its assumption of an underlying causal structure. FA is based on the assumption that covariance in the observed variable is due to the presence of one or more latent factors. In short, any change in the observed variable is due to the influence of its latent factor or latent variable is the cause of observed variables. In FA, the researcher believes that certain latent factors exist that exert causal influence on the observed variables they are studying. Exploratory FA helps the researcher to identify the number and nature of such latent factor. An example of such causal structure is shown in Fig. 9.1.

In PCA, the researcher will not make any assumption about an underlying causal structure. PCA is simply a variable reduction procedure that (typically)

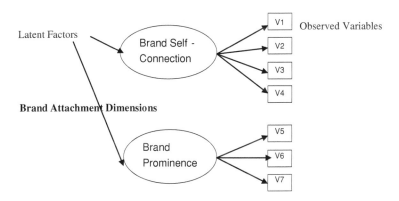

Fig. 9.1 An example of causal structure that is assumed in factor analysis

results in a relatively small number of components that account for most of the variance in a set of observed variables (i.e. groupings of observed variables vs. latent constructs).

http://www.youtube.com/watch?v=znrfcV4ZvlQ

http://www.youtube.com/watch?NR=1&feature=endscreen&v=pmMPXUtk QCc

9.3 A Hypothetical Example of Factor Analysis

Consider a construction company (ABC Builders) that is planning to build an apartment complex near a university. Suppose the company is interested in identifying the perception of the university faculties regarding the value consciousness,[2] price consciousness[3] and purchase decision involvement (PDI),[4] and sale proneness[5] that would help the company to construct and design apartments according to the target people. The company hired a marketing research firm to determine how these four major response dimensions the faculties concerned about before buying an apartment. The research firm identified the scale to measure these three constructs using some existing literature in price consciousness (3-item 5-point Likert scale), value consciousness (3-item 5-point Likert scale), sale proneness (2-item 5-point Likert scale) and PDI (4-item measure on 5-point bipolar phrases). The firm surveyed 98 randomly selected respondents (faculties), using different scales to determine the perception of the faculties with regard to the PDI, price, value consciousness and sale proneness. Table 9.2 shows the selected items for measuring the above-mentioned constructs.

Variables were labelled as V_1 through V_{12}. The data were analysed using PCA and the varimax rotation procedure. Let us begin with how this can be achieved by performing FA. Given below are the steps of SPSS operations that are adopted for performing FA.

---

[2] Value consciousness is defined as a concern for price paid relative to quality received (Lichtenstein et al. 1993).

[3] Price consciousness is the degree to which the consumer focuses exclusively on paying low prices (Lichtenstein et al. 1993).

[4] Purchase decision involvement (PDI) is defined as the extent of interest and concern that a consumer brings to bear upon a purchase-decision task (Mittal 1989). This scale considers purchase decision task as its goal object, and is considered mindset-not response behaviour.

[5] Sale proneness is defined as an increased propensity to respond to a purchase offer because the sale form in which the price is presented positively affects purchase evaluations (Lichtenstein et al. 1990).

Table 9.2 Items for measuring PDI, price and value consciousness and sale proneness

Sl. number	Variables
(V₁)	Selecting from many types and brands of this product (apartments) available in the market, would you say that
	I would not care at all as to which one I buy 1 2 3 4 5 I would care a great deal as to which one I buy
(V₂)	Do you think that the various types and brands of this product available in the market are all very alike or are all very different
	They are alike 1 2 3 4 5 They are all different
(V₃)	How important would it be to you to make a right choice of this product from ABC?
	Not at all important 1 2 3 4 5 Extremely important
(V₄)	In making your selection of this product from ABC, how concerned would you be the outcome of your choice?
	Not at all concerned 1 2 3 4 5 Very much concerned
(V₅)	I am very concerned about low prices, but I am equally concerned about product quality
(V₆)	When purchasing a product, I always try to maximize the quality I get for the money I spend
(V₇)	When I buy products, I like to be sure that I am getting my money's worth
(V₈)	I am not willing to go to extra effort to find lower prices
(V₉)	The money saved by finding lower prices is usually not worth the time and effort
(V₁₀)	The time it takes to find low prices is usually not worth the effort
(V₁₁)	When I buy Brand that's on sales, I feel that I am getting a good deal
(V₁₂)	Compared with most people, I am more likely buy brand that are on special

9.4 SPSS Procedures for Performing Factor Analysis on PDI, Price and Value Consciousness and Sale Proneness Data in Windows

Step 1 Create a data file with these 12 items either in Excel (APARTMENT.xlsx) or in SPSS directly (APARTMENT_PROF.SREEJESH.sav). For the sake of convenience, let us code each of these items in Table 9.3 as V_1, V_2, ... V_{12}. Once you have entered the data consist of all these 98 faculties, your SPSS **Data view** screen would like the one shown in Fig. 9.2.

Step 2 **Analyse => Dimension Reduction => Factor** to get Fig. 9.3.

Step 3 Once you click the option **Factor** in the second step, you would see a window of **FA** with all the variables that are listed in the SPSS variable view in the left panel (and there would a blank space in the right side **Fig.** 9.4).

Step 4 In Step 4, select all the 12 variables by clicking on them and move these variables to the right-side panel under **Variables** window (Fig. 9.5).

Step 5 Click on **Descriptives** to produce Fig. 9.4. Then click on the following: **(1) Initial solution** (under **Statistics), (2) Coefficients, (3) Determinant, (4) KMO and Bartlett's test of sphericity** (under **Correlation Matrix).** The detailed descriptions about these components are discussed below (Fig. 9.6).

Table 9.3 Example: PDI, price and value consciousness and sale proneness data for a sample of 98 university faculties

Res. number	V_1	V_2	V_3	V_4	V_5	V_6	V_7	V_8	V_9	V_{10}	V_{11}	V_{12}
1	4	3	3	3	4	4	3	3	4	2	4	4
2	3	4	3	3	4	4	4	4	4	3	3	4
3	2	2	2	3	4	4	5	2	2	2	2	1
4	4	3	4	4	4	3	4	4	4	4	3	5
5	4	5	5	4	5	4	4	3	3	4	5	4
6	3	2	3	2	4	3	4	4	3	3	4	4
7	4	4	3	4	3	3	4	4	5	4	4	4
8	5	5	5	5	5	5	4	5	5	4	5	5
9	5	4	4	4	4	4	5	4	5	4	5	5
10	5	4	4	5	4	5	5	4	4	3	5	4
11	4	4	3	4	3	2	3	2	2	3	5	5
12	4	4	5	4	4	5	5	5	4	5	4	4
13	3	2	3	2	3	4	3	2	2	2	5	5
14	4	3	3	3	3	3	4	3	4	3	4	3
15	3	3	3	3	4	4	4	4	3	2	4	4
16	5	4	4	4	3	3	3	5	5	4	4	3
17	3	4	4	4	4	4	5	4	5	3	4	4
18	3	3	2	4	3	4	4	3	5	2	3	4
19	3	4	4	4	4	4	4	4	4	3	4	4
20	3	4	4	4	5	4	4	5	5	4	5	4
21	3	4	3	3	4	3	4	4	4	3	4	5
22	2	3	3	3	3	3	3	4	3	3	4	4
23	3	3	3	2	3	3	3	5	5	4	3	3
24	3	4	4	5	4	4	3	3	3	3	5	4
25	5	5	5	3	5	5	5	2	3	2	4	4
26	5	5	5	5	4	4	4	5	4	4	4	5
27	5	5	4	5	2	4	3	5	3	3	5	5
28	2	4	4	4	3	3	2	3	2	3	3	3
29	3	3	3	3	3	3	3	3	2	4	4	4
30	3	5	5	4	4	3	3	5	4	5	5	5
31	3	2	2	2	3	3	2	3	3	3	4	4
32	2	3	2	3	4	4	3	4	4	4	4	4
33	4	3	4	4	3	3	2	3	3	4	5	4
34	2	2	2	2	3	4	3	3	4	4	4	3
35	4	4	3	4	4	4	4	5	3	3	5	3
36	4	4	4	4	4	3	3	5	4	4	4	4
37	4	3	2	3	2	2	3	3	4	3	2	2
38	4	5	3	4	4	3	3	3	4	3	4	3
39	5	4	3	2	4	4	3	5	5	4	4	3
40	3	3	3	3	3	2	2	3	2	3	4	3
41	4	3	3	4	3	2	2	2	2	3	3	4
42	4	3	2	3	3	3	2	3	3	2	3	4
43	5	4	5	4	4	3	3	4	4	5	5	4
44	5	4	4	5	5	4	3	4	4	4	4	5

(continued)

Table 9.3 (continued)

Res. number	V_1	V_2	V_3	V_4	V_5	V_6	V_7	V_8	V_9	V_{10}	V_{11}	V_{12}
45	5	4	3	4	4	4	3	4	4	4	3	4
46	5	5	4	4	4	4	3	4	3	5	4	4
47	4	5	5	5	5	5	4	4	4	4	4	4
48	3	4	3	4	3	4	3	4	3	2	3	3
49	3	4	3	3	4	3	3	3	2	3	3	5
50	3	3	4	5	4	4	4	5	5	4	3	4
51	4	5	4	5	4	4	3	5	2	3	4	4
52	3	4	3	4	4	3	3	3	4	4	5	5
53	5	4	4	5	4	5	3	4	5	3	5	4
54	5	5	5	5	4	5	4	4	4	3	5	5
55	3	5	5	5	3	2	2	3	4	2	5	3
56	5	4	2	4	4	3	3	4	5	4	4	4
57	3	4	3	4	3	3	3	3	4	4	3	4
58	3	4	5	5	4	3	2	4	4	2	4	3
59	4	5	5	4	3	4	3	4	5	3	3	3
60	4	3	3	3	4	3	3	4	3	4	4	4
61	5	5	5	5	4	3	3	5	5	5	4	5
62	4	4	3	3	3	3	2	3	2	2	2	3
63	4	3	3	3	4	4	3	3	4	2	4	4
64	3	4	3	3	4	4	4	4	4	3	3	4
65	2	2	2	3	4	4	5	2	2	2	2	1
66	4	3	4	4	4	3	4	4	4	4	3	5
67	4	5	5	4	5	4	4	3	3	4	5	4
68	3	2	3	2	4	3	4	4	3	3	4	4
69	4	4	3	4	3	3	4	4	5	4	4	4
70	5	5	5	5	5	5	4	5	5	4	5	5
71	5	4	4	4	4	4	5	4	5	4	5	5
72	5	4	4	5	4	5	5	4	4	3	5	4
73	4	4	3	4	3	2	3	2	2	3	5	5
74	4	4	5	4	4	5	5	5	4	5	4	4
75	3	2	3	2	3	4	3	2	2	2	5	5
76	4	3	3	3	3	3	4	3	4	3	4	3
77	3	3	3	3	4	4	4	4	3	2	4	4
78	5	4	4	4	3	3	3	5	5	4	4	3
79	3	4	4	4	4	4	5	4	5	3	4	4
80	3	3	2	4	3	4	4	3	5	2	3	4
81	3	4	4	4	4	4	4	4	4	3	4	4
82	3	4	4	4	5	4	4	5	5	4	5	4
83	3	4	3	3	4	3	4	4	4	3	4	5
84	2	3	3	3	3	3	3	4	3	3	4	4
85	3	3	3	2	3	3	3	5	5	4	3	3
86	3	4	4	5	4	4	3	3	3	3	5	4
87	5	5	5	3	5	5	5	2	3	2	4	4
88	5	5	5	5	4	4	4	5	4	4	4	5
89	5	5	4	5	2	4	3	5	3	3	5	5

(continued)

Table 9.3 (continued)

Res. number	V_1	V_2	V_3	V_4	V_5	V_6	V_7	V_8	V_9	V_{10}	V_{11}	V_{12}
90	2	4	4	4	3	3	2	3	2	3	3	3
91	3	3	3	3	3	3	3	3	2	4	4	4
92	3	5	5	4	4	3	3	5	4	5	5	5
93	3	2	2	2	3	3	2	3	3	3	4	4
94	2	3	2	3	4	4	3	4	4	4	4	4
95	4	3	4	4	3	3	2	3	3	4	5	4
96	2	2	2	2	3	4	3	3	4	4	4	3
97	4	4	3	4	4	4	4	5	3	3	5	3
98	4	4	4	4	4	3	3	5	4	4	4	4

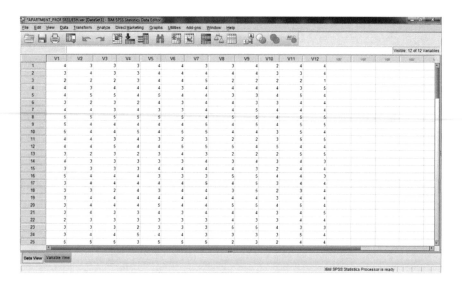

Fig. 9.2 SPSS data editor with PDI, price and value consciousness and sales proneness

1. **Initial solution** (under **Statistics**)

   The selection of this option in SPSS will produce the unrotated FA outputs such as communalities, Eigen values and percentage of variance explained. This output could be used as benchmark and compared with rotated factor solution results.

2. **Coefficients** (under **Correlation Matrix**)

   This selection will produce the output of correlation matrix (12 × 12 correlation matrix) for the 12 items, which are selected for FA. This correlation matrix summarizes the interrelationship among a set of selected variables or, as in our case, a set of items in a scale. The inadequate correlation among the selected items indicates irrelevancy of FA. The understanding of how these correlations

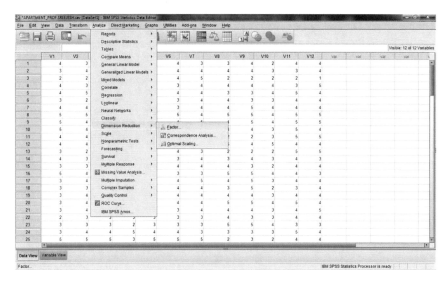

Fig. 9.3 Direction to get factor analysis in IBM SPSS 20.0

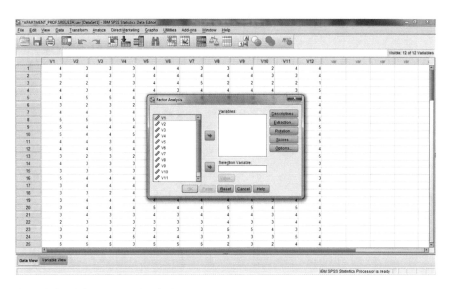

Fig. 9.4 SPSS factor analysis window

are obtained is beyond the scope of this book, and therefore, the procedure is
not discussed in this chapter.

3. **Determinant** (under **Correlation Matrix**)

This selection will produce the output of determinant of the correlation matrix.
In general, the values for the determinants of the matrices can range between

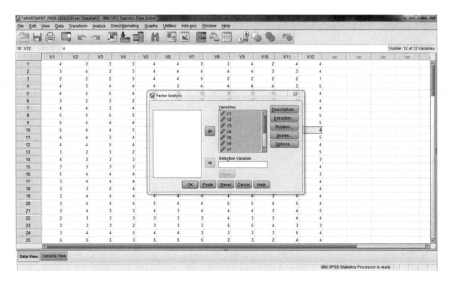

Fig. 9.5 After entering Variables into the factor analysis window

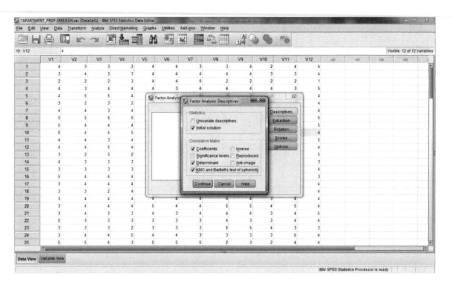

Fig. 9.6 Factor analysis descriptive window

$-\infty$ and $+\infty$. However, values for the determinant of a correlation matrix range only between 0 and 1.00. When all of the off-diagonal elements in the correlation matrix are equal to 0, the determinant of that matrix will be equal to 1. That would mean that matrix is an identity matrix and there is no correlation between the items. Therefore, FA will result into as many factors as there are items. A value of 0 for a determinant indicates that there is at least one linear dependency in the matrix. That means that one or more columns (or rows) in the matrix can be obtained by linear transformations of other columns (or rows) or combinations of columns (or rows). Linear dependency could occur, for example, when one item is highly correlated with the other (e.g. $r > 0.80$). It could also occur when one person's answers are the exact replica or are a linear combination of another person's answers. When this occurs, SPSS for Windows issues the following warning: ***Determinant** = 0.000* and ***this Matrix is Not Positive Definite***. Therefore, the ideal range of determinant in FA would be in between 0 and 1.00 (neither exact 0 nor exact 1).

9.5 KMO and Bartlett's Test of Sphericity (Under Correlation Matrix)

KMO stands for Kaiser–Meyer–Olkin and named after statisticians, and it is considered to be the measure of sampling adequacy. As a general guideline, it is considered that a value greater than 0.60 shows acceptable sampling adequacy, greater than 0.70 shows good sampling adequacy, greater than 0.80 shows very good sampling adequacy and greater than 0.90 shows excellent sampling adequacy. It means that a larger values indicates greater likelihood that the correlation matrix is not an identity matrix and null hypothesis will be rejected (null hypothesis = the correlation matrix is an identity matrix).

Once you complete the selection of these four components, click on **Continue** to go the main window of **FA.**

Step 6 In step 6, click on **Extraction** at the bottom of Fig. 9.7. In this window, select **PCA** from the **Methods** pull-down. *Select (2)* **Unrotated factor solution** (under **Display**), **Correlation matrix** and also select the **Scree plot** box, Check **Based on Eigenvalues eigen values greater than one** under **Extract**. This setting instructs the computer to extract based on eigen values greater than one criteria. Click on **Continue.**

9.6 Principle Component Analysis

The objective behind the usage of principle component analysis other than other methods is that PCA summarizes the interrelationships among a set of original variables in terms of a smaller set of orthogonal (i.e. uncorrelated) principal components that are linear combinations of original variables.

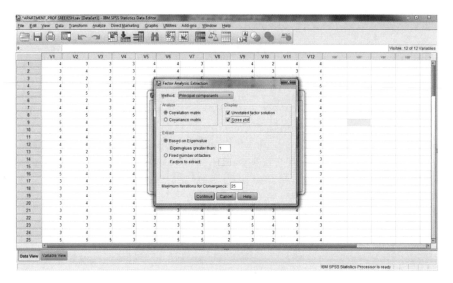

Fig. 9.7 Factor analysis extraction window

9.7 Unrotated Factor Solution

In the **Extraction** window, we selected **Unrotated factor solution** in the **Display** side (right side). This option usually selected to compare this unrotated solution with the rotated solution (the importance of rotation would be discussed in the later part of this chapter).

9.8 Scree Plot

We generally use scree plot to select the number of extracted factors. The selection of scree plot produces a graphical display in which eigen values on the Y-axis and number of factors on the X-axis. The word 'scree' typically represents a kink or distinct binding or a trailing point. For identifying the number of extracted factors, we can have look into the scree plot, in which we would consider only those factors that are present before the scree or kink begins.

9.9 Eigen Values and Eigen Values Greater than One

Eigen value represents the amount of variance in all of the items that can be explained by a given principal component or factor. In PCA, the total amount of variance available is equal to the number of items; therefore, dividing the eigen

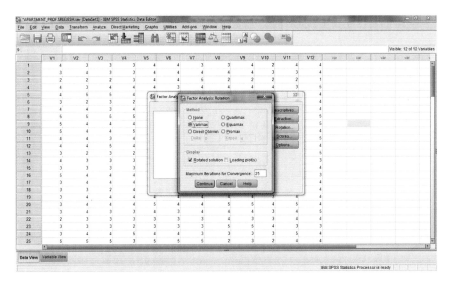

Fig. 9.8 Factor analysis rotation window

value by the number of items gives the proportion of total item variance accounted for by the given principal component or factor. The rationale for the eigen values greater than one criterion is that any individual factor should account for the variance of at least a single variable if it is to be retained for interpretation. This criterion is considered to be more reliable when the number of variables under study is between 20 and 50.

Step 7   In step 7, click on **Rotation,** which will give you Fig. 9.8. Click on **Varimax** and then make sure **Rotated solution** is also checked. Click on **Continue.**

9.10 Rotated Solution

Unrotated factor solutions achieve the objective of data reduction, but it would not provide information that offers the most adequate interpretation of the variables under examination. Therefore, for achieving more theoretically meaningful factor solution, we employ a rotational method. In most of the cases, rotation of the factors improves the interpretation by reducing some of the ambiguities that often accompany initial unrotated factor solutions.

Step 8   Click on **Options,** which will give you Fig. 9.8.
Click on **Suppress absolute values less than** and type 4 (point 4) in the box (see Fig. 9.8).
Suppressing small factor loadings makes the output easier to read.
Click on **Continue** then **OK.** Compare Output 1 to your output and syntax.

9.11 SPSS Syntax Method

```
FACTOR
  /VARIABLES V1 V2 V3 V4 V5 V6 V7 V8 V9 V10 V11 V12
  /MISSING LISTWISE
  /ANALYSIS V1 V2 V3 V4 V5 V6 V7 V8 V9 V10 V11 V12
  /PRINT INITIAL CORRELATION DET KMO EXTRACTION ROTATION
  /FORMAT BLANK (.40)
  /PLOT EIGEN
  /CRITERIA MINEIGEN (1) ITERATE (25)
  /EXTRACTION PC
  /CRITERIA ITERATE (25)
  /ROTATION VARIMAX
  /METHOD = CORRELATION.
```

9.12 Output 1: IBM SPSS 20.0 Output for Factor Analysis

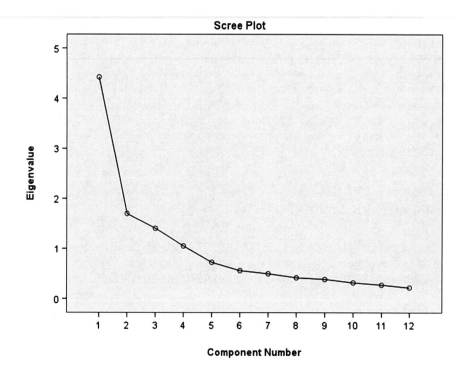

9.13 Results and Interpretation

The aforementioned steps (Figs. 9.2, 9.3, 9.4, 9.5, 9.6, 9.7, 9.8, 9.9 and 9.10) give a number of tables depending on the option selected by the researcher for doing FA in IBM SPSS 20.0. The first table in FA output is **correlation matrix.** Table 9.4: Presents 12×12 correlation matrix for the 20 items specified in the study. This correlation matrix summarizes the interrelationship among set of variables or, as in this example, a set of items in a scale. The correlation ranges between -1.00 and $+1.00$, with higher absolute values indicating a stronger relationship between two variables. A positive value indicates direct relationship between two items. In Table 9.4, for example, the correlation between V2 (*Do you think that the various types and brands of this product available in the market are all very alike or are all very different*) and V3 (*How important would it be to you to make a right choice of this product from ABC?*) was 0.734. This means that respondents who scored high on V2 also scored high on V3. A negative value indicates an inverse relationship between two items: high scores on one item are associated with low scores on the second item. Given the magnitude of correlation between variables, it is clear that the hypothesized factor model appears to be appropriate. Looking at the correlation table for larger number of variable is a tiresome job, and therefore, we have some other measures to check the adequacy of correlation or interrelationship between the factored items, and these measures are as follows:

1 The determinant

This is the determinant of the matrix (12×12), and the value is located under the correlation matrix (Table 9.4). In our example, we got a value of 0.007, its neither exact zero or exact one, which is greater than the cut-off value of 0.00001. Therefore, we can conclude that the correlation matrix is neither an identity matrix nor a singular matrix. This value confirms the assumption that there are sufficient interrelationships among our study items.

2 Bartlett's test of Spherecity and the KMO

Table 9.5 gives the results of KMO and Bartlett's test (Bartlett 1950). Bartlett's test of Spherecity tests the null hypothesis that the correlation matrix is an identity matrix (there is no relationship between items) and follows Chi square distribution. Larger the value of Bartlett's test indicates greater likelihood the correlation matrix is not an identity matrix and null hypothesis will be rejected. In this example, The Bartlett's test value (452.25) is significant (i.e. a significance value of less than 0.05); this means that we may reject the null hypothesis that our correlation matrix is an identity matrix and will conclude that the variables are correlated highly enough to provide a reasonable basis for FA. The KMO test is a measure of sampling adequacy. The KMO measure should be greater than 0.70 and is inadequate if less than 0.60. All these three measures (determinant, Bartlett's test and KMO) show the evidence that there are good interrelationships

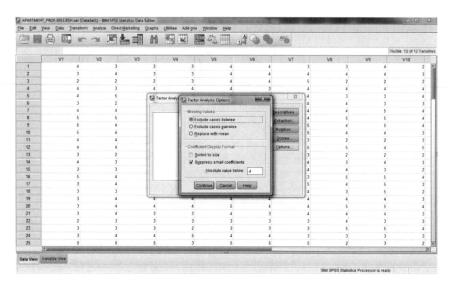

Fig. 9.9 Factor analysis options window

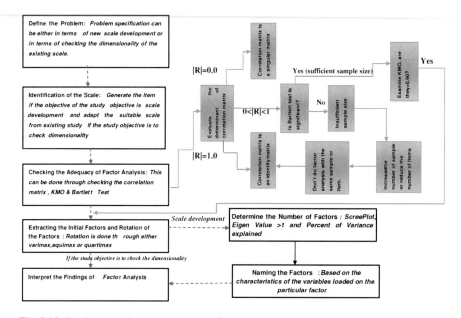

Fig. 9.10 Decision-making process behind factor analysis

between study items and measures. Therefore, we can go for extracting factors using these items.

Table 9.6 presents the communality of each item or measure to the common factor (i.e. the proportion of variance in each variable accounted for by the

Table 9.4 Correlation matrix[a]

		V1	V2	V3	V4	V5	V6	V7	V8	V9	V10	V11	V12
Correlation	V1	1.000	0.543	0.468	0.467	0.201	0.246	0.169	0.283	0.286	0.248	0.309	0.322
	V2	0.543	1.000	0.734	0.706	0.362	0.257	0.138	0.392	0.247	0.269	0.323	0.317
	V3	0.468	0.734	1.000	0.641	0.444	0.323	0.204	0.380	0.203	0.346	0.421	0.341
	V4	0.467	0.706	0.641	1.000	0.246	0.252	0.115	0.344	0.246	0.214	0.322	0.284
	V5	0.201	0.362	0.444	0.246	1.000	0.534	0.502	0.223	0.227	0.199	0.238	0.226
	V6	0.246	0.257	0.323	0.252	0.534	1.000	0.598	0.225	0.242	-0.033	0.203	0.114
	V7	0.169	0.138	0.204	0.115	0.502	0.598	1.000	0.169	0.314	0.015	0.055	0.076
	V8	0.283	0.392	0.380	0.344	0.223	0.225	0.169	1.000	0.565	0.535	0.175	0.202
	V9	0.286	0.247	0.203	0.246	0.227	0.242	0.314	0.565	1.000	0.380	0.077	0.106
	V10	0.248	0.269	0.346	0.214	0.199	-0.033	0.015	0.535	0.380	1.000	0.240	0.278
	V11	0.309	0.323	0.421	0.322	0.238	0.203	0.055	0.175	0.077	0.240	1.000	0.504
	V12	0.322	0.317	0.341	0.284	0.226	0.114	0.076	0.202	0.106	0.278	0.504	1.000

[a] Determinant = 0.007

Table 9.5 KMO and Bartlett's test

Kaiser–Meyer–Olkin measure of sampling adequacy		0.806
	Approx. Chi Square	452.251
Bartlett's test of sphericity	df	66
	Sig.	0.000

Table 9.6 Initial communalities

	Initial	Extraction
V1	1.000	0.494
V2	1.000	0.825
V3	1.000	0.745
V4	1.000	0.759
V5	1.000	0.640
V6	1.000	0.749
V7	1.000	0.759
V8	1.000	0.744
V9	1.000	0.711
V10	1.000	0.717
V11	1.000	0.715
V12	1.000	0.722

Extraction method: Principal component analysis

common factors). While using PCA for factor extraction, we could get as many factors as variables. When all factors are included in the solution, all of the variance of each variable is accounted for by the common factors. Thus, the proportion of variance accounted for by the common factors, or the communality of a variable is 1 for all the variables.

In Table 9.7, total variance is divided into 12 possible factors, because the use of PCA. In our factor extraction option in SPSS, we have selected factor extraction option as 'Based on eigen value and eigen value > 1' criteria. Which means that the factor should explains more information than a single item would have explained. Based on eigen value criteria, we have retained only four factor solution. These four factors account for 23.33, 18.07, 16.47 and 13.60 % of the total variance, respectively. That is, almost 71.49 % of the total variance is attributable to these three factors. The remaining eight factors together account for only approximately 28.51 % of the variance. Thus, a model with three factors may be adequate to represent the data. From the scree plot, it again appears that a four-factor model should be sufficient to represent the data set.

Table 9.8 shows the component matrix, it is an unrotated component analysis factor matrix. The values inside the table show correlation of each variable to the respective extracted factor. Here in our example, we have extracted four factors, the value of V1 (0.650) for the component 1 shows the correlation of item number one to the component 1. These coefficients, called *factor loadings*, indicate how closely the variables are related to each factor. However, as the factors are

Table 9.7 Total variance explained

Component	Initial eigen values			Extraction sums of squared loadings			Rotation sums of squared loadings		
	Total	Variance	Cumulative (%)	Total	Variance (%)	Cumulative (%)	Total	Variance (%)	Cumulative (%)
1	4.425	36.876	36.876	4.425	36.876	36.876	2.801	23.339	23.339
2	1.701	14.171	51.046	1.701	14.171	51.046	2.168	18.070	41.409
3	1.403	11.689	62.736	1.403	11.689	62.736	1.977	16.475	57.884
4	1.051	8.757	71.493	1.051	8.757	71.493	1.633	13.609	71.493
5	0.726	6.046	77.539						
6	0.561	4.673	82.212						
7	0.500	4.166	86.378						
8	0.422	3.515	89.893						
9	0.391	3.255	93.148						
10	0.322	2.686	95.834						
11	0.277	2.311	98.145						
12	0.223	1.855	100.000						

Extraction method: Principal component analysis

Table 9.8 Component matrix[a]

	Component			
	1	2	3	4
V1	0.650			
V2	0.786			
V3	0.807			
V4	0.718			
V5	0.592	0.492		
V6	0.519	0.672		
V7	0.412	0.763		
V8	0.617		0.597	
V9	0.509		0.652	
V10	0.498		0.535	
V11	0.531			0.504
V12	0.510			0.570

Extraction method: Principal component analysis
[a] 4 components extracted

unrotated (the factors were extracted on the basis of the proportion of total variance explained), significant cross-loadings have occurred, thus it becomes very difficult to identify which variables actually throng to each component or factor. There the role of 'rotation' comes and helps to give good and meaningful interpretation. Technically, rotation means tilting the axes of each factor toward right in order to facilitate the variables to have closer association or affinity with only a single factor.

Table 9.9 gives the Rotated Factor Matrix, which contains four loadings, is key for understanding the results of the analysis. The FA using PCA has sorted the items (V1 to V12) into four overlapping groups of items, each which has a loading

Table 9.9 Rotated component matrix[a]

	Component			
	1	2	3	4
V1	0.641			
V2	0.876			
V3	0.771			
V4	0.855			
V5		0.725		
V6		0.839		
V7		0.861		
V8			0.805	
V9			0.779	
V10			0.759	
V11				0.799
V12				0.819

Extraction method: Principal component analysis
Rotation method: Varimax with Kaiser normalization
[a] Rotation converged in 5 iterations

Table 9.10 Component transformation matrix

Component	1	2	3	4
1	0.702	0.421	0.437	0.372
2	−0.291	0.889	−0.102	−0.337
3	−0.296	−0.124	0.884	−0.339
4	−0.578	0.127	0.129	0.795

Extraction method: Principal component analysis
Rotation method: Varimax with Kaiser normalization

of |0.40| or higher (|0.40| means the absolute value, or value without considering the sign, is greater than 0.40). Actually, every item has some loading from every factor, but there are blanks in the matrix where weights were less than |0.40|, which had achieved using the suppress option in SPSS.

The loading coefficients in this table generated through an orthogonal rotation (Varimax), which shows the correlation coefficient of each item to the component or factor, so they ranges from −1.0 to +1.0. The negative loading coefficient simply means that the relationship of the respective item to the component or factor in opposite direction. As a rule of thumb, it is considered that a factor loading lower than |0.40| is considered as bad, greater than |0.40| considered as good (Table 9.10).

In summary, it can be concluded that FA has identified four factors from the list of 12 variables. In the main, these factors are represented by the specific statements written to reflect the four different perception constructs: Product decision involvement, price consciousness, value consciousness and sales proneness.

9.14 Key Statistics

Communality. Communality is the amount of variance a variable shares with all the other variables being considered. This is also the proportion of variance explained by the common factors.

Correlation matrix. A correlation matrix is a lower triangular matrix showing the simple correlations, r, between all possible pairs of variables included in the analysis. The diagonal elements, which are all one, are usually omitted.

Eigen value. The eigen value represents the total variance explained by each factor.

Factor loadings. Factor loadings are simple correlations between the variables and the factors.

Factor-loading plot. A factor-loading plot is a plot of the original variables using the factor loadings as coordinates.

Factor matrix. A factor matrix contains the factor loadings of all the variables on all the factors extracted.

Factor scores. Factor scores are composite scores estimated for each respondent on the derived factors.

KMO measure of sampling adequacy. The KMO measure of sampling adequacy is an index used to examine the appropriateness of FA. High values (between 0.5 and 1.0) indicate that FA is appropriate. Values below 0.5 imply that FA may not be appropriate.

Percentage of variance. The percentage of the total variance attributed to each factor.

Residuals. Residuals are the differences between the observed correlations, as given in the input correlation matrix, and the reproduced correlations, as estimated from the factor matrix.

Scree plot. A scree plot is a plot of the eigen values against the number of factors in order of extraction.

9.15 Review Questions

1. Discuss the possible reasons for the use of FA with the data (**FACTOR**).
2. Produce a correlation matrix for the 12 variables (scale items). Does it appear that FA would be appropriate for these data?
3. Do a principal component analysis (with rotation if necessary for interpretation) using the data. How many factors should be retained? What is the percentage of variance accounted for each factor? Interpret the factors.

Reference

Hair JF Jr, Black WC, Babin BJ, Anderson RE (2010) Multivariate data analysis: a global perspective. Pearson, London

Chapter 10
Cluster Analysis

Cluster analysis is a group of multivariate techniques whose major objective is to combine observations/object/cases into groups or clusters, such that each group or cluster formed is homogeneous or similar with respect to some certain characteristics and these groups should be different from other groups with respect to same characteristics. In cluster analysis, the researcher can classifies objects, such as respondents, products or other entities and cases or events, based on a set of selected variables or characteristics. Cluster analysis works based on certain set of variables, called "Cluster variate", which form the basis for comparing the objects in the cluster analysis. In cluster analysis, the selection of cluster variate is very important, because in cluster analysis the focus is for comparing the objects in each cluster based on variate, rather than the estimation of the variate itself. This difference makes cluster analysis different from other multivariate techniques. Therefore, the researcher's definition of the cluster variate plays a crucial role in cluster analysis.

10.1 Steps for Conducting the Cluster Analysis

The process of performing cluster analysis involves six integrated processes, as shown in Fig. 10.1.

S. Sreejesh et al., *Business Research Methods*,
DOI: 10.1007/978-3-319-00539-3_10,
© Springer International Publishing Switzerland 2014

Fig. 10.1 ICICLE plot

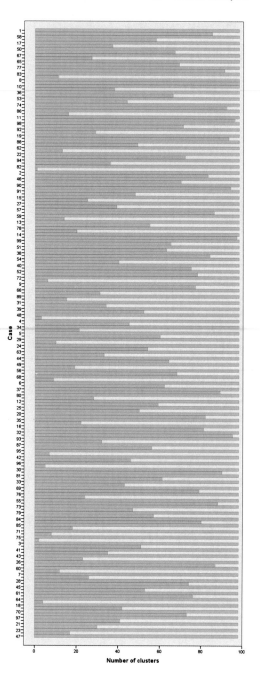

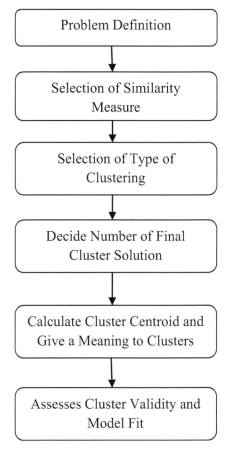

The following section details the steps for performing cluster analysis in detail using an example.

10.1.1 Step 1: Problem Definition

The first and crucial step in the cluster analysis is to define or formulate the problem in a precise manner in terms of properly defined variables. For understanding the cluster analysis in detail, let us formulate a problem. A famous supermarket chains in the country want to identify exploratory buying behaviour tendencies[1] of its loyal customers. As part of its research, the company identified and prepared the list of its 99 customers from its customer

---

[1] Exploratory buying behaviour tendencies can be defined as the differentiating variable of people's disposition to engage in buying behaviour.

database. For understanding the exploratory buying behaviour of its customers, the company administered a questionnaire to the 99 loyal customers. The questionnaire consists of seven exploratory buying behaviour statements that were measured on a 7-point rating scale with 1 strongly disagree and 7 strongly agree. The detailed description about the statements used in the survey is given as follows:

V1: Event though certain food products are available in a number of different flavours, I tend to buy the same flavour which I have been using (*Reverse coded*).
V2: When I see a new brand on the shelf, I am not afraid of giving it a try
V3: I am very cautious in trying new or different products (*Reverse coded*)
V4: I enjoy taking chances in buying unfamiliar brands just to get some variety in my purchase
V5: I do not like to shop around just out of curiosity
V6: I like to shop around and look at displays
V7: I do not like to talk to my friends about my purchases.

The data file attached with this note gives the scores obtained by these 99 loyal customers for seven statements to determine the exploratory buying behaviour.

10.1.2 Step 2: Selection of Appropriate Distance or Similarity Measure

It has already been discussed in the introduction that cluster analysis works based on distance or similarity. Thus, it is essential to select an appropriate distance measure by which the similarity between the cases or subjects can be identified, to club similar object in a cluster.

There are two main widely accepted and used distance measures for measuring similarity between objects, *Squared Euclidean Distance and Euclidean Distance*. The squared Euclidean distance is the sum of squared differences between the values for each variable. Euclidean distance is the square root of the sum of squared differences between the values for each variable. There are other different methods of distances are available, but it is beyond the scope of this book, and therefore, in the example aforementioned, we will limit the distance measure to either Squared Euclidean Distance or Euclidean Distance.

10.1.3 Step 3: Selection of Clustering Type

There are two major types of cluster analysis: (1) **Hierarchical Cluster Analysis** and (2) **Non-Hierarchical Cluster Analysis**. Hierarchical cluster analysis involves n-1 clustering decisions, in which n equals number of observations. This type of cluster analysis combines observations into a hierarchy or tree-like structure. Hierarchical clustering technique can be again classified into **Agglomerative Clustering** and **Divisive Clustering**. In an agglomerative method of clustering, a hierarchical process follows and clustering starts with each object or observation as a single cluster, or with N number of clusters and end up with a single cluster. For example, if we want to cluster 100 observations using hierarchical procedure with agglomerative type, clustering initially starts with 100 individual clusters, each includes a single observation. At first step, the two most similar objects are being combined, leaving other 99 clusters. At the very next step, clustering happens for the other most similar objects, so that there would be around 98 clusters. This process continues until the last step where the final two remaining clusters are combined into a single cluster. Divisive clustering is the opposite of agglomerative clustering in which clustering starts with single cluster and end up with N number of clusters or each object is a single-member cluster. There are five major approaches in agglomerative clustering, and these are the following:

1. **Single Linkage or Nearest Neighbourhood Method**
   This method of agglomerative clustering procedure based on the principle of shortest distance. In this method, the similarity between clusters as the shortest distance from any object in one cluster to any object in the other.
2. **Complete Linkage or Farthest Neighbourhood Method**
   This method of clustering is similar to single linkage algorithm, except that cluster similarity is based on maximum distance between observations in each cluster. In this method, all objects in a cluster are linked to each other at some maximum distance.
3. **Average Linkage**
   In This method of clustering, similarity of any two clusters, is the average similarity of all individuals in one cluster with all individuals in another. This method of clustering is most preferred among linkage methods, because it avoids taking two extreme members while considering the distance between the two clusters. The other advantage for this method is that it considers all the objects of the cluster rather than two extreme members of the clusters.
4. **Centroid Method**
   In this method of clustering, the similarity between two clusters is the distance between the cluster centroids. The term cluster centroid explains the mean values of the observations on the variables in the cluster variate. In this technique, every time individuals are grouped, and a new centroid is computed.
5. **Ward's Method**
   This kind of clustering follows a variance-based approach. In this method of clustering, within cluster variance is to be minimised. In Ward's method, the distance is the total sum of squared deviation (error sum of squares). In this technique, at each stage, two clusters are joined to produce smallest increase in the overall sum of the squared within the cluster distances.

10.2 SPSS Output Interpretation for Hierarchical Clustering

Table 10.1 shows proximity or similarity matrix of first eight cases. It is a data matrix that represents the squared Euclidean distance measure of pairs of objects. The value of case number 1 versus 2 is 29.0, and it shows the sum of squared differences between the values for each variable of these two cases or the extent of dissimilarities between these two cases. Larger value indicates larger difference or dissimilarity between the pairs of objects. This table shows the initial information about clustering of cases.

Table 10.2 presents the agglomeration schedule for the first 20 stages of clustering. Agglomeration schedule is a table which gives information about how the subjects are joined at each stage of the cluster analysis. In this table, column one indicates the **stages** of clustering. For 99 cases, there would be 98 stages of clustering. The second column **Cluster combined**, under that there are two sub-columns, **Clusters 1** and **2** show the stages at which the two cases combined. For example, in this study, out of 98 stages, cluster analysis start with clubbing case numbers 10 and 8. The third column **Coefficients** show the distance. In our example, the distance between case numbers 8 and 10 is 0.00, and it is the lowest value among all other pairs. Therefore, case numbers 8 and 10 are considered to be the first cluster solution. In the second stage, case number 14 and 99 is being clubbed so as to form second cluster, because the coefficient value is 0.500, it is the second lowest among all other cases. The fourth column **Stage Cluster First Appears**, under this column, there are two subcolumns, which indicate the stage at which the respective cases have been clustered previously. For example, in the first row (stage 1), the corresponding value of two zeros in **Cluster 1** and **Cluster 2** signifies that in the first stage, the cases (8 in cluster 1 and 10 cluster 2) have not clustered previously. In stage 18 of **Stage Cluster First Appears** column, a number (4) is mentioned under subcolumn cluster 2, it explains that in stage 18, clusters 16 and 32 are combined, in that the cluster 2 (case 32) already been

Table 10.1 Distance measure for first eight cases

Proximity matrix

Case	Squared Euclidean distance							
	1	2	3	4	5	6	7	8
1	0.000	29.000	30.000	26.000	35.000	13.000	61.000	11.000
2	29.000	0.000	5.000	9.000	16.000	12.000	22.000	18.000
3	30.000	5.000	0.000	10.000	11.000	11.000	13.000	19.000
4	26.000	9.000	10.000	0.000	13.000	5.000	15.000	9.000
5	35.000	16.000	11.000	13.000	0.000	10.000	14.000	12.000
6	13.000	12.000	11.000	5.000	10.000	0.000	20.000	4.000
7	61.000	22.000	13.000	15.000	14.000	20.000	0.000	32.000
8	11.000	18.000	19.000	9.000	12.000	4.000	32.000	0.000

Table 10.2 Agglomeration schedule for first 20 stages of clustering

Agglomeration schedule

Stage	Cluster combined		Coefficients	Stage cluster first appears		Next stage
	Cluster 1	Cluster 2		Cluster 1	Cluster 2	
1	8	10	0.000	0	0	61
2	14	99	0.500	0	0	34
3	11	98	1.000	0	0	28
4	32	93	1.500	0	0	18
5	90	91	2.000	0	0	29
6	19	88	2.500	0	0	50
7	74	86	3.000	0	0	55
8	77	83	3.500	0	0	30
9	30	81	4.000	0	0	38
10	37	80	4.500	0	0	37
11	55	73	5.000	0	0	52
12	26	60	5.500	0	0	76
13	57	59	6.000	0	0	60
14	1	58	6.500	0	0	41
15	38	54	7.000	0	0	36
16	2	46	7.500	0	0	29
17	20	35	8.000	0	0	49
18	16	32	8.833	0	4	67
19	84	85	9.833	0	0	42
20	69	76	10.833	0	0	56

clustered in fourth stage. In the last column, **Next Stage** indicates at which stage the cases are clustering again. For example, in stage one, under **Next Stage** the value mentioned is 61, it is nothing but the stage at which the first stage cluster (cases 8 and 10) is clustering again with another case/clusters.

Another way to identify the formation of clusters in hierarchical cluster analysis is through icicle plot as mentioned in Fig. 10.1. The plot resembles a row of icicles hanging from eaves. Figure 10.1 mentioned a vertical icicle plot, in which the rows of the plot represent the cases (here 99 cases) that are being clustered and columns represent the stages involved in the formation of clusters. The vertical icicle plot should be read from "left to right". Once we read from left to right, in between case numbers 8 and 10, there are no *white spaces*. That is, it supports the agglomeration schedule that cases 8 and 10 are clustering in the first stage. As we go again to the right, we can see in the plot that in between case numbers 14 and 99 a little bit white space. Therefore, we can infer that in second stage, case numbers 14 and 99 are clustering in the second stage. This process continues until all the cases are identified, which belong to a single cluster.

Yet, another graphical way to identify the number of cluster solution is through looking at the dendrogram as shown in Fig. 10.2. It is a tree diagram, considered to be a critical component of hierarchical clustering output. This graphical output displays a relative similarity between cases considered for cluster analysis. In

Fig. 10.2 Dendrogram

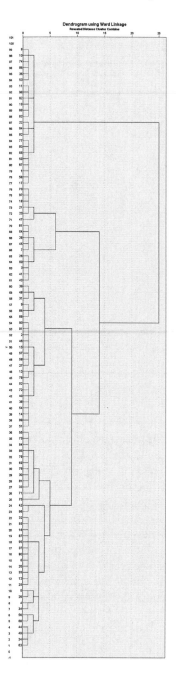

Fig. 10.2, looking at the dendrogram, we can interpret the clustering through reading the diagram from "left to right". In the upper part of the diagram, it is represented as "Rescaled Distance Cluster Combine". This shows that cluster

distances are rescaled to get the range of the output from "0 to 25", in which 0 represents no distance and 25 represents highest distance.

10.2.1 Step 4: Decide Number of Clusters to be Retained in the Final Cluster Solution

In hierarchical cluster analysis, the prominent part is to decide the number of clusters. There are no hard and fast rules for final cluster solution, and there are few guidelines that can be followed while deciding the number of cluster. The following are some of the general guidelines for deciding number of clusters (Table 10.3):

Tables 10.4, 10.5, and 10.6 show relative cluster size or frequency distribution of two, three, and four cluster solutions, respectively. From the tables, it is evident that in case of cluster 4, the distribution is more or less equal.

Table 10.3 Cluster solution determination

Theoretical base	Agglomeration schedule	Dendrogram	Relative cluster size
In this method, use the theoretical base or experience of the researcher can be used to decide the number of clusters	This method of cluster determination is not possible in all the cases. In good cluster solution, while reading agglomeration schedule coefficients, a sudden jump appears. The point just before the sudden jump appears in the coefficient column is the point of stopping point for merging clusters	Drawing an imaginary vertical line through dendrogram will show the number of cluster solution. Looking at the number of cut points, one can assess the number of clusters. If there are four cut points, then we can say that there are four clusters	In this case, one can restrict the clusters to a limited number (e.g., 3 or 4 or 5), so that we will get a series of cluster solutions from 2 to that number. Then draw the relative frequency of cases in each cluster. Finally, one can select that cluster in which the relative frequency distribution of cases is almost equal across clusters

Table 10.4 Two clusters

	Frequency	Percent	Valid percent	Cumulative percent
Group 1	23	23.2	23.2	23.2
Group 2	76	76.8	76.8	100.0
Total	99	100.0	100.0	

Table 10.5 Three clusters

	Frequency	Percent	Valid percent	Cumulative percent
Group 1	23	23.2	23.2	23.2
Group 2	60	60.6	60.6	83.8
Group 3	16	16.2	16.2	100.0
Total	99	100.0	100.0	

Table 10.6 Four clusters

	Frequency	Percent	Valid percent	Cumulative percent
Group 1	23	23.2	23.2	23.2
Group 2	24	24.2	24.2	47.5
Group 3	16	16.2	16.2	63.6
Group 4	36	36.4	36.4	100.0
Total	99	100.0	100.0	

10.2.2 Step 5: Calculate Cluster Centroid and Give Meaning to Cluster Solution

After the determination of final cluster solution (here in this example, the final cluster solution is 4), it is very important to find the meaning of the cluster solution in terms of importance of cluster variate. It can be achieved though the determination of cluster centroids. Here, we have generated cluster centroid using a multiple discriminant analysis. Table 10.7 shows the results generated through discriminant analysis. From the results, it found that the group 1 or cluster 1 people are showing high importance to all the seven variables. We can call them as "severe exploratory consumers". The second group of consumers are showing a buying tendency, which is above average, so we can call them as "superior exploratory consumers". The third group of people are showing a buying behaviour tendency, which is mediocre. Therefore, we will call them as "Mediocre consumers". Finally, the last group is the lowest in this category, so we will call them as "stumpy consumers".

10.2.3 Step 6: Assess the Cluster Validity and Model Fit

The following are some of the suggestive procedures for confirming validity and model fit in cluster analysis.

1. Run cluster analysis on the same data with different distance measures and compare the results across distance measures. In addition, researcher can use different methods of clustering on the same data, and later on, results can be analysed and compared.

Table 10.7 Group statistics

Four clusters		Mean	Standard deviation	Valid *N* (listwise)	
				Unweighted	Weighted
Group 1	V1	4.6957	0.82212	23	23.000
	V2	5.3043	0.70290	23	23.000
	V3	5.7826	0.42174	23	23.000
	V4	5.1739	0.65033	23	23.000
	V5	5.0000	0.95346	23	23.000
	V6	5.4348	0.66237	23	23.000
	V7	5.0435	0.63806	23	23.000
Group 2	V1	3.6250	0.57578	24	24.000
	V2	4.0833	0.71728	24	24.000
	V3	4.0417	0.69025	24	24.000
	V4	3.0000	0.93250	24	24.000
	V5	3.9583	0.62409	24	24.000
	V6	4.5417	1.14129	24	24.000
	V7	4.0000	0.78019	24	24.000
Group 3	V1	2.9375	0.77190	16	16.000
	V2	3.7500	1.23828	16	16.000
	V3	3.9375	1.18145	16	16.000
	V4	3.1875	0.98107	16	16.000
	V5	3.8750	0.95743	16	16.000
	V6	1.7500	0.77460	16	16.000
	V7	2.8750	1.14746	16	16.000
Group 4	V1	4.5000	0.73679	36	36.000
	V2	4.8056	0.82183	36	36.000
	V3	5.1944	0.66845	36	36.000
	V4	3.8889	1.00791	36	36.000
	V5	4.6111	1.20185	36	36.000
	V6	3.3889	1.04957	36	36.000
	V7	4.1111	0.91894	36	36.000
Total	V1	4.0808	0.96549	99	99.000
	V2	4.5758	1.01107	99	99.000
	V3	4.8485	1.03375	99	99.000
	V4	3.8586	1.21227	99	99.000
	V5	4.4242	1.06991	99	99.000
	V6	3.8788	1.54704	99	99.000
	V7	4.1010	1.09260	99	99.000

2. Divide the data into two parts and perform cluster analysis for these two halves. Cluster centroids can be compared for their consistency for the split samples.
3. Add or delete the original set of variables and perform cluster analysis and compare the results for each set of variables.

10.3 SPSS Procedure for Hierarchical Cluster Analysis

=>Open the data

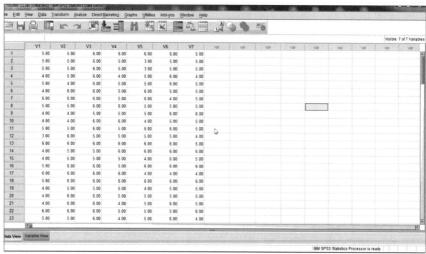

=> Analyse =>Classify =>**Hierarchical Cluster Analysis**

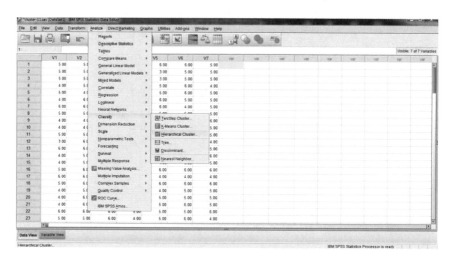

=> Select all the seven variables and place it on the **Variables** box

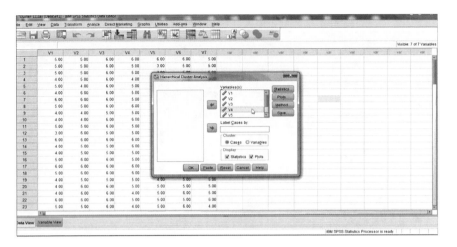

=> Statistics =>Click on **Agglomeration Schedule** and **Proximity matrix,** then click **Continue**

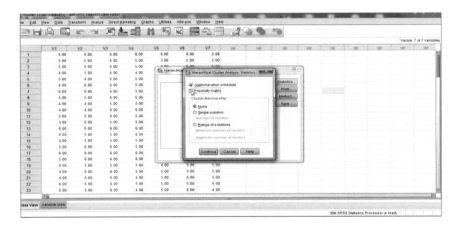

=>Click on Plots =>**Dendrogram**, **All Clusters** and from Orientation **Vertical,** then click **Continue**

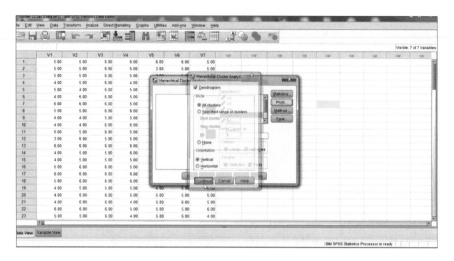

=>Cluster method =>Select **Ward's Method** and **Squared Euclidean Distance**, then Click **Continue**

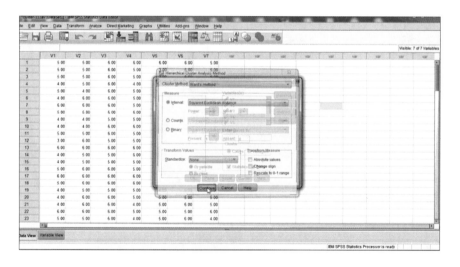

Click **Ok** to get the results of Hierarchical Cluster Analysis

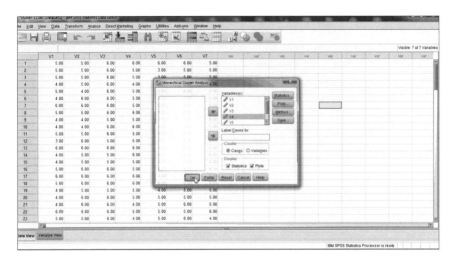

10.4 Questions

1. Segmentation studies in Marketing will employ which of the following statistical techniques?

   a. Regression
   b. Discriminant analysis
   c. **Cluster analaysis**
   d. Conjoint analaysis
   e. *T*-tests

2. The logic of _____ is to group individuals or objects by their similarity or distance from each other.

   a. **Cluster Analysis**
   b. Factor analysis
   c. Discriminant analysis
   d. Regression analysis
   e. Bivariate analysis

3. Which method of analysis does not classify variables as dependent or independent?

   a. Multiple regression analysis
   b. Discriminant analysis
   c. Analysis of variance

d. **Cluster analysis**

e. Simple regression analysis

4. A _____ or tree graph is a graphical device for displaying clustering results. Vertical lines represent clusters that are joined together. The position of the line on the scale indicates the distances at which clusters were joined.

a. **Dendrogram**

b. Scattergram

c. Scree plot

d. Icicle diagram

e. Histogram.

Chapter 11
Binary Logistic Regression

11.1 Chapter Overview

This chapter discusses a methodology that is more or less analogous to linear regression discussed in the previous chapter, *Binary Logistic Regression*. In a binary logistic regression, a single dependent variable (categorical: two categories) is predicted from one or more independent variables (metric or non-metric). This chapter also explains what the logistic regression model tells us: Interpretation of regression coefficients and odds ratios using IBM SPSS 20.0. The example detailed in this chapter involves one metric- and four non-metric-independent variables.

11.2 Logistic Regression

Logistic regression is considered to be a specialized form of regression. In regression equation, the researcher explains the relationship between one metric-dependent and one or more metric-independent variables. In logistic regression, we can predict a categorical dependent variable (non-metric) in terms of one or more categorical (non-metric) or non-categorical (metric) independent variables. The coefficients that we derived from both the equations are more or less similar, in a way that it explains the relative impact of each predictor variable on dependent variable. In discriminant analysis, the non-metric dependent variable is predicted based on metric-independent variables and categorizing the members or objects in each group based on discriminant Z scores. It requires the calculation of cutting scores and based on that we will assign the observations to each group. The major differences between these three methods are shown Table 11.1.

S. Sreejesh et al., *Business Research Methods*,
DOI: 10.1007/978-3-319-00539-3_11,
© Springer International Publishing Switzerland 2014

Table 11.1 Differences among three methods

Major differences	Regression analysis	Discriminant analysis	Logistic regression
Dependent variable	Metric (non-categorical)	Non-metric (categorical)	Non-metric (categorical)
Independent variable	Metric (non-categorical)	Metric (non-categorical)	Metric or non-metric
Assumptions	All major assumptions like linearity, normality, equality of variance and no multicollinearity	Normality, Linearity, equality of variance and covariance	Not based on these strict assumptions except multicollinearity. Robust even if these assumptions are not met

11.3 Logistic Curve Versus Regression Line

Figure 11.1 shows logistic regression curve to represent the relationship between dependent and independent variables. The logistic regression uses binary-dependent variable and has only the values of 0 and 1, and metric- or non-metric-independent variable, and predicting the probability (ranges from 0 to 1) of the dependent variable based on the levels of independent variable. At very low levels of independent variable, this probability approaches to zero, but never reaches to zero. In a similar fashion, as the independent variable increases, the probability of the dependent variable also increases and approaches to one but never exceed it. The linear regression line in Fig. 11.2 shows one to one relationship (linear) with metric-dependent and metric-independent variable could not explain non-linear relationships (0 or 1). At the same time, logistic regression follows binomial distribution instead of normal distribution, and therefore, it invalidate all the statistical testing based on the assumptions of normality. Logistic regression also creates instances of hetroscedasticity or unequal variances as it works in dichotomously

Fig. 11.1 Logistic regression curve

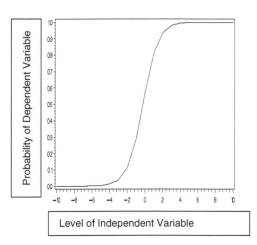

Fig. 11.2 Linear regression curve

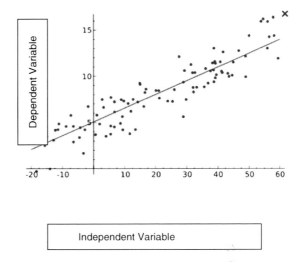

(categorical) dependent variable. In linear regression, the predicted value could not restrict in a range (0–1) as we discussed in the case of logistic regression.

Logistic regression achieves this restriction (0–1) in two steps. In first case, it transforms probability of the event as **_Odds value_**. **Odds**—it is the ratio of the probability of the two outcomes or events $\left[\left[\frac{Prob_i}{1-Prob_i}\right]\right]$. Representing the probability of a 1 as **p** so that the probability of a zero is $(1-p)$, then the odds is simply given by $p/(1-p)$. For example, assume that the purchase probability of product A is 0.50, then the odds ratio product A is the ratio of the probability of the two outcomes (purchase versus non-purchase) $= 0.50/1-0.50 = 1$. In this way, probability would be stated in metric form. Any odds value can be converted back into a probability that falls between 0 and 1.

In the second stage, the Odd ratio is converted into **_logit value_**. Logit value is calculated by taking the logarithm of the odds. This is mainly to achieve or keep the odds values from going below zero, which is the lower limit of the odds. The following Table 11.2 shows the relationship between Probability, Odds value and Logit value.

Odds value less than 1 will have a negative logit value and greater than 1 will have a positive logit value. Once we get the logit value from the Odds value, we

Table 11.2 Relationship between probability, odds and logit value

Probability	Odds	Log odds (Logit value)
0.00	0.00	Cannot be calculated
0.10	0.111	−2.197
0.30	0.428	−0.847
0.50	1.00	0.000
0.70	2.333	0.847
0.90	9.00	2.197
1.00	Cannot be calculated	–

can always transform this value back into Odds and then into probability, and this would restrict the problem of Odds value going below zero.

11.4 Hypothetical Example of Logistic Regression: Defaulter Prediction

The data in Table 17.1 come from a factious study. A total of 609 account holders were studied to determine and predict how credit defaulting behaviour is dependent on the other variables observed.

In the last few quarters, one of the public sector bank in India (let's call it ABC Bank) observed that the default rate in its credit card portfolio has gone up and this is causing a rise in Non-Performing Assets (NPA) of the bank. In order to reduce the risk, the bank is interested in constructing a model to predict and differentiate its defaulter and non-defaulters. The bank has classified the customers into two categories, that is, clear category (non-defaulter) and default category. Now the bank is interested in knowing the repayment behaviour of the customers based on information collected from their applications for credit cards. The information collected was age of the customer, income of the customer, number of dependents, nature of job of the account holder (permanent versus temporary), education of the account holder and possession of other loans. The information is collected from first 20 account holders and is shown in Table 11.3.

The researcher used the Logistic regression for the purpose of predicting future defaulters versus non-defaulters.

11.5 Logistic Regression Equation for Defaulter Prediction

$$LOGIT_i = \ln\left[\left[\frac{Prob_{defaulter}}{1 - Prob_{defaulter}}\right]\right]$$
$$= \beta_{10} + \beta_{11}Age + \beta_{12}Gender + \beta_{13}Income + \beta_{14}Legal\ Issues$$
$$+ \beta_{15}Number\ of\ Dependents + \beta_{16}Job + \beta_{17}Education$$
$$+ \beta_{18}Other\ Loan \tag{11.1}$$

11.6 SPSS Procedures for Performing Factor Analysis on Defaulter Prediction

Step 1 **Analyse => Regression => Binary Logistic** to get to Fig. 11.3

Step 2   Move repayment behaviour into the **Dependent variable** box and age, income, number of dependents, job, education and other loan into **Covariates box**_Make sure **Enter** is the selected Method. (This enters all the variables in the covariates box into the logistic regression equation simultaneously)._ See Fig. 11.4

Step 3   If you have categorical independent variable in the study, click on **Categorical** and move all the categorical independent variables from the left panel window of **Covariates** to right panel window of **Categorical Covariates** to get Fig. 11.5. Then click on **Continue to** get back to **Logistic Regression** window

Step 4   Click on save to produce probabilities and group membership, which will give Fig. 11.6. Then click on **Continue to** get back to **Logistic Regression** window

Step 5   Click on Options to produce Fig. 11.7. Click on **Classification Plots** and **Hosmer–Lemeshow Goodness of Fit**. Then click on **Continue to** get back to **Logistic Regression** window. Then Click on **OK** to get the output window

Table 11.3 Defaulter prediction data (First 20 samples)

Account number	Repayment behaviour	Age	Gender	Income	Number dependents	Job	Education	Other_loan
21.00	0.00	56.00	0.00	20.00	0.00	0.00	0.00	0.00
31.00	0.00	43.00	0.00	25.00	0.00	1.00	0.00	0.00
51.00	1.00	56.00	1.00	6.00	1.00	1.00	1.00	1.00
71.00	0.00	64.00	1.00	40.00	0.00	1.00	1.00	1.00
74.00	0.00	49.00	0.00	42.00	0.00	1.00	0.00	0.00
91.00	0.00	46.00	0.00	8.00	0.00	1.00	0.00	0.00
111.00	1.00	52.00	0.00	26.00	1.00	1.00	0.00	0.00
131.00	0.00	63.00	0.00	6.00	0.00	0.00	0.00	0.00
141.00	0.00	42.00	0.00	43.00	0.00	1.00	0.00	0.00
191.00	0.00	55.00	0.00	23.00	1.00	0.00	1.00	0.00
201.00	0.00	74.00	0.00	26.00	0.00	0.00	1.00	0.00
241.00	0.00	53.00	0.00	10.00	0.00	0.00	0.00	0.00
251.00	0.00	58.00	0.00	40.00	0.00	1.00	0.00	0.00
261.00	0.00	56.00	0.00	30.00	0.00	1.00	0.00	0.00
271.00	0.00	69.00	0.00	10.00	0.00	0.00	1.00	0.00
283.00	1.00	51.00	1.00	32.00	1.00	0.00	1.00	1.00
291.00	0.00	43.00	0.00	12.00	0.00	1.00	0.00	0.00
311.00	0.00	64.00	1.00	41.00	1.00	0.00	1.00	1.00
312.00	0.00	44.00	0.00	23.00	0.00	0.00	1.00	0.00

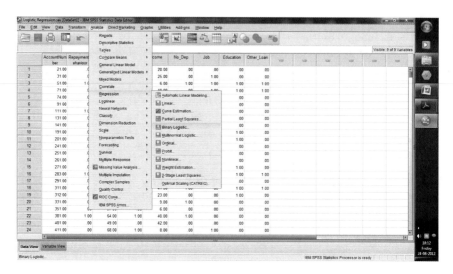

Fig. 11.3   IBM SPSS 20.0 binary logistic selection

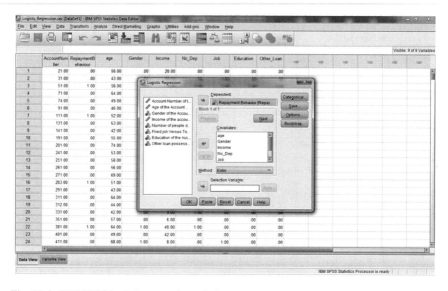

Fig. 11.4   IBM SPSS logistic regression window

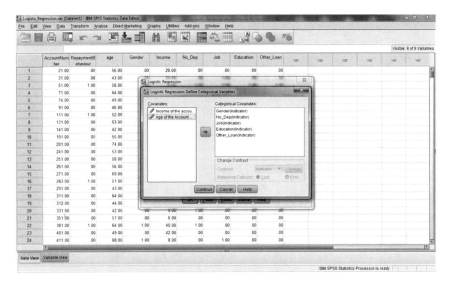

Fig. 11.5 Defining of categorical independent variables

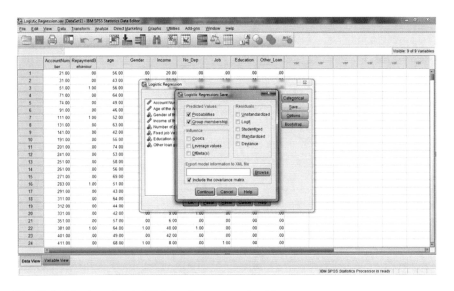

Fig. 11.6 Selection of probabilities and group membership

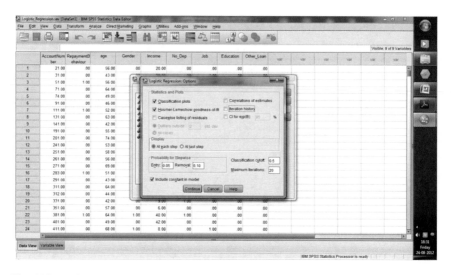

Fig. 11.7 Logistic regression option window

11.7 IBM SPSS 20.0 Syntax for Binary Logistic Regression

```
GET
  FILE = 'G:\LIBRARY\I-BOOK DEVELOPMENT\Logistic Regres-
sion.sav'.
  DATASET NAME DataSet1 WINDOW = FRONT.
  LOGISTIC REGRESSION VARIABLES RepaymentBehaviour
  /METHOD = ENTER age Gender Income No_Dep Job Education
Other_Loan
  /CONTRAST (Gender) = Indicator
  /CONTRAST (No_Dep) = Indicator
  /CONTRAST (Job) = Indicator
  /CONTRAST (Education) = Indicator
  /CONTRAST (Other_Loan) = Indicator
  /SAVE = PRED PGROUP
  /CLASSPLOT
  /PRINT = GOODFIT
  /CRITERIA = PIN(0.05) POUT(0.10) ITERATE(20) CUT(0.5).
```

11.8 IBM SPSS 20.0 Output for Logistic Regression

Table 11.4 shows the number of observations **Included in Analysis** and the number of observation used (**Total**) in the analysis. The number of observations **Included in Analysis** may be less than the **Total** if there are missing values for

Table 11.4 Case processing summary

Unweighted cases[a]		N	Percent (%)
Selected cases	Included in analysis	609	100.0
	Missing cases	0	0.0
	Total	609	100.0
Unselected cases		0	0.0
Total		609	100.0

[a] If weight is in effect, see classification table for the total number of cases

Table 11.5 Dependent variable encoding

Original value	Internal value
Defaulter	0
Non-defaulter	1

Table 11.6 Categorical variables codings

		Frequency	Parameter coding (1)
Other loan possessed by the account holder	Yes	511	1.000
	No	98	0.000
Number of people depended on Account holder	2 or <2 dependents	443	1.000
	More than 2 dependents	166	0.000
Fixed job versus temporary	Permanent Job	222	1.000
	Temporary Job	387	0.000
Education of the account holder (School vs. College)	School education	354	1.000
	College education	255	0.000
Gender of the account holder	Male	487	1.000
	Female	122	0.000

any variables in the equation. By default, SPSS does a listwise deletion of incomplete cases. In the current example, both are same, because there are no missing values.

Table 11.5 shows the categorical representation for the dichotomously dependent variable-Repayment Behaviour. 0 used for defaulter category and 1 for non-defaulter category.

Table 11.6 explicitly shows the labelling used by the researcher to represent the categorically independent variables.

The **Classification Table** shown in Table 11.7. As mentioned earlier, it is common practice to use 0.5 as the cut-off for predicting occurrence. That is, to predict non-occurrence of the event of interest whenever $p < 0.5$ and to predict occurrence if $p > 0.5$. The Classification table indicates how many correct and incorrect predictions would be made for a wide range of probability cut-off points used for the model. In this case, 88.3 per cent of the cases are correctly classified

Table 11.7 Classification table[a,b]

Observed			Predicted		
			Repayment behaviour		Percentage correct
			Defaulter	Non-defaulter	
Step 0	Repayment behaviour	Defaulter	538	0	100.0
		Non-defaulter	71	0	0.0
	Overall percentage				88.3

[a] Constant is included in the model
[b] The cut value is 0.500

Table 11.8 Variables not in the equation

			Score	df	Significant
Step 0	Variables	Age	11.819	1	0.001
		Gender(1)	16.246	1	0.000
		Income	17.302	1	0.000
		No_Dep(1)	7.483	1	0.006
		Job(1)	5.429	1	0.020
		Education(1)	11.536	1	0.001
		Other_Loan(1)	6.775	1	0.009
	Overall statistics		49.121	7	0.000

Table 11.9 Omnibus tests of model coefficients

		Chi square	df	Significant
Step 1	Step	46.798	7	0.000
	Block	46.798	7	0.000
	Model	46.798	7	0.000

using the 0.50 cut-off point, which is similar to 'Hit Ratio' in discriminant analysis.

Table 11.8 shows how individually these independent variables predict the dependent variable. In this study, all the variables are found to be significant at 5 per cent ($p < 0.05$).

In SPSS, we can adopt different methods to prove the contribution or predictability of this independent variable on the dichotomously dependent variable. One of the test that SPSS follows is **Omnibus Tests of Model Coefficients** in Table 11.9. This test will give an inference that, when we consider all the independent together, the model specified is significant or not. In this example, it found that all the variable taken together the specified **Model** is significant ($X^2 = 46.79$, $df = 7$, $N = 75$, $p < 0.001$).

11.9 Assessing a Model's Fit and Predictive Ability

There are several statistics printed by SPSS that can be used to assess model fit. The important among them are as follows:

(i) The R^2 table, which is the Cox and Snell R^2, generalized coefficient of determination. The closer the values of R^2 to 1, the better the fit of the model. Cox and Snell R^2 may not achieve a maximum value of 1. The second R^2, Nagelkerke R^2, is a better one to use (Table 11.10).

(ii) Observe the Hosmer and Lemeshow tables shown in Table 11.11. SPSS computes a Chi square from observed and expected frequencies in the Table 11.12. Large Chi square values (and correspondingly small p-values) indicate a lack of fit for the model. In our example, the Hosmer and Lemeshow Chi square test for the final model yields a p value of 0.225, thus suggesting a model with satisfactory predictive value. Note that the Hosmer and Lemeshow Chi square test is not a test of importance of specific model parameter

In Table 11.13, **Estimates** are the binary logit regression estimates or coefficients for the **Parameters** in the model. The logistic regression model models the

Table 11.10 Model summary

Step	−2 Log likelihood	Cox & Snell R^2	Nagelkerke R^2
1	391.761[a]	0.074	0.144

[a] Estimation terminated at iteration number 6 because parameter estimates changed by <0.001

Table 11.11 Hosmer and lemeshow test

Step	Chi square	df	Significant
1	13.636	8	0.092

Table 11.12 Contingency table for Hosmer and Lemeshow test

		Repayment behaviour = defaulter		Repayment behaviour = non-D		Total
		Observed	Expected	Observed	Expected	
Step 1	1	62	60.404	0	1.596	62
	2	59	59.536	3	2.464	62
	3	60	57.839	1	3.161	61
	4	57	57.967	5	4.033	62
	5	51	56.241	10	4.759	61
	6	55	55.491	6	5.509	61
	7	54	54.302	7	6.698	61
	8	57	51.725	4	9.275	61
	9	46	47.489	15	13.511	61
	10	37	37.006	20	19.994	57

Table 11.13 Variables in the equation

		B	S.E.	Wald	df	Significant	Exp(B)
Step 1[a]	age	0.035	0.015	5.194	1	0.023	1.036
	Gender(1)	-1.536	0.526	8.511	1	0.004	0.215
	Income	0.010	0.004	7.510	1	0.006	1.010
	No_Dep(1)	-0.244	0.298	0.672	1	0.412	0.784
	Job(1)	-0.681	0.307	4.922	1	0.027	0.506
	Education(1)	-0.861	0.331	6.786	1	0.009	0.423
	Other_Loan(1)	1.749	0.616	8.053	1	0.005	5.749
	Constant	-4.118	1.056	15.195	1	0.000	0.016

[a] Variable(s) entered on step 1: age, Gender, Income, No_Dep, Job, Education, Other_Loan

log odds of a positive response (probability modelled for Non-Defaulter = 1) as a linear combination the predictor variables. This is written as follows:

$$LOGIT_i = \ln \frac{Prob_{Non-defaulter}}{1 - Prob_{Non-defaulter}}$$
$$= -4.118 + 0.035 * Age - 1.536 * Gender + 0.010 * Income$$
$$- 0.244 * Number\ of\ Dependents - 0.681 * Job$$
$$- 0.861 * Education + 1.749 * OtherLoan$$

SPSS will give the output of both logistic coefficients and exponentiated logistic coefficients. According to Hair et al. (2010), the original logistic coefficients are most appropriate for determining the direction of the relationship and less useful in determining the magnitude of relationships. Exponentiated coefficients directly reflect the magnitude of the change in the odds value. Because they are exponents, they are interpreted with slight difference. The exponentiated coefficients less than 1.0 reflect negative relationships, while values above 1.0 denote positive relationships.

Age: This is the estimated logistic regression coefficient for the variable age, given the other variables are held constant in the model. The difference in log-odds is expected to be **0.035** units higher for non-defaulter compared with defaulter, while holding the other variables constant in the model. We got an exponentiated coefficient value of 1.036 for age. For assessing magnitude, the easier approach to determine the change in probability from these values is:

Percentage change in odds = (Exponentiated coefficient-1.0) * 100
= (1.036−1) * 100 = 3.6 %

which means if the exponentiated coefficient is 1.036, a one unit change in the independent variable will increase the odds by 3.6 %.

Gender (1): This is a dichotomous independent variable and we considered male group (male = 1, female = 0) as our reference category. The value we estimated is the estimate logistic regression coefficient for a one unit change in gender, given the other variables in the model are held constant. The logit coefficient for gender is -1.536 for the reference category (males) in terms of females. The coefficient value is negative, which means the reference category will have a negative impact on non-defaulter or the male group decreases the likelihood of being a non-defaulter compared with females. The percentage of change in odds is 78.5 %, which means the exponentiated coefficient is 0.215; a one unit change in the independent variable (males) will decrease the odds by 78.5 %.

Intercept: This is the logistic regression estimate when all variables in the model are evaluated

Note: Interpretation of the remaining coefficients in the same manner.

Standard Error: These are the standard errors of the individual regression coefficients. They are used in both the **95 % Wald Confidence Limits**.

The **Wald** Chi square test statistic is the squared ratio of the **Estimate** to the **Standard Error** of the respective predictor. The **Wald** value follows a central Chi square distribution with degrees of freedom given by **DF**, which is used to test against the alternative hypothesis that the **Estimate** is not equal to zero. The probability that a particular **Wald** test statistic is as extreme as, or more so, than what has been observed under the null hypothesis is defined by **Pr > ChiSq**.

DF: This column gives the degrees of freedom corresponding to the **Parameter**. Each **Parameter** estimated in the model requires one **DF** and defines the Chi square distribution to test whether the individual regression coefficient is zero, given the other variables are in the model.

Chi Square and **Pr > ChiSq:** These are the test statistics and p-values, respectively, testing the null hypothesis that an individual predictor's regression coefficient is zero, given the other predictor variables are in the model.

11.10   Questions

1. Which of the following is true?

    (a) Binomial logistic regression is the same as multiple regression
    (b) Binomial logistic regression can only be used with scores.
    (c) Binomial logistic regression is not at all like multiple regression
    (d) **Binomial logistic regression is analogous to multiple regression**

2. The logit value in logistic regression is

    (a) Is the cube root of the sample size
    (b) Is an instruction to record the data
    (c) Is a logarithm of a digit
    (d) **Is the natural logarithm of the odds ratio**

3. In binary logistic regression, the dependent variable is

   (a) Metric and non-categorical
   (b) **Non-metric and dichotomous**
   (c) It can be metric or non-metric
   (d) None of these

4. Logistic regression follows a distribution of

   (a) Normal
   (b) **Binomial**
   (c) Poisson
   (d) Skewed-Normal

5. The shape of logistic curve is

   (a) S-Shaped
   (b) L-Shaped
   (c) U-Shaped
   (d) Inverted U-shaped

Part V
Data Presentation

Chapter 12
Business Research Reports

Market researchers and decision makers conduct research on various problems/
opportunities and base their future decisions on the findings of the research. Unless
the research results are properly communicated in the reports, they would be of
little use to managers. Managers cannot take valid and effective decisions unless
the entire research findings are presented to them in a systematic manner.
A business research report contains many items including findings, analysis,
interpretations, conclusions and at times recommendations. These can be presented
to the management either in a written form or communicated orally. For the
research findings to be useful to the managers, the research report needs to be
meticulously designed, with all the necessary contents properly arranged and
presented.

This chapter deals with the fundamentals of report writing and presentation.
The chapter begins with a description of the types of research reports, provides
an insight into the various components of the written business research report
and concludes with a description of the features of written and oral
presentation.

12.1 Types of Research Reports

12.1.1 Short Reports

Short research reports usually run into 4–5 pages and are prepared for those
researches, which have a well-defined problem, limited scope and employ a clear-
cut methodology. These reports usually start with a concise statement regarding
the approval for the study, followed by the objective of the study, that is, the
problem definition and the research overview, which contains concisely, the main
part of the research, such as the methodology used. This is followed by conclusions based on the findings and recommendations, if any. The underlying basis for

S. Sreejesh et al., *Business Research Methods,*
DOI: 10.1007/978-3-319-00539-3_12,
© Springer International Publishing Switzerland 2014

these types of reports is to make information available, to all those concerned, in an easy-to-use format. Short reports are prepared even for small clients who have inexpensive projects.

12.1.2 Long Reports

As the name indicates, long reports are more detailed than the short reports. They can be further subdivided into technical and management reports based on the objectives of the researchers' and the end users'. Technical reports (TRs) are primarily meant for researchers. Management reports are meant for managers (as end users), to aid their decision-making.

12.1.2.1 The Technical Report

A TR should focus on a specific topic logically pertaining to the research objective. The report should include the following: a descriptive title, author name and information, date, list of keywords, informative abstract, body, acknowledgments, list of references and appendices. The introduction of each TR should clearly identify its thesis and an organizational plan for the same.

The body should consist of sources of data, research procedures, sampling design, and data collection methods, instruments used, and data analysis arranged into a standard format under motivation, methods, results and discussion. The TR should include sufficient procedural information for other users to replicate the study. Therefore, it should explain what was done, why it was done, what was discovered and what was significant in the findings. The report should identify clearly what is original about the work, and how it relates to past knowledge.

There is no minimum or maximum length requirement for a TR. However, usually they are of 10–15 pages. A good quality TR should have the conclusions and recommendations in line with the findings. While all necessary details should be referred to, it should avoid the inclusion of non-essential information and oversimplification.

12.1.2.2 The Management Report

Managers and decision-makers want information quick and straight to the point. Therefore, they show little interest in knowing the technicalities of the research. They are more interested in the ultimate findings and conclusions, which can act as a base for their decisions. As the management reports are meant for a non-technical audience, there should be very less use of technical jargons and wherever jargons are used, they should be explained using a footnote or in the appendices. The language of a management report should be such that it is easy to understand. Some of the other features of a good management report are as follows:

- Short and direct statements
- Underlining relevant parts for better emphasis
- Pictures and graphs accompanying tables
- Graphics and animations accompanying the presentation of the report

12.2 Components of Research Reports

Be they short or long, formal or informal, routine or special, public or private and daily/weekly/monthly/annual, research reports have a set of specified components. A typical research report has the followings sections:

- Prefatory information:

  - Letter of Transmittal
  - Title Page
  - Authorization Statement
  - Executive Summary
  - Table of Contents

- Introduction:

  - Problem Statement
  - Research Objectives
  - Background

- Methodology:

  - Sampling Design
  - Research Design
  - Data Collection
  - Data Analysis
  - Limitations

- Findings
- Conclusions and Recommendations
- Appendices
- Bibliography

12.2.1 Prefatory Information

The prefatory information contains the letter of transmittal, the title page, authorization statement, executive summary and table of contents.

Letter of Transmittal. The letter of transmittal is a sort of authorization by the client organization, citing approval for the project. This becomes necessary when the relationship between the researcher and the client is formal. A transmittal letter consists of a salutation of the person who commissioned the report, the objectivity of the letter, a brief synopsis of the report, acknowledgements and follow-up action expected of the reader.

Title Page. The title page should include the following:

- The title of the report
- The date
- Name of the client
- Name of the organization and the researchers
- The nature of the project in a precise and succinct manner

The title should incorporate the following elements: the variables taken into account in the study, the type of relationship between the variables included in the study and the target population for whom the results can be useful. A short informative title can be effective.

Authorization Statement. A letter of authorization is a letter from the client to the researcher approving the project and specifying some of the details. Such letters usually accompany the research reports to federal and state governments where detailed information about authorization factors is required. At times, a reference to the letter of authorization in the letter of transmittal is deemed enough. The letter not only helps in identifying the sponsor, but also outlines the original request.

Executive Summary. This functions as a miniature report. The key findings are very concisely presented in the executive summary running into 100–200 words or a maximum of two pages. The major thrust of the executive summary should be on highlighting the objective, salient features and analysis of the results including the recommendations. Recommendations should be given if the client wants them, else should be avoided. This is because some decision-makers do not want their thought process to be limited to the recommendations given. As the executive summary is the gist of the whole report, it is framed only after the report is completed. Conclusions should be supported later and graphics should be used if necessary.

Table of Contents. The table of contents lists the divisions and sub-divisions of the report with appropriate page numbers. Shorter reports can suffice with the main headings only. As the table of contents lists the topics covered, it is preferable to take the headings from the headings in the report. A linking row of dots should connect the topics with the page number. The list should be in the same sequence as it appears in the original report. The list of tables, charts and graphs follows the table of contents.

12.2.2 Introduction

The introduction gives an overview of the report. It highlights parts of the project like problem definition, research objectives, background material and the findings. It lays down the plan for the development of the project.

Problem Statement. This highlights the basic problem for the research will probe into. It explains the reason why the research is being conducted and is usually followed by a set of objectives.

Research Objectives. Research objectives form the heart of the study. They address the purpose of the project. Every research follows a set of well-planned objectives. Therefore, the general and specific objectives should be stated. These can be adjusted for sequencing without changing their basic nature. The research objectives can take the form of questions and statements. The objectives influence the choice of research methodology and the basic structure used to report the findings.

Background. Background information may include a review of the previous research or descriptions of conditions that caused the project to be authorized. It may entail preliminary results from an experience survey or secondary data from various sources. The references from secondary data, definitions and assumptions are included in this section. Background material depending on whether it contains the literature reviews or information relating to the occurrence of the problem is placed either after the research objectives or before the problem definition, respectively.

12.2.3 Methodology

For short reports and management reports, it is not necessary to have a separate section on the methodology used. This can be included in the introduction section and details can be accommodated in the appendix. However, in the case of a TR, methodology needs to be explained as an independent section and include the following.

Sampling Design. The researcher in this section defines the target population and the sampling methods to use. This section contains other necessary information such as:

- Type of sampling (probability or non-probability) used
- Type of probability sampling (simple random or complex random) or non-probability sampling (quota sampling or snowball sampling) used
- The factors influenced the determination of sample size and selection of the sampling elements
- The levels of confidence and the margin of acceptable error

The sampling methods used should be explained and calculations should be placed in the appendix rather than in the body of the report.

Research Design. The research design has to be custom-made to the research purpose and should contain information on:

- Nature of the research design
- Design of questionnaires
- Questionnaire development and pre-testing
- Data that were gathered
- Definition of interview and type of interviewers
- Sources (both primary and secondary) from which data were collected
- Scales and instruments used
- Designs of sampling, coding and method of data input
- Strengths and weaknesses

Copies of materials used and the technical details should be placed in the appendix.

Data Collection. The contents of this section depend on the research design. As the name implies, data collection pertains to the information about:

- Time of data collection
- Field conditions during data collection
- The number of field workers and supervisors
- The training aspects of supervisors and workers
- Handling of irregularities, if any
- Subject assignments to various groups
- Administration of tests and questionnaires
- Manipulation of variables

If any secondary data were used, then the relevance of that data should be given. Details of field instructions and any other necessary information should be given in the appendix.

Data Analysis. This section provides information on the different methods used to analyse the data and the justification for choosing the methods. In other words, it should justify the choice of the methods based on assumptions. It provides details on:

- Data handling
- Groundwork analysis
- Rational statistical tests and analysis

Limitations. Certain researchers tend to avoid this section, but this is not a sign of professionalism. There should be a tactful combination of reference and explanation of the various methodologies and their limitations or implementation problems. The limitations need not be explained in detail. Details of limitations do not belittle the research. They help the reader in acknowledging its honesty and validity.

12.2.4 Findings

Most of the space in the report is devoted to this section. It presents all the relevant data but makes no attempt to draw any inferences. The section attempts to bring the fore any pattern in the industry. Charts, graphs and tables are generally used to present quantitative data. It is better to report one finding per page and support it with quantitative data.

12.2.5 Conclusions and Recommendations

Conclusions should be directly related to the research objectives or hypotheses. Conclusions are inferences drawn from the findings. The researcher should always present the conclusions as he has first-hand knowledge of the research study. It is wrong to leave the inference of the conclusions on the reader.

Recommendations on the other hand are a few corrective actions presented by the researcher. They highlight the actions the report calls for as per the researcher. The recommendations should be in line with the results of the report and should be explicit. They may even contain plans of how future research for the same can proceed. However, recommendations ought to be given only if the client is interested. It may happen that the client does not want any recommendations on the findings. In such a case, the report should not carry any recommendations.

12.2.6 Appendices

Appendices are optional. They should be used to present details that were part of the research but were not necessary to the presentation of the findings or conclusions.

Appendices include raw data, calculations, graphs, copies of forms and ques-tionnaires, complex tables, instructions to field workers and other quantitative material that would look inappropriate in the main text. The reader can refer to them if required. However, care should be taken that they do not exist in isolation and reference to each appendix is given in the text.

12.2.7 Bibliography

A list of citations or references to books or periodical articles on a particular topic is known as a bibliography. It contains all the works consulted in the preparation of the report, not just those referred to in the text. A consistent reference format should be used all through the section.

12.3 Written Presentation

12.3.1 Pre-writing Concerns

The effectiveness of a research report depends on how well it is presented. A report has many parts and all parts should display interconnectivity. This interconnectivity is possible only with a meticulous organization of the different parts of the report. This organization should be reflected in the initial sections of the report. A good researcher spends significant amount of time in designing this initial section wherein he tries to relate the purpose of the report, the audience it is meant for, the technical background and the limitations under which the report is written.

Customizing the report to the tastes of different audience is necessary. The gap arising due to degree of difference between the subject knowledge of the writer and the reader should be taken into account. The technical knowledge of the end-users may not match that of the researcher so the report should be written in a simple manner with less technical jargons. This would enable the readers to understand the theme of the project and relate the conclusions to the specific objectives outlined in the report. In fact, all parts of the report should coherently pursue the research problem. This means that the conclusions and findings when integrated backwards should show some connection with the research objectives, which were framed in line with the problem situation. This unified structure assists the reader to understand how the research problem was probed into and how the project was accomplished. As the final organized report is written after the research is over, the researcher can relate the facts and present the findings in a manner that would appeal to the reader. Pre-writing concerns, therefore, play an important role in designing the research report. Pre-writing entails the following sections:

- Outline
- Bibliography

Outline. The best way to organize a report is to develop an outline of the main sections. The outlining stage gives a natural progression to the various stages of report writing. The outlining stage concentrates on how it should be presented to make an impact on the readers. In trying to establish the relation among the various parts, the outline should introduce the complete scope of the report. As said earlier, the outline should contain the main headings of the various sections along with their sub-headings and sub sub-headings. This task is now made easy with the help of special software that helps in drawing a proper outline for a project report.

Two styles of outlining can be generally identified, that is, the topic outline and the sentence outline. The topic outline includes a key word or phrase that reminds the writer of the nature of the argument represented by the keyword. The sentence outline on the other hand gives a description of the ideas associated with the specific topic. A traditional outline structure for a TR is shown below.

(1) Major Topic Heading

   (A) Main Sub-topic Heading

      (1) Sub Sub-Topic Heading

         (a) Further Details.

A newer form of outlining is the decimal form. Decimal form of outline is shown below.

(1) Major Topic Heading

   1.1 Main Sub-topic Heading

      1.1.1 Sub Sub-Topic Heading

   1.2 Main Sub-topic Heading

      1.2.1 Sub Sub-Topic Heading

Bibliography. As defined earlier, bibliography is a list of citations or references to books or periodicals on a particular topic. It is necessary to provide the details of the secondary sources used to prepare the technical or long report. Special software can help in searching, sorting, indexing and formatting bibliographies into any required style. This software helps to cite the references from online sources and translate them into database records, which can be used for future referrals.

12.3.2 Writing the Draft

Different authors have different styles of presenting their work. Some prefer to write the report themselves doing the additions/deletions, while others depend on a good editor to transcribe their reports into the required format. The quality of a report depends upon the following:

- Readability and Comprehensibility
- Tone
- Final proof

Readability and Comprehensibility. A report has to be properly understood by the readers to achieve high readership. Therefore, a researcher should take into account the needs of the reader before preparing the report. The basic requirements of a report are readability and comprehensibility. The following points should be noted in this context:

- It is necessary to avoid ambiguous statements.
- The report should be checked for grammar.
- As far as possible, simple words that convey the meaning clearly should be used.
- Sentences should be reviewed and edited to ensure a flow from one statement to another.
- Larger units of text should be broken down into smaller ones without altering the original meaning.
- Visual aids should be provided wherever required for better understanding.
- Visuals should not be inserted at the end of a section. They should be placed within the section for better comprehensibility.
- Each paragraph should contain only one idea.
- Underlining and capitalization should be used to differentiate and emphasize the important ideas from the secondary and subordinate ideas.
- Technical terms and jargons should be avoided wherever possible. Wherever unavoidable, they should find a reference in the footnotes.
- Each reference should include the name of the author, article title, journal title, volume, page numbers and year. Journal titles and book titles should be in italics. Book references should also include the publisher's name.
- Symbols, abbreviations, diagrams and statistics should find a reference, if necessary.

Tone. Proper use of tone is essential for better reading effects. This highlights the attitude of the writer and reflects his understanding of the reader. The report should make tactful use of details and generalizations. It should focus on facts and not the opinions of the writer. The report should make use of passive voice as far as possible and should avoid the use of first person. Recommendations should not undergo any sort of alterations to give them a positive image.

Final proof. Final editing of the draft should be taken up after a gap of at least a day. This helps in identifying mistakes, if any, better and correcting the mistakes. Final editing requires various questions to be answered pertaining to the organization, contextual and layout of the final report. This can be done a couple of times and looking at the report with a different focus each time. The executive summary follows the final stage of editing.

12.3.3 Presentation of the Research Report

A business researcher can present the findings of the research either in an electronic format or as a printout. Irrespective of the medium the researcher chooses to present his report, he should ensure that the findings are presented in a professional manner to the end-user. Some of the important aspects that should be considered for presenting a report are listed below.

- Reports should be typed or printed using an ink-jet, laser, or colour printer.
- The report should have a uniform font.
- The findings of the research study should be placed under appropriate headings and sub-headings.
- Leave ample space between the lines and on all sides for better reading. Overcrowding creates problems and is stressful for the eyes.
- Split larger text paragraphs into smaller paragraphs.
- Use bullet points to list specific points.
- Ensure that appropriate labels are assigned to every table, figure and graph that appears in the report.

12.4 Oral Presentations

The findings of the research may be presented orally. Such presentations are made to a small group of people (decision-makers/managers) who are more interested in the critical findings of the report. Therefore, unlike written reports that are elaborate, oral presentations are only briefings. Oral presentations are known to continue for 20–30 min, but presentations extending beyond an hour are not uncommon. Such sessions are interactive where the audience clarifies their doubts at the end of the presentation. Some distinctive features of oral presentation are explored in the subsequent sections.

12.4.1 Initial Planning

This basically requires the speaker to preplan certain strategies for a better presentation. For this, the speaker gets in touch with the organizers to determine the following:

- The type of speech expected of him/her. Whether the interaction will be an informal chat or a formal discussion.
- Whether the audience will consist of general or specialist clients and their numbers.
- Whether the time allotted will be sufficient for an exploratory presentation or whether the presentation will have to be a short one consisting of only the major points.
- The expected content of the presentation. This is to have an idea of what the audience expects of the presentation, so as to get prepared in advance.
- The type of audio-visuals to be used to facilitate the presentation.

- Whether a memorized speech or an extemporaneous presentation will create a better impact.

12.4.2 Preparation

Once the content of the presentation is decided, the next step involves planning how to present it. For the presentation to be well constructed and tidy, it has to be prepared well in advance. The preparation should include framing a time bound outline and a proper homework of the content in advance. The following points need to be taken into account:

- The content collected should be jotted down in big, bold letters highlighting the problem, its importance and steps to be taken.
- The outline of the presentation should be such that it keeps the interest of the audience alive throughout the presentation.
- Sentences should be short and appropriately arranged to follow a logical sequence.
- Determine the content that has to be supported by visual aids.
- The presenter should get a feel of the room and the equipment, if possible 1 day in advance.
- The presenter should do a thorough rehearsal of the presentation. This can be done in the presence of colleagues to get their feedback and make corrections if necessary.

12.4.3 Making the Presentation

This involves the execution of all that is rehearsed. It should start with a warm welcome or a greeting to the audience. The execution of the presentation would consist of the following:

Opening. The opening should be as brief as possible using not more than 15 % of the allotted time. The opening section should provide an overview of the entire presentation. It should include the reasons for the initiation of the project and its objectives. It is necessary to start the presentation with a startling fact, a pertinent question, or an interesting statistical figure to grab the attention of the audience. *Findings and Conclusions.* Findings and conclusions should immediately follow and it should be ensured that each conclusion is in line with the research objectives. The speaker should spend 60 % of the allotted time in explaining the details of this section.

Recommendations. The recommendations should appropriately follow the conclusions thus maintaining the flow of the presentation. After the presentation is over, it can be thrown open to the audience for questions.

The following points need to be taken into account during the presentation:

- Be ready with the opening statement when being introduced by the host.
- Use a natural, moderate rate of speech and use automatic gestures.
- While using laser pointers, remember not to point them at the audience.
- If lights need to be turned off, do it but not completely and for long.
- Try to interact with the audience and maintain eye contact.
- Try to have an impressive and memorable summary.
- While doing all this, keep a strict eye on the time factor. It is good to finish before time; never overshoot the time limits.

12.4.4 Delivery

An oral presentation is said to be effective when the content of the presentation is accompanied by the positive approach of the speaker. Therefore, the dress, speed of speech and tone and pitch of voice of the speaker play an important role in the success of a presentation. First time or inexperienced speakers may get nervous and this nervousness comes in the way of an effective presentation. Taking a few deep breaths, before starting the presentation helps in overcoming the nervousness. The presenter can arrive early and greet people as they walk in and have a chat. This creates a relaxed atmosphere. The following problems should be taken care of:

- Vocal Problems

  - Try to speak loud enough to be heard by the audience.
  - Avoid speaking too fast and give a pause after every sentence, but not a long one.
  - Vary the volume, tone according to the content.
  - Use appropriate language. For example, get the right level of formality/ informality.
  - Watch out for too much 'uh,' 'you know', 'okay' and other kinds of nervous verbal habits.

- Physical Behaviour

  - Avoid habitual behaviour (pacing, fumbling change in pocket or twirling hair).
  - Use hands to emphasize points but do not indulge in too much hand waving.
  - Do not turn your back to the audience and neither keep looking at a single individual. Try to maintain eye contact with all.
  - Avoid being a barrier between the audience and the OHP or the display screen.
  - Do not fumble with visuals. Arrange them in order, in advance.

- Handling Questions

  This is the most important section of the oral presentation. This session evaluates the interaction abilities of the speaker. A few points are worth considering in this regard.

  – Postpone questions aimed at resolving specific problems (or arcane knowledge). This is particularly important if the answer is expected to distract either the presenter or the audience away from the flow of the presentation.
  – The presenter should repeat the question so that the entire audience knows about the question and the presenter gets time to understand the question.
  – The presenter should not interrupt the questioner in the middle and try to answer. He should wait for the question to be complete.
  – Take a pause before starting to answer.
  – If the presenter is not able to answer the question, he should say so.
  – The presenter can offer to research an answer and then get back to the questioner later or ask for suggestions from the audience.
  – The presenter should avoid prolonged discussions with one person, extended answers and especially arguments.

12.5 Visual Aids

12.5.1 Tables

A research report more often than not contains quantitative data to substantiate the various findings. These quantitative findings if presented in a narrative form would go unnoticed by the reader. Therefore, a better way of representing them is to make use of tables to present the statistics. Tables save the writer from being caught in details, which can be boring. Data in the form of tables form a vital part of the report and makes the comparisons of quantitative data easier.

There are two types of tables based on their nature: general and summary. General tables are large, complex and exhaustive. As they are very comprehensive, they are usually reserved for the appendix. Summary tables, on the other hand, are concise and contain data that are closely associated with an explicit finding. This form of table can be customized to make it appealing. This can be done by retaining such important details only that will aid the reader in understanding the contents of the table. Tables should be used when graphs or figures cannot make the point.

A table should have the following features:

Title and Number. The title should be brief and yet all-inclusive of the information provided. It should be comprehensive enough to explain the subject of the table, the data classification and the relationship between the column and row headings.

It may also include a sub-title, if required. The sub-title usually includes the measurement units used. If different measurement units are used in different parts of the table, it should be appropriately mentioned. All tables in a report should be numbered and a reference for each should be given in the text. The table title and number usually appear at the top.

Bannerheads and Stubheads. Bannerheads are the identifying criteria for the contents of the columns. Bannerheads specify the contents of the columns, that is, what data the column holds. Stubheads perform the same function for the contents of the rows.

Footnotes. Any special reference to or explanation that cannot be incorporated in the table is given in the form of footnotes. Letters and asterisks instead of numbers are used to spot footnotes, as they help to avoid confusion with data values. Footnotes as they appear at the bottom of the page are also used to explain unfamiliar abbreviations to the reader.

Source. Tables derived from secondary sources cannot be deemed to be original. Therefore, they should bear a source note that acknowledges the table to the original source. A source can be anything from a published or printed material to company websites. The source is generally given at the bottom of the table.

12.5.2 Charts and Graphs

Charts and graphs in a research report tend to translate numerical information into visual form for better understanding of the subject matter. Like tables, charts and graphs also have a number and a title, labels for parts of the figure and sources and footnotes. Graphs and charts which depict a general trend are accompanied by a statement as 'not to scale' to avoid any confusions. Charts can be of the following types:

- Line Graphs
- Pie Charts
- Bar Charts

12.5.2.1 Line Graphs

A type of graph that highlights trends by drawing connecting lines between data points is known as a line graph. A line graph is a bar graph with the tops of the bars represented by points joined by continuous lines. This presents an eye-catching way to illustrate trends and changes over long, continuous intervals. A line graph takes statistical data presented in tables and represents them in rising and falling lines, steep or gentle curves. Line graphs have an X-axis (horizontal) and a Y-axis (vertical), both labelled. When a time variable is used, the X-axis is numbered for the time period, which is the independent variable, and the Y-axis is numbered for what is being measured, which is the dependent variable. Line graphs represent data that change with time, such as cycles, fluctuations, trends, distributions, increases and decreases in profits, employment, energy levels and temperatures. A line graph shows trends in data clearly, and hence, it is possible to predict the future trends for which data have not been collected.

12.5.2.2 Pie Charts

A type of presentation graphic in which percentage values are represented as proportionally sized slices of a pie is known as a pie chart. These charts are used to display the sizes of parts of some total quantity at a particular time. They can be used to compare different parts among themselves or with the whole. Therefore, they are represented in percentages. Before drawing a pie chart, it should be ensured that the sum of the different parts to be included totals 100. This is because the pie chart is a circle. The slices of varying percentages are arranged proportionately in a descending order, in a clockwise direction, with the largest slice occupying the 12 o'clock position in the circle. Different parts in the pie are shaded with different colours for better identification. Each slice is labelled horizontally and its appropriate percentage of the whole is also mentioned. As pie charts are round figures, they are usually labelled outside the circle. Pie charts can be misrepresented if parts of the whole are left out and if the whole is not defined as to what it stands for.

12.5.2.3 Bar Charts

A bar graph demonstrates the magnitude, sizes of several items or emphasizes the difference at equal intervals of time. Each bar represents a separate quantity, and multiple bars may be grouped and displayed horizontally or vertically. It shows the changes in the value of the dependent variable plotted on the Y-axis at discrete intervals of the independent variable plotted on the X-axis. Bar graphs are similar to line graphs with the difference that instead of using points, horizontal or vertical rectangular bars are used. Use of bar graphs makes it easier to point out differences among several items in a chart with multiple variables, over a time period. They tend to emphasize the rise or fall of one variable under the influence of another. Bar charts are of various types like pictogram/histogram grouped bar charts, segmented bars or deviation bar charts.

12.6 Summary

The essence of a business research report is the way it is presented, be it in the written format or orally. This makes it imperative for the report to be inclusive of all the necessary details. These details may vary according to the specific requirements of the clients. Business reports are of two types, that is, short and long. Short reports are concise and are made for those researches that have a well-defined problem, limited scope and employ a clear-cut methodology. Long reports are detailed and usually comprise of technical and management reports. The various components of these reports are as follows: prefatory information, introduction, methodology, findings, conclusions and recommendations, appendices and bibliography. While preparing a written report, the following points should be taken care of:

- Pre-writing concerns which consist of preparing, organizing and formatting the outline and bibliography.
- Writing the draft that requires adapting the tone of the report to the tastes of the audience for better readability and comprehensibility.
- Presentation considerations, which include the type of writing to be used, font of the words, formatting and preparing the cover of the report.

An oral presentation generally concentrates on the summary of the project with emphasis on the findings, conclusions and recommendations. Therefore, the essential criteria for a successful oral presentation are as follows:

- Initial planning, where the speaker plans certain strategies in advance regarding what to include in the report for a better presentation.
- Preparation, where he decides how to assemble the necessary items to maintain a flow in the presentation.
- Making the presentation, where he actually concentrates on presenting the essential findings of the report and the conclusions based on the objectives.
- Delivery, which provides essential tips on points to be taken care of during a presentation.
- Visual aids, which bring out the various ways in which the statistical findings can be presented for a better impact of the presentation.

Index

S. Sreejesh et al., *Business Research Methods*,
DOI: 10.1007/978-3-319-00539-3,
© Springer International Publishing Switzerland 2014

Printed by Publishers' Graphics LLC